# GEORGES CLEMENCEAU

**LONGMANS, GREEN AND CO.**
55 FIFTH AVENUE, NEW YORK
221 EAST 20TH STREET, CHICAGO
TREMONT TEMPLE, BOSTON
128 UNIVERSITY AVENUE, TORONTO


**LONGMANS, GREEN AND CO. LTD.**
39 PATERNOSTER ROW, E C 4, LONDON
53 NICOL ROAD, BOMBAY
6 OLD COURT HOUSE STREET, CALCUTTA
167 MOUNT ROAD, MADRAS

# GEORGES CLEMENCEAU

By JEAN MARTET

Translated by
Milton Waldman

LONGMANS, GREEN AND CO.

London • New York • Toronto

1930

MARTET

GEORGES CLEMENCEAU

SECOND EDITION

*To*

NICOLAS PIÉTRI

J. M.

# TRANSLATOR'S PREFACE

EVERY time a celebrated political personage dies one, two or a host of his surviving intimates and associates fill their fountain-pens, send out for writing paper, hire secretaries and make contracts with publishers to the end that their dead friend or master may be suitably recorded for those who already knew all about him. Occasionally posterity is taken into account, but not often or seriously. The biographer's principal intention is to write an extended obituary notice, pointing out the deceased's virtues, the so frequent occasions on which he was right and his enemies wrong, and, if possible, to produce hitherto unpublished documents wherewith to support new, interesting, and perhaps sensational revelations.

This book has no such purpose. The impulse which led to its writing and the circumstances under which it was written are fully set forth by the author in his first chapter and need not be elaborated here. His unique contact with Clemenceau led to an unrivalled opportunity for knowledge of him, particularly during those nightmare days of the last year of the war. That knowledge, as in the case of countless others, led to respect and boundless admiration; but in the case of M. Martet, this admiration went a step further and became a deep and lasting affection — an affection which its subject but rarely commanded in his active and pugnacious career.

But it is an affection which frankly stops short of idolatry.

No one can mistake the love and reverence which M. Martet felt for his chief; but, equally, no one can fail to penetrate the author's careful self-suppression and perceive the half-sympathetic, half-sardonic smile with which he regards so many of the activities which occupied his hero's life — separation of Church and State, universal male suffrage, ideals of Justice and Patriotism, all the panaceas which the native philosopher Clemenceau came to discard but which the congenital philosopher Martet could never from the beginning have taken seriously.

So when the author sets himself to the task of recording his hero, as he explains in the opening pages of his book, he is not concerned with reopening closed debates and giving temporary life to dead issues. His sole idea is to make the world see that unique man Clemenceau as he saw him, in three dimensions (with a suggestion of a fourth), Clemenceau speaking, breathing, scolding, eating, philosophizing, haggling, and musing over the sculptures and pictures which he so deeply and passionately loved. The old political quarrels are allowed to lie — Clemenceau is not made to argue them over again with Thiers and Gambetta. Who cares? It is more important to know that he loathed Thiers and why, that he respected Gambetta and why, that he adored Claude Monet more than any politician he had ever known. The sole exception to this general rule is the controversial matter which still remained open between Clemenceau and his contemporaries Foch, Poincaré, the enemy statesmen and the allied statesmen at Versailles. Those issues were still living and active when these conversations took place, and Clemenceau speaks his mind about them as an advocate of his own views. No one will regret hearing his restatement of them or reading the documents and the new evidence he adduces.

The task that M. Martet set himself, then, was not that of the journalist, whose business it is to discuss, but that of the artist, whose task it is to present. How far he has succeeded the pages that follow will show. In the preparation of this translation I have read his manuscript through with care three times, and have been struck anew each time with the fact that here was a work of art which partook of the nature, though it did not perhaps attain the degree, of Boswell's portrait of Johnson or Plato's of Socrates. All three make their heroes acquainted to us in the only way that it is possible for man to know his fellow human-beings — by observing what they did, what they said, what they felt. And again, in kind though not in degree, he shared this advantage with them — that his subject was a man of rare and formidable stature. No one who probes to the depth of Clemenceau's mind and follows and studies the contours of his intelligence, who sympathizes with his enthusiasms for the greatness of man's achievements, who appreciates the strength of his hate, the violence of his scorn, the power of love and loyalty that could be aroused in him, the unselfishness of his patriotism (though in itself it may be excessive) and of his sense of justice, will fail to recognize that here was a man who would have been distinguished even if he had not given his life to action and his name had not been spread daily across the newspapers of the world. For there was nothing in which he was interested which he was unable to illuminate with an original and characteristic thought couched in a striking and memorable phrase — and there were few things in which he was not interested. The arts and sciences, history, archæology, sculpture, painting, geology, the humanities — the manifestations of man's effort and his stupidity in the realm of politics, religion, economics, and sociology. With all these he familiarized himself and pursued their study with intensity.

In these pages there appears also the story of his life. Owing to the form which these conversations took, as the author explains in his first chapter, there is no set chronology of events.

Clemenceau talked as ideas and memories came to him, making no effort to attain to the effect of a formal statement, and wisely not being encouraged to do so by Martet. Ideas suggested images and images ideas, and in the course of these talks, which were spread over nearly two years, he tells of his family, the stout Vendée yeomen who grew to be landed proprietors in the course of the centuries; of the corner of France in which he was born, on 28th September 1841, which he loved and returned to all his life and where in the end he was buried, on 25th November 1929; of his relatives, especially his father and mother, and of their part in forming his ideas.

The next period of his life, the scholastic, is given in some detail, especially his study of medicine, a profession which he was destined to follow because it had been followed (somewhat inattentively, we gather) by his father, his grandfather, and his great-grandfather. We follow him through his medical course at Nantes and Paris, and how early and how ardently he threw himself into the materialistic philosophy so fashionable amongst the youth of his time, a philosophy to which he gave its final expression in his last important work, *Au Soir de la Pensée.*

The next event of his life was his journey to America in 1865, "to see how Democracy worked over there." With many cases of books and a most elegant wardrobe (this latter passion seems to have left him in middle life) he went to New York and looked about him, eking out the meagre allowance which his father was able to give him by teaching French and riding to young ladies in a Stamford, Connecticut, school. He married in America a Miss Plummer of Springfield, Massachusetts, heard Dickens lecture, and came back with a vast indignation against America because of the way the whites treated the blacks — his feeling in this respect coloured many of his subsequent opinions of the United States, as more recent events in the book show.

Returning to Paris in 1866 he began, with moderate success, the practice of medicine. But very early it was obvious that his life-work was to be politics. An ineffaceable impression was made on him by his father's arrest in 1858 on an unjust charge of conspiracy against the Second Empire — the protests of his fellow-townsmen obtained old Dr. Clemenceau's release just as he was being transported to Algiers, the experience costing the reason of one of his daughters. The young Georges vowed to avenge his father, and within four years was imprisoned for an anti-Imperialist demonstration in the Place de la Bastille.

His actual political career began with his appointment as Mayor of Montmartre in September of 1870 — Napoleon III had been driven out, the Third Republic had replaced him, and the victorious Germans were infesting Paris. The appointment was confirmed a short time later in the popular election. Hence, during the fearful and bloody uprising of the Commune, it was the young Mayor's duty to keep order in his troublesome arrondissement. What his problems were will appear in a lengthy document which he himself compiled in 1872 and which is here published for the first time. Briefly it may be said that he had to suppress insurrection on behalf of a government he disliked, and frustrate the patriotic rebels of the Communards with whom to a large extent he was in sympathy; as a result both sides distrusted him, and the document referred to is his answer to the accusation later brought that he had duplicitously connived at a shocking double assassination.

From then on he remained one of the conspicuous figures of the Third Republic, a thorn in the side of successive governments through the papers he edited, two of which are particularly referred to, *La Justice* and *L'Homme Libre*. So troublesome did they find him that extreme measures were very nearly resorted to. Grave charges were brought against him — a dramatic scene in the Chamber of Deputies is described, when a Prime Minister, declaring that his colleagues were all afraid of Clemenceau's tongue, pen, and sword, hurled the direct charge of treason because one of the backers of *Justice,* Cornelius Herz, was a German-born American. On another occasion a plot was formed to inculpate him in treasonable dealings by means of a forgery. And his magnificent defence of the unfortunate Alfred Dreyfus, the victim of that celebrated *cause célèbre* which convulsed France for nearly a decade, called down on him as well as on his colleague Zola, the execration of a host of the respectable, whom his sturdy opposition to priestly influence in the State had already made his enemies.

Then during the early years of this century came a period of comparative quiet, during which he sat in the Senate and edited his paper. He travelled widely, usually departing from the beaten track, and collecting impressions which are peculiarly, often amusingly his own. In 1906 he became Prime Minister, or President of the Council, an office he held during the Casablanca crisis, and which he handled with characteristic firmness. An entertaining incident of that crisis is here discussed. But being strong-willed, unable to brook opposition, contemptuous of the abilities of such colleagues as the Constitution and political necessity compelled him to include in his cabinet, he fell in 1909 — having, as he remarks, brought down every government for thirty years, he ended by bringing down his own.

At the outbreak of the war he was editing *L'Homme Libre* and playing a minor part in the political situation. He still held his seat in the Senate and became a member of the Military Committee. But the way in which the war was conducted daily aroused his wrathful contempt, and the successively falling Ministries, even the President of the Republic, quivered under the darts of his mordant sarcasm. The censorship attempted to restrain him by deleting his editorials; his answer, more pointed than any invective, was to change the name of *L'Homme Libre* to *L'Homme Enchainé*.

The day came when it was obvious that he and he alone could end the war successfully. The military situation was desperate; part of the army was in mutiny; the public was restive, and defeatists were gathering the courage to become articulate. Even those who hated him realized that it was to him that France must turn if she was to win through. And so in November of 1917, Poincaré, the man he distrusted and had refused to truckle to, summoned this modern Cincinnatus to power. And to real power, the only kind he would accept. For this fighting democrat had all his life been by temperament an autocrat, and in his view the situation now demanded nothing short of despotism.

The rest of his history is too familiar to require repetition. He announced his policy in one word 'Victory' — the 'Tiger' became known to his countrymen as 'Père de la Victoire.' Ruthlessly, arrogantly, but with supreme self-confidence he pressed to his goal. He supported the unified command, as he explains though he disliked the commander — a bitter pill for him to swallow, but a necessary one. And he achieved victory — it is fairly safe to say that no one else in his place could have done as much. He wrangled, bargained, threatened, even compromised his way through the peace negotiations. Then he resigned, and fell quickly into oblivion. It will seem sad as well as surprising to many who read these pages that the hard-bitten, disillusioned octogenarian cared so deeply because the crowning honour of the Presidency had been withheld from him — here he admits the fact.

His life had more of action, of success and defeat, triumph and disappointment, worship and loathing in it, than fell to the lot of any other man of his time. Yet in the end he remains apart from it all. His real life was in his mind, the rest was only a process of illusion and disillusion. I can only repeat that had he done none of the things he did, merely thought the thoughts that were his, he would have been a greatly distinguished person. He was a Greek of the Periclean age in his passion for ideas, his ironic attitude towards his fellowmen, his love for his country — a worthy subject for a book which should become a permanent contribution to biographical literature.

MILTON WALDMAN

# CONTENTS

xvi CONTENTS

# LIST OF ILLUSTRATIONS

[Where not otherwise stated the illustrations have been reproduced from material kindly supplied by the Editor of *L'Illustration*.]

*Paris, 18th May* 1928

MY DEAR MARTET,

I have been criticized and attacked. I shall be again. In order to answer these attacks it is possible that you will have need of certain documents. I am giving them to you, leaving you free to make what you judge to be the best use of them.

Here is, first, a collection of documents relating to certain facts and notably those of the 18th March 1871.

Here is, secondly, another collection which will enable you to make clear certain events of yesterday:

1. A note from Mordacq about Foch, beginning with the words, '1st October 1918, the Marshal states . . .'

2. A memorandum by me (. . . pages) on my relations with Foch.

3. A letter from Mangin dated 2nd December 1917.

4. A letter from me to Tardieu, dated 24 November 1923, relating to the left bank of the Rhine.

Yours

G. CLEMENCEAU

*Monsieur Jean Martet, G.C.*

# GEORGES CLEMENCEAU

## I

### How This Book Came to be Written

I BECAME Clemenceau's secretary in February 1915. The war
had been going on for six months. Clemenceau was a Senator, member of the Military Committee and of the Committee for Foreign Affairs, besides which he edited a daily
newspaper called, before the war, *L'Homme Libre* — after the
institution of censorship the name was changed to *L'Homme
Enchaîné*.

In November 1917 Clemenceau took office and made me
chief of his private secretariat. I held this position until the
fall of the ministry. In January 1920, Clemenceau had once
more become a private citizen, having given up his seat in the
senate and resigned the editorship of his newspaper.[1] I there-
upon resumed my duties of personal secretary and continued
to exercise them for two or three years. When I was compelled to leave him, I remained his friend and retained his
friendship until the day of his death.

In July 1927, Clemenceau was very seriously ill; one day,

[1] The day that the Clemenceau Cabinet was formed *L'Homme Enchaîné* became
once more *L'Homme Libre*.

having gone to the Rue Franklin,[2] I had so strong an impression of being in the presence of a dying man that upon my return home I made a memorandum of what I then believed to be his last words and his last views. He recovered his health. I continued, however, to keep a record of his views. Why in the name of Heaven, I asked myself, had I not undertaken this simple task in the beginning? What treasures should I then have accumulated! But from 1915 to 1920 there was the war, and within this period came his ministry. At that time one scarcely thought of taking notes, of collecting documents for future books — one knew so little of what the morrow would bring forth.

Beginning with 1920 I might perhaps have been in a position to undertake this task. But I had my daily bread to consider; I scarcely had time to think of the future. But I must say that the twenty-four months which I had just passed in the Rue Saint-Dominique [3] with a Clemenceau for whom nothing existed but action and struggle; a Clemenceau who seemed, in the grip of this superhuman necessity, daily more devoid of all 'humanity'; a Clemenceau whom the armistice perhaps left a little drunk with victory . . . those twenty-four months assuredly did not cause me to lose my admiration for him — quite the contrary, for I had seen him at work and I had seen how in one year, from November 1917 to November 1918, he wrested victory from the tragic and desperate situation in which matters stood when he assumed office — yet the filial affection which I bore him when he was solitary, beaten, and hated was somewhat diminished. For 'one should only write about what one loves.'

In 1927 he again found himself alone and beaten; if he was not hated, it was only because he had been forgotten. It is, possibly, one of the most incredible facts of history, that this

[2] He lived at 8 Rue Franklin in Passy.
[3] The old building of the Ministry of War is situated in the Rue Saint-Dominique.

man, who had saved his country, saw himself abandoned by everyone less than ten years after his triumph, thrust into a loneliness for which I fervently hope France will one day blush. By 1927 the stupidity and ingratitude of his fellow citizens had brought together those who during the years of war and victory had seen him as the machine rather than the man, who had admired rather than loved him.

It was at this time that I began to make notes of these conversations. I went to see him, and we talked, or more accurately, he talked, for he was always very fond of expressing himself with the spoken word, believing that it frequently guided and gave strength to his thoughts. When I returned home I set down as faithfully as I could all that I had been listening to, including not only the general substance, but also the turns of phrase, the colour, intonation, the fire that he had given it. I shall probably be charged with having put in Clemenceau's mouth words which he never uttered. Well, if that accusation is made, I shall answer that I may have been, in fact that at times I certainly have been, inexact in reproducing these conversations; but never in the way of adding, only in curtailing. That seemed to me proper. I thought it right to distinguish between what was actually said to me and what was thought aloud in my presence. Everything that I have written was spoken, and nearly always to the exact word, to the comma almost; I may have made mistakes in names or dates, may have heard incorrectly or remembered imperfectly, but if so I should be surprised; my hearing and my memory are both quite good.

I have recorded all this without the least desire to intrude myself. I did not even want to correct certain ungrammatical turns of phrase which he used, nor to read into various rather superficial reflections what Clemenceau had disdained to put into them. Some will say perhaps 'hackneyed, commonplace.' I should indeed like to hear the ultimate truths which fall from *their* lips when they are prattling with a friend. . .

The reader will notice that from the very beginning these conversations develop at random. I do not attempt to give them one direction rather than another. Clemenceau passes from M. Poincaré to the *Soir de la Pensée*,[4] from the *Soir de la Pensée* to his little cottage in the Vendée,[5] and so on. But one day, the 12th of May 1928, Clemenceau sent for Piétri[6] and myself, and turning to me said: 'I am nearly ready to leave the scene. I am going to talk to you about certain "crimes" of which I have been accused; it is right that you should know how to answer.'

These 'crimes' were the Commune; the assassination of the generals, Lecomte and Clément Thomas;[7] Cornélius Herz;[8] the Dreyfus affair.

After Clemenceau had told me what he remembered of these bygone events, I remarked that as a matter of fact there were other 'crimes' even more recent which were being dragged out and hurled at him oftener; his attitude towards Monsieur Poincaré, towards Marshal Foch, the way in which he had conducted the war, concluded the Peace, etc. Clemenceau gave his views on all these issues; afterwards he told me the story of his life. He 'spoke' his memoirs to me. I trust that no one will be surprised at the desultory and irregular course of these talks; they are only conversations — not a formal cross-examination. Probably some contradictions will

---

[4] It was in 1927 that Clemenceau published his large philosophical work in two volumes, where he set forth his conception of the universe.

[5] Clemenceau was the tenant of a little farm house in the Vendée at Saint-Vincent-sur-Jard, where he passed his summer months.

[6] Executor of Clemenceau's estate. His best friend and the one who showed him the warmest and most disinterested affection (see later).

[7] On the 18th March 1871, Generals Lecomte and Clément Thomas were killed by the Communards in Paris. Clemenceau was Mayor of Montmartre at that time and was accused of having a hand in this assassination.

[8] In 1892 when Clemenceau was editor of *Justice*, he was accused of having put his paper at the disposal of Germany through the instrumentality of one of his backers, Cornélius Herz.

be found and perhaps some unjust and over-strong statements; but this could not be avoided, for it would be impossible to eliminate these statements unless I ignored certain lapses and portrayed a Clemenceau who wasn't really Clemenceau.

Henry Bernstein has said: 'The life of Georges Clemenceau is the finest contemporary work of art. What a poem ! What subject in tragedy can surpass in pathos the fate of this contemporary of ours ?' Perhaps I should apologize to the memory of Clemenceau since this is the point of view that I have desired to take in writing these pages. He is great because he won a war which seemed destined to end in stalemate. He is perhaps greatest of all for having lived as he did in the midst of passion, hazard, danger, hate, contumely. He fought for liberty and for justice and for even more deceptive chimeras. Not a day passed which was not for him a day either of defeat or of victory. He was loved to adoration, ignored to oblivion. Those who were his partisans one day became his adversaries the next. He was accused of everything and worse than everything. He made men and then unmade them. He formed parties and later spurned them with disgust. He revelled in the intoxication of action and yet saw the vanity of it.

Who was right: he or Gambetta? he or Jules Ferry? he or Poincaré? he or Briand? It matters little — even Briand and Poincaré would grant that ! Even when wrong his mistakes were on the grand scale, noble, splendid — and useful. The hatred which he bore to his last day toward the opponents of his ideas and his methods was of value to them, and could not but increase their capacity for action and for thought. A man never finds his real strength until he is in the opposition.

Accordingly I hope that I shall be pardoned for having tried to keep alive the echo of a voice which has not always sounded agreeably in people's ears: for the sake of humanity's records I have not the right to leave this chronicle in my drawer.

I hope also that the reader will forgive me for having so often brought myself on the scene in the course of the following pages. The 'myself' who turns up at nearly every instant will perhaps in the end become tedious. But in order that Clemenceau might talk it was necessary that there should be someone to listen to him. I was that listener; that is all that I was, and beyond that I have no vanity in the matter.

# II

## The Dying Man

I am at my desk. Bernier [1] is speaking to me on the telephone:

'Hello! is that you? I have just been brought a news agency despatch. I'm going to read it to you. . . Are you listening?'

'Go ahead.'

' "M. Georges Clemenceau, who has grown weaker during the last fortnight and had to keep to his room, has become noticeably worse in the last 48 hours." '

'Go on.'

' "Professor Laubry and Dr. Florand, the former Premier's usual doctors, have been called in consultation. We are informed that, though they do not consider the condition of the illustrious patient critical, they at least thought it advisable to inform his family that his condition might give cause for serious uneasiness." Do you hear me?' asks Bernier.

'Continue. . .'

' "In consequence M. Albert Clemenceau, brother of the former Premier, his son M. Michel Clemenceau and his daughter Mme. Jacquemaire, have been notified, and have gone at

---

[1] Editor of *L'Homme Libre*. Bernier lived for many years on terms of closest friendship with Clemenceau.

once to the Rue Franklin.  His other daughter, Mme. Jung, who is taking a cure, will arrive shortly.

' "No definite illness is affecting M. Clemenceau.  Certain organs, especially the heart and the lungs, are still functioning perfectly; but a noticeable decline in the mental faculties of the former president can be noticed." '

I start.  'What's this nonsense !  Decline in his mental faculties ?  They've written *that* ?'

'Let me finish,' says Bernier.  ' "However, a slight improvement was noticed yesterday, and M. Clemenceau has been able to take light nourishment." '

'Is that all ?'

'Yes. . . When did you last see him ?'

'Not a month ago.  He was in perfect health and his spirits were livelier than those of three-quarters of the men of our own age. . .'

'Oh, my dear fellow !  My dear fellow !' says Bernier, on the point of tears.

'He spoke of a voyage which he wanted to make to the coast of Asia Minor.[2]  A fortnight ago I received a most enthusiastic letter from him. . . Today his mental faculties are failing !'

'Try to get some information.  Telephone the Rue Franklin. Tell me what's going on, won't you ?'

'Yes.  Good-bye.'

I telephone the Rue Franklin.  Passy 98–82.  A number which I am getting to know. . . A thick, peevish voice answers — Brabant's, the chauffeur.

'Is Albert[3] there ?'

'Yes.'

---

[2] Clemenceau intended, for a short while, to write a book on the Ionians and Dorians.  He saw in them certain bases of comparison with the age in which we are living.  It was on March 24th that he first spoke to me of his project.  'That sea . . . that parliament of islands !  Will you come ?  I'll take you.'  His ideas shortly took another turn, and the project was abandoned.

[3] The valet.  He was the most perfect and devoted of Clemenceau's servants.

'Let me speak to him.'

And when Albert is at the end of the wire: 'Now then, what's happening ? Is Clemenceau ill ?'

'Yes. . .'

'Seriously ill ?'

'Well . . . Things aren't going. . .'

'But are they feeling uneasy ?'

'Does Monsieur wish to come ? I will tell him. . . He will be able to see Monsieur. Three minutes. . .'

Taxi.

Rue Franklin.

Albert opens the door for me.

'Well ?'

'Well, he's been ill for five or six days, very ill. His memory's going. In the evening he no longer remembers the people he saw in the morning. He has become much thinner; he can't stand on his legs any more.'

'Can I see him ?'

He shows me into the study. Once again I glance at the room — full of books, full of Indian, Chinese, Japanese objects; all showing a kind of heavy blatancy, and giving the illusion of having come from the remotest points of space and time in order to find here a billet where they could be traversed in the twinkling of an eye . . . I see again the Daumier,[4] the Monet.[5] Above the door the enormous pale mask of Queen Taiae[6] smiles mysteriously. On one of the book shelves the Tegea[7] head looks with serenity towards the Infinite.

---

[4] In 1919 the Ministers of Clemenceau's Cabinet had given their President this lovely Daumier which represents Don Quixote and Sancho Panza.

[5] A landscape. It is well known that Claude Monet was a great friend of Clemenceau's. In 1928 Clemenceau wrote a monograph on the work of this great painter.

[6] The original of this cast is in the Cairo Museum.

[7] A head of a Goddess of the finest period of Greek sculpture. The original is in the Museum of Tegea.

Albert returns to fetch me. I cross the little hall, also crammed to the ceiling with books, atlases, old magazines, loose papers, dictionaries. I hear a dismal cough — his. I enter the room. He is there, fully dressed, wearing his grey jacket, swallowed up in the sofa, which a furniture dealer had offered him at the time of Cottin's attempt at assassination.[8] He is hemmed in, shut off — sullen. His face is hollow, his eyes half-shut. He extends a lifeless hand which at once falls limp. With a flicker of his eyelids he indicates a seat.

I ask him: 'Are you coughing ? Do you have bronchitis ?'

A vague gesture. 'I cough . . . I do not cough . . . I don't know anything about it. You know . . . What God does . . . He has His own ideas.'

'What treatment have they prescribed for you ?'

'Oh ! Little stories, fantasies; that's none of my business. My business is to be ill.'

'I thought you had left for the Vendée.'

'Yes, but at the last moment I changed my opinion about my health.'

(Not a bad phrase on the tongue of one whose 'mental faculties were declining.')

He is silent. I don't know what to say. I don't want to speak to him of himself. I speak of myself, idiotically . . . of my work, of my troubles. . .

'What,' he says, 'did I hear you remark that there were several sluts running about the streets ? There are indeed. That's necessary for the picturesque aspect of things.'

Again silence. I venture this question:

'Have you seen Mandel ?'[9]

'Yes. Who hasn't seen Mandel ? He pierces walls . . . I

---

[8] It will be remembered that in 1919 Clemenceau received a bullet wound from a man named Cottin.

[9] A deputy. Formerly head of Clemenceau's Cabinet.

find him from time to time . . . there, in front of me . . . on a sofa, in a chair. He tells me things. I do not listen. He is satisfied.'[10]

'Are you suffering from diabetes at the moment ?'

'It's possible . . . I have everything and nothing. These village witch-doctors try to put little tickets on my diseases. They exert themselves quite uselessly. My own impression is, chiefly, that I am 86 years old. . . Ah, Martet ! Martet ! What do you think of all this ?'

'Of all what, sir ?'

'Of life ? Of men ?'

I can no longer see anything in his eyes but a little steely flame. Not a word which does not bear the mark of a strong will and a scoffing sanity—to their extreme limit. But he is tired, so tired ! I should like to say a friendly word to him, but I am afraid lest he suspect my anxiety. As a matter of fact it would not frighten him. He feels he is dying; he weighs oblivion with an amused look, as if saying: 'So that's the hole I'm about to jump into ? Let's see what's at the bottom of it.'

With a gesture of his grey-gloved hand he shows me a letter on the table: 'There's an Englishman who has written to remind me that it will soon be ten years since I came into power. He would like to know if I have any impressions about it. I haven't. I haven't even any memories . . . Have you any memories ?'

'That is all I have, sir.'

'Even that is too much. Forget, Martet. Let's forget, let's be men of our own time.'

[10] Clemenceau was always fond of these witticisms about Mandel. On July 23 he wrote to me: 'I see from the papers that Mandel has been operated on for anthrax and that the English are going to fortify Singapore. Although there is no connection between them, both phenomena are equally deplorable. I can see the intervention of Gosset [the surgeon] in the first case. But no sign of the League of Nations in the second.'

Then, as I extend my hand to take my departure:

'Tell your Poincaré . . . tell him I have nothing to say to him.'

Albert is waiting for me behind the door.  He escorts me out.  We exchange a couple of words.  The doctors have said that he ought not to receive any visitors.

'How do you find him ?' Albert asks me.  I shrug my shoulders.

Outside a storm has broken noisily.  I want to telephone Bernier, but all the telephones in the neighborhood are out of order.  The rain falls in a warm shower.  Lightning flashes from the steely sky.  There is something Æschylean, something which seems in harmony with the spirit of the dying man.  For he is about to die . . . and he was so great, so great !

FORGET ?  How can I ?  The coming to power in November 1917 — I remember it as I lived it, in a kind of stupor; I remember how inevitable and yet how unexpected it was at the same time.

For many, many months, M. Clemenceau's intimates had advised him to adopt an attitude of conciliation towards M. Poincaré.  Mandel repeated it to him every evening at *l'Homme Enchainé,* and very frequently returned the next morning to the Rue Franklin to reiterate it once more.

'But pardon me, Mr. President, what would M. Guizot or M. Thiers [11] in similar circumstances have. . .'

'Lay off it, Mandel !  You look at everything like a politician !'

As for myself — although I made it a habit not to interfere too much in these things — I could not help saying to M.

---

[11] Mandel always expressed himself in the most academic phraseology and talked through his nose.  I shared the same room with him at the War Office for over two years, and I know his eloquence.

Clemenceau in our morning conversations[12] what I thought of all this.

'In your today's article you still take a line against M. Poincaré. You reproach him with not wanting to know and not knowing what he wants. . .'

'Yes, because it's true. Oughtn't it to be said ?'

'I don't know if it ought to be said or not. But I do know that in saying it you take away from M. Poincaré all desire to entrust you with power. . .'

'Well ?'

'The war will end without you, and I am afraid that in consequence it will end very badly. . .'

'It will end as it began and as it is being prosecuted. . .'

'Exactly ! I am sure that M. Poincaré is only waiting for a sign from you in order to appeal for your co-operation. For the love of God, make that sign !'

Clemenceau stopped joking and looked at me with sardonic eyes:

'No, Martet,' he said to me, 'I shan't make that sign — you can do what you like. I shan't do it, for this reason: that, far from seeking power like all these worthy people, I'm afraid of it. I am terribly afraid of it. I would give anything to escape from it ! You have merely to look at me and see clearly that I'm a goner: seventy-six years old, rotten with diabetes. . . How do you expect me to pull it off ? Secondly, I'm not at all sure that we could pull it off in the pass to which we've come.'

'You think that Germany can't be beaten ?'

'I think it's a job, a difficult one . . . not because Germany is Germany; German strength has its limits: the Boche is stupid, narrow. But because France is France. My unhappy country frightens me. I look about on all sides: I see noth-

[12] In 1917 I went to the Rue Franklin in the morning and to the office of *l'Homme Enchaîné*, 13 Rue Taitbout, in the evening.

ing. I see . . . Parliament bewildered and enslaved, a press
. . . preposterous, a public opinion unbalanced, distracted . . .
and beyond all that just words. Ah! those magnificent words.
Never have such beautiful speeches been heard! A pity that
that isn't enough for victory!'

'But, nevertheless, if M. Poincaré tendered you office?'

'But do you really mean that he will offer it to me? Despite
everything, alas! Despite everything!'

'What shall you do?'

'I shall accept. One cannot refuse office. But I shall not
have sought it. There will be nothing to reproach me with:
not the wink of an eye, not the shuffle of a foot. Then the
power that will be offered me will have this new and special
quality about it, that it will be real power.'

During this time M. Clemenceau wrote such things as:

9th September: 'The President of our Republic has not
made much more than a beginning. . .' It was the day after
the fall of the Ribot Cabinet, at the height of the ministerial
crisis.

13th September: 'M. Poincaré himself ended up by understanding that there is a public opinion in France.'

8th October: My correspondent has concluded, 'Of what
is M. Poincaré thinking then?' I answered, 'Of himself.'
Etc., etc.

Painlevé's Cabinet falls.[13]

On the 15th November M. Clemenceau was still writing his
daily article: Bernier must have the text of this in his archives,
and probably Clemenceau tacked on to it with his own vitriolic

[13] The ministries from 1914 onwards were:

    1st   Viviani (June 13th to August 26th, 1914).
    2nd Viviani (August 26th to October 29th, 1915).
    1st   Briand (December 12th, 1916, to March 20th, 1917).
    Ribot (March 20th to September 12th, 1917).
    Painlevé (September 12th to November 16th, 1917).

Not to mention minor changes.
Since the outbreak of war there had been six War Ministers: M. Messimy, M.
Millerand, General Galliéni, General Roques, General Lyautey, M. Painlevé.

and savage pen a footnote directed against 'l'homme de l'Elysée.' But the article did not appear. For in the afternoon of the 15th Clemenceau, who had already been called by the President of the Republic on the afternoon of the 14th, was again summoned by M. Poincaré, who tendered him office.

Clemenceau accepted. In the issue of *l'Homme Enchainé* of the 16th Clemenceau's article was replaced with an article by M. Camille Picard, deputy for the Vosges, 'Why We Shall Hold On.' It was no longer just a question of 'holding on.' . . . Save for the title one would have known instantly that Clemenceau had dropped his pen.

On leaving the Elysée on the 15th Clemenceau began his visits, calling on M. Antonin Dubost, President of the Senate, and M. Deschanel, President of the Chamber. On the 16th the Cabinet is formed. Clemenceau presents his colleagues to M. Poincaré: M. Nail, who holds the Portfolio of Justice, M. Pichon, of Foreign Affairs, and so forth. The papers say, 'Speed record.' The reason was that the Clemenceau Ministry had been formed well before Painlevé's was overturned.

## III

## THE DYING MAN COME TO LIFE AGAIN

*12th July* 1927

I TELEPHONE the Rue Franklin. Albert tells me: 'He passed a good night, this morning he has been able to eat. Florand came: he's satisfied.'

*22nd July*

I WAS compelled to leave Paris for several days. I wrote to Albert. He answered: 'I am happy to be able to tell you that M. Clemenceau is well on the way to a complete cure. The doctors are allowing him to leave for the Vendée . . . but he doesn't dare undertake the trip. His great weariness persists and the vigour which you have always known him to have isn't there any longer. You can write to him. . . But if he answers you himself it will be with difficulty. Words do not flow easily from his pen any more and it is often necessary to re-write the addresses on his letters.'

I write a letter to Clemenceau over which I take a great deal of trouble and in which I try not to show my anxiety.

Then one fine morning the following appeared in the papers:

'*Louveciennes, 30th July.* — M. Georges Clemenceau, former President of the Council, was present this morning at the

16

marriage in the Mairie of Louveciennes,[1] of his grandson, M. Georges Clemenceau,[2] to Mlle. Jeanne-Lucie Roseneau.

'The witnesses were: for the groom, M. Georges Clemenceau, his grandfather; for the bride, M. Loweanthal.

'The ceremony took place in the strictest privacy.

'The two families and a few guests went on foot from the Château de Louveciennes to the Mairie.

'M. Georges Clemenceau, who seemed very vigorous and very cheerful, left Louveciennes at once after the ceremony and returned to Paris by car.'

And I receive this card from Albert:

*Saint-Vincent,[3] the 2nd*

Monsieur Martet,

I am very glad to notify you of the arrival in the Vendée of the President after an excellent journey which has not in the least tired him. His health is as good as it could be at the moment and I notice that he is working regularly now.

Believe me, etc. . .

*15th August*

The newspapers announce:

'Dr. Antoine Florand, honorary physician to the hospitals of Paris, Commander of the Legion of Honour, has just died.'

It was — if I may say so — a dramatic stroke of the kind whose tragic humour Clemenceau so deeply appreciated. Death was unable to do anything with him, therefore he carried off his physician.

[1] A small place near Paris.
[2] The elder of Michel Clemenceau's two sons.
[3] Saint-Vincent-sur-Jard (Vendée). It was here — at the seaside — that Clemenceau had a house called Bel-Ebat.

## IV

### 'A MIXTURE OF ANARCHIST AND CONSERVATIVE'

*20th September* 1927

THE papers announce: 'M. Clemenceau has left Saint-Vincent-sur-Jard by road for Paris, where he will remain several days. He will also return by road.'

*21st September*

I telephone the Rue Franklin. It is the cook who answers: 'M. Clemenceau is back. But the flat is undergoing repairs and he has gone to stay with M. Piétri.'[1]

2 Avenue de Messine. A large room with two windows on the Avenue and the Boulevard Haussmann. Albert shows me in at the same time as an American whom I have just met on the landing.

And Clemenceau is there, erect and solid, returned from afar.

CLEMENCEAU: Come in! [*To the American*] How are you? You're looking very well. [*To me*] And you? What

---

[1] Piétri had known Clemenceau in 1917. In 1921 he took him to Corsica. From there Clemenceau wrote to me: 'Corsica is a place where you can always hear a hullabaloo in every direction. You can't go and pick a rose without a rifle and several pistols in hand. You're usually forced to lie prone on the ground before daring to go down into your garden. You soon get used to it however.'

has become of you ? It's odd. I often look for your name in the papers, but I never see it. . .

MYSELF: There must be *some* shrinking violets. [*I notice on the mantelpiece an enormous Browning automatic conspicuously in view, very black against the white marble.*] Huh ! What's that for ?

CLEMENCEAU: What ?

MYSELF: That instrument over there.

CLEMENCEAU: Oh ! That, Martet, is simply because I don't allow anyone to stand in front of my car on the road with the idea of preventing my passing.

MYSELF: If he does, you fire on him ?

CLEMENCEAU: Rather !

MYSELF: But if it's a policeman ?

CLEMENCEAU: Specially if it's a policeman ! [*To the American*] I must tell you that I am a mixture of anarchist and conservative, in proportions which still remain to be determined. [*To both of us*] Sit down. [*We sit down. The American utters a few words in English. Then, suspecting that I do not understand, he changes over politely to French, which he speaks very well.*]

THE AMERICAN: But you look as if you were going on marvellously.

CLEMENCEAU: Yes. I have decided not to die this time: 86 years . . . My life would have been too short. I must be allowed a little more time. When I left Paris I was practically a goner. I had laryngitis with a kind of diabetic bronchitis. . . Now I look myself over — it's all right. I left the Vendée yesterday morning, and before leaving I made three appointments here for 3:0, 3:5 and 3:10. At seven minutes to three I was climbing these stairs. Not bad, eh, for a dead 'un ?

MYSELF: Then you are settled here ?

CLEMENCEAU: Yes. They're making a devil of a mess at

my place, tearing off the wallpaper and taking up the carpets. They tell me it was dirty. Was it dirty?

MYSELF: Yes, it was a little dirty.

CLEMENCEAU: Ugh! Then they're cleaning. I think that you are satisfied with our foreign policy?

MYSELF: Sir, I. . .

CLEMENCEAU: You have reason to be. M. Briand believes in peace, so that's all right. There *is* a man who believes in it perhaps a little less: I mean President Hindenburg.[2] Mark well what I'm telling you: in six months, in a year, five years, ten years, when they like, as they like, the Boches will invade us. I don't know if you recently saw in the *Journal* that extraordinary picture — it represented all the ministers in the park at Rambouillet, at a meeting of the Cabinet, frolicking with a swan. That picture reassured me. We are well defended.[3]

THE AMERICAN: And the Vendée? How is it there? Did you have good weather?

CLEMENCEAU: Yes, it rained all the time.

MYSELF: You love the rain.

CLEMENCEAU: I do. It is the one divinity which really does good. Thanks to the rain I now have in my garden, in front of my windows, plants as high as that [*indicating with his hands*] between myself and the sea. Ah! Martet, when I'm there, seated on my bench, I am happy.[4] [*To the American*]

[2] It was at the time of the Tannenburg speech.

[3] The silence of Clemenceau since 1920 was caused in large part by this hopeless pessimism. He wrote to me in 1922: 'We are marching to catastrophe so complete that it is impossible for me to find a way out of it. The worst of it is that these puppets who have brought us to this point are only in part responsible. They have given themselves away. The country has tolerated everything. Even today all it can do is to wring its hands. The defeat of Germany was crushing. You see how she rebounded. Amongst us I only see the lowest kind of ambition in the midst of a complete collapse into apathy. As far as I am concerned I am ready to act. But I should like to know if it is a question of having oneself sacrificed all alone for good government, or if it is possible to obtain a concentration of energies.'

[4] Clemenceau wrote to me from the Vendée on July 27, 1923: 'With my

CLEMENCEAU TELLS A STORY TO A FEW FRIENDS

Left to right: Clemenceau; M. Wormser, his former Chief-of-Cabinet; Martet, the Editor of *L'Illustration*

I must tell you that your Coolidge is an extraordinary specimen. You will have got on very well with your debts by the
time you have ruined us. You will be a little more alone in
the world than you are today. As for England. . .

THE AMERICAN: England will always be England !

CLEMENCEAU: I should think there are very good chances
of it ! As for Japan, it is useless to talk of her. If she could
only swallow you ! And then ? There was France. We
didn't hate you. We loved you rather. We are such a
funny people. When we find ourselves face to face with
people who allow us to live at all we always want to fling
ourselves on their necks. When we are no longer here what
will you do ? Towards whom will you turn ? But you get
angry with me when I say that.

THE AMERICAN: No. We are never angry with you. We
forgive you even when you haven't a very high opinion of us.
We have a very high opinion of you.

CLEMENCEAU: Yes, I know you. You applaud me, you
send me flowers, and when my back is turned. . . Oh, well,
there are a few good Americans, I suppose.

THE AMERICAN: Thank you.

MYSELF: What have you come to Paris for ?

CLEMENCEAU: Oh, a very sad business. I have come because of my sister.[5] She is seventy-seven years old and has
contracted a disease about which nothing can be done, and
she knows it. Which does not prevent her from writing
everybody letters as calm and serene as if she were as well

books, my flowers and the sea, I am in a very comfortable nook. I have not
budged from my window for a week.'

8th *August* 1925.

'I am in a bath of flowers and I am slogging away at animal psychology, now
watching my dog who is eating his leash (thereby showing his superiority to many
of us humans), now putting my own questions to shrimps and sardines, who make
no reply. . . The weather does not matter here. There is sunshine in my "soul,"
whatever happens. The proof is that at the prize distribution at the Saint-Vincent
school I made a speech which astonished myself even. I am discovering myself
every day.'

[5] Mlle. Adrienne Clemenceau.

as you or I. I've come to look up a nursing home for her.
I thought at first of the Sisters in the Rue Bizet,[6] but they told
me there: 'We only accept people for operations. But wait a
moment. We will ask the Mother Superior.' Then I left. I
went to the Rue Antoine Chantin, to Gosset's nursing
home. . . Chantin ?  Do you know anything about him,
Martet ?

MYSELF:  He is probably some great man or other.

CLEMENCEAU:  There are too many of them. One gets lost
amongst them.[7]  In a few days I shall go back to the Vendée.  Not for long, though. She has only a few months to
live . . . [*Sighs*] God deceives me !

MYSELF:  Fortunately you still have men left.

CLEMENCEAU:  Fortunately we still have men left.

[*Enter Albert*]

ALBERT:  There is a man here who would like to see you,
sir.  He says he is the son of M. Momus of Lourdes.

CLEMENCEAU:  M. Momus of Lourdes ?

ALBERT:  Yes, sir.

CLEMENCEAU:  Don't know him. I know one Momus: he
is the hero of the little rhymes. Maybe it's he. Martet, you've
been my secretary. Carry on as if you still were. See this
hero, squeeze the juice out of him and toss him away.

[*I go out. Albert says: 'I think he's off his head.' I come
face to face in the doorway with a man whose eyes burn with
alarming brilliance.*]

THE MAN:  M. Clemenceau ?

MYSELF:  He has just gone out.

THE MAN:  They told me he was here.

MYSELF:  They were wrong. What do you want of him ?

---

[6] It was here that M. Clemenceau had had an operation on the prostate gland.
[7] Clemenceau's little joke about the Parisian passion for naming streets for the
latest celebrity, major or minor.—*Translator's note.*

THE MAN: It is about a family affair. I have come to find him because I know he's got some 'pep.' I have my rights to vindicate. I also have 'pep,' and I have a Browning in my pocket with six bullets in it.

MYSELF: I might have suspected it. If you have anything to communicate to M. Clemenceau, write me a note. I will consider it, I will speak to M. Clemenceau about it, and if he judges that he ought to and can interfere, he will do so.

THE MAN: There's a good deal of 'if' in all this.

MYSELF: I can't do any more than that.

THE MAN: What's your name?

MYSELF: Martet.

[*He writes the name on a newspaper which he takes from his pocket, and offers me his left hand; his right hand is bandaged. I push him gently towards the door.*]

THE MAN: I should have preferred to see M. Clemenceau.

MYSELF: Write to me. It's the same thing.

THE MAN: So you say. [*He goes out.*]

MYSELF [*to Albert*]: Who is the American?

ALBERT: He is Colonel Bonsal, who accompanied us during our visit to America.[8]

[*I go back into the room.*]

CLEMENCEAU: Well?

MYSELF: It's a man who asserts that he has rights to vindicate. . .

CLEMENCEAU: Oh! I'm not so keen about that. . .

MYSELF: . . . and has a Browning with six bullets in his pocket.

THE AMERICAN: Oh!

CLEMENCEAU [*who has seen others like that*]: Good! Would you like me to tell you about my last love affair?

THE AMERICAN: Not the last: the most recent.

CLEMENCEAU: Yes, but I don't like to boast. I was in the

[8] In 1922.

Vendée with two or three young women who had come to see me. . .

THE AMERICAN: That's quite a habit of yours, isn't it ?

CLEMENCEAU [*to me*]: You know one of them — little Bensa.[9] One day, taking advantage of the fact that I had gone for a walk, and seeing on what terms of familiarity we were, little Bensa and I, another young woman undertook to question her on what I did and what I was. I came up from behind without making any noise and said, 'There's one further bit of information which Mme. Bensa would not be able to give you — when I am in bed I always kick.'

THE AMERICAN [*smiling*]: A detail to chronicle for History.

CLEMENCEAU: And can you also guess who has arrived in the Vendée ? I had a visit from Mandel !

MYSELF: It isn't possible !

CLEMENCEAU: That surprises you ? You find that Mandel appears rarely in my life ?[10] He stayed an hour. He talked to me about heaps of things which I didn't catch very well. Then it occurred to me that I hadn't asked him to lunch.

MYSELF: Oh, and poor Florand ! You took very bad care of him.

CLEMENCEAU: Ah ! Yes, poor old Florand ! A bit dull perhaps. Florand probably was not . . . a very . . . an extraordinarily good doctor. They think a lot of themselves. . . But what a nice fellow !

One day he gave me a drug to swallow. I asked him, 'What's in it ?' He answered, 'My word of honour, I haven't the least idea.' I therefore took the stuff on his word of honour. It did me good. Why not ?

MYSELF: You have not yet entrusted me with any commission for M. Poincaré.

---

[9] M. Clemenceau's goddaughter.
[10] Pure irony. The reproach has often been brought against M. Clemenceau that Mandel — with whom not everyone sympathized — did not appear 'rarely' enough in his life.

CLEMENCEAU: Yes. Tell him this. When I made the Peace I asked Wilson for the left bank of the Rhine. A little fiction to keep Foch happy.[11] He refused to give it to me. He said, 'I am going to give you something much more useful than that: an agreement to come to your help in case of aggression. Naturally with the reservation that Congress consents.' But congress said no. [*With a gesture.*] That was the end. It was necessary to begin all over again! They preferred to agree to everything.

MYSELF: But why didn't you tell all this yourself, sir?

CLEMENCEAU: Oh, Monsieur Martet! I have the habit of speaking only when there are ears to hear me.

[11] *Histoire de faire plaisir au Foch* in the original. — *Translator's note.*

# V

## THE AMERICAN LEGIONAIRES

THE newspapers announce that Clemenceau received a delegation from the American Legion this morning. The American Legionaires have been in France for some time. Yesterday, the 22nd, at the instance of Mr. A. Piatt Andrew, the Committee of Resolutions placed before the Convention the following motion, which was carried unanimously:

'The Convention of the American Legion, having learnt of the arrival in Paris of the man who was Prime Minister of France at the time when we ranged ourselves on the side of the Allies, sends to M. Georges Clemenceau its fraternal greetings and assures him that the memory of the great part he played in the victory has remained vividly in the minds of the Legionaires. The latter send him their best wishes for his health and prosperity.'

This morning at 10 o'clock a delegation proceeded to the Avenue de Messine. It was led by General Pershing and Messrs. Savage and Piatt Andrew. Colonel Stephen Bonsal presented the delegates to Clemenceau. Friendly words were exchanged. Then General Giguilliat, Superintendent of the Military Academy at Culver (Indiana), offered Clemenceau a little set of shelves upon which were arranged thirteen volumes, specially printed for the purpose under the editorship of the University (of Paris). Thirteen volumes, amongst which were: *The Life of John Marshall,* by Albert Beveridge, *Jefferson and Hamilton,* by Claude G. Bowers, etc. All the great Americans.

After which the Legionaires, drawn up on the pavement of the Avenue de Messine, cheered lustily — Clemenceau has shown himself on Piétri's balcony, has thanked them with a wave of his hand. They are good friends.

Pershing makes a speech: 'Always the same! Always young!' Clemenceau glances at Pershing and murmurs: 'I wonder how old he thinks I am, anyway!'

# VI

## From Cécile Sorel to Cottin

I RETURN to see Clemenceau with my wife; he is still at Piétri's. Albert shows us into the drawing-room. On the divan is the charming little set of shelves presented by the American Legionaires. On a three-legged table is a bouquet of enormous and gorgeous chrysanthemums.

ALBERT [*showing me the flowers*]: They are from Cécile Sorel. Monsieur thanked her in a letter in which he said, 'Thanks for the wonderful flowers with which it has pleased you to humiliate my old age.'

MYSELF: Is he doing well now ?

ALBERT: Very well. He has entirely recovered. He is working.

MYSELF: And the Vendée ?

ALBERT: The garden is splendid. There are flowers everywhere. Unfortunately it's an old shanty, you know; the rooms let in water and everything is rotting.

MYSELF: Do many people come to see Clemenceau both in the Vendée and here ?

ALBERT: Very few, sir, very few. [*He goes out. Five minutes elapse. Clemenceau enters, looks at my wife.*]

CLEMENCEAU: Ah ! Well, well ! How nice you look — like someone whose body and soul are in excellent state.

28

MY WIFE: My husband says that I haven't got a soul.

CLEMENCEAU: That's very exaggerated. Come this way. [*He makes us lead the way into his bedroom.*]

MY WIFE: How nice it is here !

CLEMENCEAU: It's all right. All my life I have been pretty lucky. Sit down. But not on that sofa — it's a little hard. Piétri has plenty of good qualities, but really you do wear out your backside on his sofas. Sit here. That's it. Are you all right ?

MY WIFE: Very well, thank you.

CLEMENCEAU: You have to get a move on in this world in order to get your share of comfort. You don't know if you'll be able to get it in the next one. The data are missing.

MYSELF: How are you, sir ?

CLEMENCEAU: Normal. I went to bed yesterday at nine o'clock. I got up at four and began to work. It's going well — I'm satisfied. You know, when the phrases hang together neatly it is because your blood is circulating as it ought. But it's odd — I don't care.

MYSELF: About what ?

CLEMENCEAU: About living. They might say to me, 'You're still good for twenty-five years,' and I've no idea how I should take it. I have seen everything, Martet ! All that passes before my eyes at this moment is only a series of depressing repetitions.

MYSELF: I used to believe that no one man resembled another. . .

CLEMENCEAU: Perhaps, when you take the trouble to look at them. But men don't amuse me any more. I find that they attach an exaggerated importance to themselves. It's like those people who consecrate their entire lives to making a collection of beetles. They end up by never seeing anything in the world but beetles. There should be something else, all the same.

MY WIFE: But what's left, then ?

CLEMENCEAU:  Nothingness, dear lady.

MY WIFE:  Do you believe that in the long run Paradise. . .

CLEMENCEAU:  Oh, Paradise is not nothingness.  I don't know who had the first idea of Paradise.  He must have found life too short, that fellow.  Happy man !  He wanted it to go on with a less stupid government and with more amusing diversions. . . Nothingness is really superior to Paradise.  Paradise is an improvement — Nothingness is perfection.[1]  With nothingness everything arranges itself perfectly.  I am seeing my poor sister. . .

MYSELF:  How is she ?

CLEMENCEAU:  As one is when one is done for and knows it and is suffering.  The saddest thing is that she still has months of it to bear.  This morning I went to see her with my brother Albert.  On leaving I said to her, 'I am going to shake hands with Gosset now, and then I will come up again to say good-bye to you.'  She answered, 'It's no good coming back again: you might have to tell me lies.'  I didn't answer — what was there to say ?  I didn't go back. . . Of us all she was my father's favourite.  I was very fond of her. Nevertheless she is associated with a very disagreeable date in my life.  They sent me to school when she made her first appearance in the world.  Until then it was my mother who taught me my lessons.

MYSELF:  Are you working ?

CLEMENCEAU:  Yes, Monsieur Martet.  I am preparing a new edition of the *Démosthène* which will be illustrated by

---

[1] Clemenceau wrote to me once: 'I will not try to hide from you that the state in which one would seem to me the most likely to be happy is the vegetable, if it were not for the cruel ferocity of the browsing animals to the dandelions.  I should vote therefore at the final reckoning for the mineral state, if it was not always in danger of finding itself threatened by the first mishap of the sun.  I shall therefore turn my desire to the atomic state which, according to Henri Poincaré, is a hole in the ether; consider me therefore henceforward fixed.  As it is not forbidden for two holes to get together I hope to meet you in the next catastrophe, which cannot be long delayed.'

Bourdelle.[2] Bourdelle is an odd sort, eh! He didn't do it badly. One of his stunts turned out pretty well. It is true, of course, that he did it according to my instructions. It is the one where Demosthenes is leaning his head against a column and looking at Attica, like this . . . simply. . .

MYSELF: What a funny idea to have a book illustrated by a sculptor!

CLEMENCEAU: He is making a kind of small bas-relief, and afterwards the engravings will be cut. The idea sounds a bit revolutionary, but that doesn't mean that it's stupid.

MYSELF: And what about *Au Soir de la Pensée*?

CLEMENCEAU: Ah! [*Rummages amongst his papers and hands me a letter from M. Gruber, 'not the brewer' but the former German professor at Lyons.*] This fellow Gruber claims that *deus* is not a brother of Theos. I want to answer that and tick off Gruber. Unfortunately I have only too much to say . . . would you answer it for me?

MYSELF: Me? But I don't know anything about it.

CLEMENCEAU: All the more reason. That's what's wanted. At least you have a little sense.

MYSELF: Humph!

CLEMENCEAU: At any rate you have got as much as a professor, haven't you?

MYSELF: In what way do you want me to answer him?

CLEMENCEAU: In whatever way you like. The important thing is to get rid of him. I have such a horror of all these people. Because in a moment of intoxication someone flung a diploma at them. . . Will you do it?

MYSELF: All right.

CLEMENCEAU: Do you know there are still people who write to me? Oh, not many, perhaps three or four, when it rains. . .

MYSELF: There is no reason why anyone should write to

2 The sculptor.

you or think of you any longer. You saved France — but that was ten years ago !

CLEMENCEAU: That is indeed obvious. I am not complaining . . . what could they say to me in fact, the poor things ? No one has anything to say. All the same there is a woman who wrote to me: 'I am very Catholic but I have your photograph hanging up in my house.' It's very decent of her, what ? Those who touch me the most are those who don't sign their letters. They don't want anything. There are others who sign and who ask me for heaps of things — ribbons and gold lace. But I look 'round in vain. I don't see anyone I could recommend for them. I don't know anyone any more. At times it's frightening. Frightening like the desert — and marvellously delightful, like the solitude of high peaks. Those who haven't left me I've eliminated, gently pushing them by the shoulders and making them understand that . . . no . . . it wasn't . . . wasn't any longer the same thing . . . that I'm no longer on their planet. . . They understood. They left very gracefully.

MYSELF: Don't you ever see your former ministers even ?

CLEMENCEAU: I'm going to tell you something interesting, Martet. I should be hard put to it to say who were my ministers and who weren't. There are those who come to see me from time to time . . . or who write to me. I look at them or I look at their signatures. I ask myself, 'Wasn't he minister for something or other in my Cabinet, that fellow ?' Hold on ! There is one . . . do you remember that chap who had a nose like this ?

MYSELF: A nose like that ?

CLEMENCEAU: A nose in the air. . . I've never seen a nose so much in the air. . .

MYSELF: Albert Favre ?

CLEMENCEAU: Yes. What was Albert Favre ?

MYSELF: Under-Secretary of State for Internal Affairs.

CLEMENCEAU: Do you mean to tell me that he had anything to do with Internal Affairs, the poor fellow? And will you also tell me why I chose Albert Favre? It must be another of Mandel's doings. He brought around a lot of people like that. . . The funniest thing about it is that Albert Favre was a member of the opposition before entering my Cabinet; once in, he remained a member of the opposition. He had it in his blood. Pams . . . the man who was at the Ministry of Justice and who was run over: Nail . . . Pichon . . . Nice fellows! They had only one fault: they were too decent. They weren't made for war: things are different when you're looking into the jaws of the Boche.

MY WIFE: Monsieur, do you think we shall always have war?

CLEMENCEAU: I can't say, dear lady. Perhaps there will come a day when the peoples will come together in a fraternal embrace to the sound of the flute, when, alone amongst all things who are born, live, and die, man will live out his allotted time in peace. It isn't probable; it's possible. Only, the question is not whether we shall never again have war and whether in a more or less distant future all this or that will come to pass. . . It is — to know whether between today and tomorrow we can have confidence in the people who up to now have done nothing but lie to us. Suppose Pierre has stuck a knife into my back. He says today, 'I'll never do it again.' Ought I then to give him back his knife or ought I rather to buy a revolver?

MY WIFE: Well, it's a nice lookout.

CLEMENCEAU: What do you want me to do? I can understand that it worries you. Think of something else. Do as I do: go to the Vendée and look at the waves.

MYSELF: Are you returning to Saint-Vincent soon?

CLEMENCEAU: On Tuesday or Wednesday.

MYSELF: By road?

CLEMENCEAU: Naturally! [*To my wife*] He puts such stupid questions, your husband. Have I a head to catch a train? I detested M. Thiers fervently, and the sentiment was quite mutual. But we agreed on one thing: we couldn't bear railways. I shall be back in a fortnight; I've an appointment with some Americans. I want to talk to them about the debts. They irritate me with their debts. There are several things which ought to be said to them. I shall say them.

[*Albert Enters.*]

ALBERT [*announcing*]: M. Thiébault-Sisson.[3]

CLEMENCEAU: Show him into the drawing-room. [*Albert goes out.*] He is charming, Thiébault-Sisson. Just think: he has read *Au Soir de la Pensée*. He wants me to write my name in the book. He wrote me in verse. . .

MYSELF: No! Why?

CLEMENCEAU: Because he loves me. When one loves, one writes in verse. Martet, I must tell you that this morning while having my breakfast I took stock of myself. And I realized that I am not annoyed any longer with anybody.

MYSELF: H'm!

CLEMENCEAU: Yes, Martet. It is true. I still have little fits of anger now and then, but they do not really come from the depths of my soul. There is nothing left in me essentially but peace and forgetfulness. Briand, Poincaré . . . René Renoult[4] . . . all those fellows are fading away into pale shadows. In that way the *Soir de la Pensée* has done me a lot of good. It has forced me to climb and see other worlds. Looked at from Vega in the Lyra constellation, the greatest of our statesmen do not seem to deserve so much hate. [*To my wife*] Do you happen to need a dog?

[3] The *Temps* art critic.
[4] A Senator. Formerly Minister for Justice.

MY WIFE: Thank you, monsieur. I already have a husband and a daughter.

CLEMENCEAU: Yes, that is a good deal. But I don't know what to do with my Aberdeen, now that my flat in the Rue Franklin has been redecorated. These animals have a magnificent contempt for anything like carpets, divans, sofas. . .

MYSELF: And the legs of beds. You once gave me one: and in no time at all he had devoured the two front legs of our bed. We were compelled to pass him on to a friend.

CLEMENCEAU: You ought to have waited until he absorbed the two hind legs: that would have restored your bed to an even keel.

MYSELF: After *Au Soir de la Pensée* what are you going to do next ?

CLEMENCEAU [*with a wink*]: I have an idea !

MYSELF: I know what it is. You remember that you wanted to visit the coast of Asia Minor ?

CLEMENCEAU: Yes, I gave that up. I have something much better in mind.

[*Albert comes back again.*]

ALBERT: M. Thiébault-Sisson is getting impatient. He has a train to catch.          [*I make a move to get up.*]

CLEMENCEAU: Will you kindly stay where you are ! I forbid you to move ! [*He goes out, goes to Thiébault-Sisson, who is waiting in the entrance, and comes back with a copy of 'Au Soir de la Pensée' wrapped and tied. I remove the string and paper: he scrawls some words on the delicate blue cover. He goes out and reappears an instant afterwards.*

*We go on talking — about a fellow who is called Marin . . . Maurin . . . Maurois ! and who has written several volumes that are 'thoroughly amusing' about the English — and about Fleury's book on the private life of Louis XV. . .*

CLEMENCEAU: Ah ! That Louis XV ! To think that we had that ! That we stood for that !

[. . . *of Versailles and the little staircase which goes from the apartments of Louis XV to those of the Dubarry. . .* ]

CLEMENCEAU: It is at the bottom of that staircase that Damiens made a pass at Louis XV with his knife. I have seen that knife. It is in the Archives. It is a little gadget about as big as this. They put the poor lunatic through the most horrible tortures. . . And those little girls whom they brought to Louis XV that he might amuse himself with them! Louis XIV had more of a way with him all the same . . . and he supported Molière.

[*Albert brings in a card.*]

CLEMENCEAU [*glancing at it*]: Mme. Pezon? I know who it is. Put her in the drawing-room.

[*We get up. He accompanies us. Whilst crossing the salon Clemenceau says to Mme. Pezon:*]

CLEMENCEAU: I should never have known you. You have become a fat matron.

MME. PEZON [*with a smile which is touching and a little sad*]: I should have recognized you. You haven't changed.

CLEMENCEAU: They have been telling me that for fifty years, my dear. [*To my wife*]: Au 'voir. Thanks for coming to see somebody who cannot even change any more. [*To me*] Au 'voir. My regards to Cottin.

I TAKE this last word away with me — Cottin. At home I turn the pages of this already old dossier. . . Clemenceau still carries the bullet in the mediastinum, and from time to time it draws a dry little cough from him. But except for him who else remembers? Who else remembers that eight years ago a man wanted to punish him for having tried to save France? He himself even does not remember except to make a joke of it. . . 'Regards to Cottin!'

The first act took place on Wednesday, the 19th of February 1919. At that moment Clemenceau, seated between England and the United States, having Germany face to face with him, was engaged in painfully hammering out the peace.

That morning, then, he left the Rue Franklin at about nine o'clock on his way to the Rue Saint-Dominique and the Ministry of War. He was in his car, unaccompanied, but on the front seat was a military chauffeur and a footman. The car had just turned the corner of the Rue Franklin and was entering the Boulevard Delessert when a man who had kept himself hidden in a public urinal leapt out, took a step towards the car, which had slowed down in order to turn, and fired a first bullet through the carriage door.

It was Cottin.

The chauffeur had accelerated and the man soon had nothing but the back of the car as a target. He continued to fire —clack, clack—I don't know how many bullets, three or four, which passed over the car from rear to front and went out through the windscreen.

The car was hastening towards the Trocadéro when Clemenceau, who knew himself to be wounded, rapped on the window and the chauffeur made a half swing and returned to the Rue Franklin.

An officer from the Aviation Headquarters in the Boulevard Delessert, who was passing at the moment, leapt on the running board, opened the right-hand door and entered the car. Clemenceau said to him: 'He was a bad shot!'

Arrived in front of No. 8 Rue Franklin, the car stopped. Supported by the chauffeur and the officer, Clemenceau got down, crossed the courtyard, and, as the chauffeur made an awkward movement, said: 'Look out! You're hurting me.'

In the meantime the passers-by had thrown themselves on Cottin who, seeing himself surrounded, threw away his revolver and put up his hands. Two policemen secured him. The crowd nearly lynched him and attacked the policemen who were trying to protect him. He was taken to the police station of the Mairie of the 16th arrondissement in the Avenue Henri Martin.

First aid was given to Clemenceau by his valet. Gosset arrived at ten minutes past nine, followed by Tuffier. At 11:30 a first bulletin was issued, signed by Tuffier, Gosset and Laubry: 'A deep wound in the posterior portion of the right shoulder blade with no vital injury. General and local condition excellent.'

Then all Paris flocked together: M. Poincaré, Marshal Foch, all the ministers, etc.

When I arrived in the Rue Saint-Dominique they told me the news, 'Clemenceau is wounded!' I jumped into a car and arrived at the Rue Franklin, where I found Clemenceau seated, his face yellow and shrivelled; he said to me: 'It is the one sensation which I hadn't yet had. I had never yet been assassinated.'

The morning passed. Telephone calls . . . telegrams. . . Sarah Bernhardt got me to take him this little message written on her own monogrammed card: 'I beg you, let me have some news of you. It is for me! For me alone! Thanks with all my heart!'

Towards one o'clock Clemenceau was seized with a slight hæmoptysis which, as the bulletin published on the following day said, 'indicates that the bullet has entered the lung.' The wounded man underwent a radioscopic and radiographic examination, and the bullet was discovered in the mediastinum . . . His temperature was normal. I did not answer Sarah Bernhardt, and she wrote me again, 'Will you please forgive me, but I so much want to have news; I feel myself utterly unnerved by the rumours. Just now Clemenceau is France. I have always loved him, and since this war I devoutly worship him. . .' [5]

[5] The great actors have always had a lyrical admiration for Clemenceau. Lucien

CLEMENCEAU ARRIVING AT THE CHAMBER OF DEPUTIES
TO DEFEND HIS POLICIES

The next day, the 20th of February, it was learnt that Cottin had been handed over to the military authorities. The prosecution was assigned to Captain Bouchardon. Cottin, who had been incarcerated at the Santé, entrusted his defence to Me. Oscar Bloch, the former defender of Hélène Brion, the pacifist propagandist. Clemenceau, whose temperature and pulse remained normal, joked with his physicians, shook his head at their diagnoses, examined with the corner of his eye Dr. Paul, the expert in medical jurisprudence, who declared before the X-ray examination that the bullet, of which no trace had yet been found, had entered the flesh, struck the shoulder blade, glanced off and gone out by the same hole. . . Clemenceau had already begun to get the better of Cottin's bullet.

And so, on the 27th February, eight days after the assault, Clemenceau, with the bullet in his mediastinum, resumed his place as President of the Committee of the Great Powers at the Peace Conference.

On the 14th March Cottin appeared before the Third Military Tribunal of Paris and was unanimously condemned to death. On the 8th April the newspapers published this paragraph:

'The President of the Council and Minister for War has today submitted a report to the President of the Republic which, after recalling the circumstances of Cottin's crime, continued as follows: "The members of the court martial having signed no recommendation to mercy, the Government Commissioner and the Military Governor of Paris are of the opinion that justice should take its course. But the President of the Council and Minister for War has appealed to the head of the State for clemency on behalf of the condemned.

Guitry wrote to him on November 18th: 'I am sending you a flag which was used on Gambetta's gun-carriage and at the lying-in-state of Victor Hugo at the Arc de Triomphe. It will be so suitable at your window. Mr. President, we owe our France to you — just that — and with heartfelt respect I greet you.'

In consequence he recommends that the death penalty pronounced on Cottin should be commuted to ten years solitary confinement." Accordingly the President of the Republic has signed a decree for the commutation of the sentence.'

Three years pass. On the 31st January 1922, Me. Oscar Bloch writes to Clemenceau,

MONSIEUR LE PRÉSIDENT:

You were kind enough three years ago to associate yourself with my efforts to obtain a commutation of sentence for my client Emile Cottin, who was condemned to death for his attempt to assassinate you. I should like once more to express my gratitude, at the same time making a fresh appeal to your generosity. Cottin is serving his ten years at Melun; his conduct leaves nothing to be desired, according to the information that I have gathered on the spot. But his health, which has always been poor, has been greatly undermined by his imprisonment; his unhappy parents, now very old people, are longing to see him again and are greatly in need of his material as well as moral aid.

You will not refuse us your intervention, Monsieur le Président ? It will be of enormous assistance to us in the appeal for mercy which we have submitted to the President of the Republic, and will serve at the least to obtain a commutation from solitary confinement to ordinary imprisonment and reinstatement to civil status.

You will appreciate better than I what would be the most efficacious form of appeal, but if you will be so good as to send me a letter written in this spirit I should be very happy to be able to add it to my documents.

In conclusion, allow me to tell you how much I dare to count on your affirmative response: you have defended anarchists guilty of political crimes too eloquently with pen and word not to make allowances for my client, whose youth

**moreover** might be pleaded in his favour. Do you remember the compassionate words which you were kind enough to addressto his mother in my presence: politics should give way to humanity ?

If you would be so good as to grant me an audience I would gladly supply you with all the information you might desire.

Believe me, Monsieur le Président, etc., etc.

OSCAR BLOCH

'Martet,' says Clemenceau to me, showing me this letter, 'if you ever kill anybody don't hire this Bloch to defend you. He hasn't got the right words. . . "Cottin's conduct leaves nothing to be desired." Maybe they've taken away his gun. "His parents are in need of his *moral* aid." Where next will morality build its nest ? "Politics should give way to humanity." It seems that in exposing myself to Cottin's bullet I was playing politics.'

Cottin stayed in prison.

But not for long.

On the 12th of July 1924 the Chamber was discussing the question of a legal amnesty. M. André Marty [6] mounted the rostrum and asked, 'Will the Minister for Justice inform us what is the condition of Cottin, who is at Melun. I beg you to make a demonstration in favour of his release from prison. If I allow myself to be insistent on this subject, it is because the assassin of Jaurés [7] is free, and it is hard for the proletariat to understand why the man who only wounded M. Clemenceau still remains in prison, especially since he has already been there five years.'

Applause from the Left and the Extreme Left.

M. Maurice Viollette, who brought forward the bill, said:

---

[6] A Communist deputy.

[7] It will be remembered that Jaurés was assassinated on the eve of the outbreak of war by a man named Vilain, who was brought before the Assize Court and acquitted.

'It is a matter for the Government to decide whether in inter-
preting the amnesty law, as the Chamber asks it to do, it
would not be wise to take into consideration the amount of
time that the prisoners have already served, and whether it
would be compatible with certain natural sentiments of
humanity, etc.'

Then M. René Renoult, the Keeper of the Seals, Minister
for Justice,[8] said:

'I undertake to examine *in a most sympathetic spirit,* the
individual cases [9] which have been quoted.'

Then, when M. Ernest Lafont pressed him on the point: 'I
am convinced that the Government will keep the promise
which it has just made and carry it out in circumstances where
the long detention of the prisoners who have been mentioned. . .'

M. RENÉ RENOULT: 'I said *"a most sympathetic spirit."* '

And the *Officiel's* report ends abruptly: 'M. le Président:
"No one else wishes to speak ?" '

No one !

On the 22nd of August 1924 the newspapers announced:
'Cottin was set free yesterday.'

It was all quite meaningless. Four and a half years in
prison for having tried to kill the man who had saved his
country.

----

[8] On November 16, 1919, M. René Renoult had been defeated at the Parliamentary elections. M. Clemenceau made it possible for him to return to political
life by giving him his seat as senator for the Var, which elected M. René Renoult
on January 11th of the next year.

[9] There had been mention of a certain number of other individuals sentenced
for various crimes.

# VII

## ON THE ROAD

*6th October* 1927

THE newspapers say:

'Yesterday, at five o'clock in the morning, just as day was breaking, M. Clemenceau left Paris by car for the Vendée. He wore a voluminous ulster and a grey cap. He seated himself in the car, Albert climbed up by the side of Brabant, and off they went.'

At three o'clock in the afternoon M. Clemenceau was at Bel-Ebat, 'happy to be back in his long low house with its gleaming white walls, its gable surmounted by a weathercock, . .' etc.

# VIII

## 'I Am With Hammurabi'

*23rd October* 1927

I RECEIVE a letter from Clemenceau:

*Paris,* 17*th October* 1927

MY DEAR BOY,

Come along and see me one day and exchange a few profound thoughts:

1. On the etymology of Theos-deus.
2. On two polishers[1] which have been found on a large
stone near my village.

Ever yours,
G. CLEMENCEAU

I go to see him in the Rue Franklin. The flat has been
completely redecorated. Wilton carpets and expensive wall-
papers. I enter his room.

---

[1] For several years M. Clemenceau had taken a keen interest in palæolithic
and neolithic studies. He wrote to me on August 8th, 1925: 'Thank you for
your letter painting the joys of your archæology. I am delighted to tell you that
my joys are just as great, for during a walk in Jeanneney's garden (Jeanneney was
a Senator) near Vesoul, amongst the coarse gravel I made a unique find: a stone
hollowed out into a cup, undoubtedly by the hand of man. I invite you to come
and view it at the beginning of October. We can easily find out where the gravel
came from. I am sure there will be other finds to make.' It is superfluous to add
that there was no trace of man's handiwork on the stone in question.

CLEMENCEAU: Hullo there! What has become of you? Have you turned Poincarist by any chance?

[*I put in front of him on the open book which he has been reading a neolithic 'scraper' of flint which I found in the fields.*]

CLEMENCEAU [*extremely interested*]: Hold on. Don't say a word. [*He takes the object, turns it round and round in a sort of fierce, enraptured curiosity.*] What in the world is this knick-knack? It isn't what Captan[2] calls a slinging stone, is it?

MYSELF: It is a sort of scraper, a lovely little scraper.

CLEMENCEAU: So it scrapes, does it, this little gadget?

MYSELF: It is with that sort of thing that our ancestors made their knives, their cutting tools. . .

CLEMENCEAU: You don't say so! You do discover the most admirable things! How do you do it? Just by stooping down! Well, just think, in the Vendée I found a kind of dolmen with traces of cuttings, grooves. . . I wonder if that wasn't a polisher's tool. Tell me, what is a polisher?

MYSELF: You know as well as I do. It is a stone on which axes are ground. . .

CLEMENCEAU: Are there any grooves in it?

MYSELF: Yes, there are. Grooves of different lengths and different widths, according to the shape and thickness of the axes, or the work which they were meant to do, etc.

CLEMENCEAU: That's it then! I have found a polisher and I'm rather proud of it! Can these things be seen in the museums?

MYSELF: There are some at Saint-Germain.[3]

CLEMENCEAU: Will you take me to Saint-Germain? Who is the curator out there?

MYSELF: M. Salomon Reinach.

[2] A specialist in the prehistoric period.
[3] In the Musée Archéologique.

CLEMENCEAU: What, in the name of the God of Abraham, the Glozel man ? What a colossal joke ! With their bricks on which they amused themselves playing at noughts and crosses. . . How the scholars plunged in ! There is nothing in the world more ludicrous than a scholar !

MYSELF: There is one who plunged a little less than the others: Jullian [4]. . .

CLEMENCEAU: Not at all ! Not at all ! He plunged like all the rest. They all plunged. Reinach saw in them palæolithic historical records; Jullian saw witches' spells. It's all the same humbug.

MYSELF: Jullian is so much more subtle, so much more intelligent.

CLEMENCEAU: I know. You have a weakness for Jullian. One day you took me to his lecture in that dungeon at the Collège de France. I listened to him. He said various things — quite nice — he is a poet. But you don't know what he has done in the meantime. He has just written me a letter telling me that I ought to go and hear Father Sanson [5] preach. . . Really. . . Do you ever read the papers, Martet ?

MYSELF: Well, it happens now and then. . .

CLEMENCEAU: And the news that you get out of them fills you with joy, no doubt . . . what ? Rather nice what they're doing, isn't it ? Politics in France today is a great game. [*With a shrug of the shoulders.*] Oh, yes, I know. Our folly does not date from our own time. There was already a germ of it in the mad schemes of Louis XIV. . . How dreary it all is ! And the elections ? [6] Are they going to let them go on like that ? Isn't anyone going to say what ought to be said ?

MYSELF: They are waiting for you to say it.

[4] Camille Jullian and Salomon Reinach have both written a great deal about the famous Glozel discoveries.
[5] A fashionable preacher.
[6] The legislative elections of May 1928.

CLEMENCEAU: Me? Just now I am with Hammurabi, who was a man in every way to be recommended and whom I have unfortunately neglected too much up to now. What I say about him in *Au Soir de la Pensée* should be carried further. I am doing it. Do you see? It's not making decisions that requires intelligence. There are heaps of people about who are making heaps of decisions — it's seeing them through. I have decided to keep quiet. Still, it will only begin to be interesting if I really do keep quiet.[7]

MYSELF: But France?

CLEMENCEAU: If she does not understand my silence she is no more likely to understand my words. Besides, it is at least as necessary that I follow up the sun and Vega. I said in *Au Soir de la Pensée* that the sun was moving in the direction of Vega. A man wrote to me: 'In my time they taught that it was moving towards Hercules. . .' The Vega theory is the result of more mature calculations, I shall answer him.

MYSELF: How's your sister getting on?

CLEMENCEAU: It's frightful. There's simply nothing to do but wait. They are giving her hypodermics, two every evening. Her hand and arm are swollen. I hope it'll soon be over.

MYSELF: When did you return from the Vendée?

CLEMENCEAU: Sunday. At Gosset's there were crucifixes everywhere. They are amusing with their 'good Gods.' God, God. Can you stick God up on a wall? One day you will see me becoming a believer just to show you how God ought to be loved. And Bolshevism, how is that getting on? Progressing nicely?

MYSELF: And Germany?

CLEMENCEAU: Germany is coming back. Doesn't anyone

[7] He changed his mind in April 1929, in order to answer Foch's attacks.

see what is going to happen ? Isn't anyone afraid ? Everybody is sitting about quite comfortably. Well, Martet, there it is.

[*I get up. Clemenceau accompanies me to the door.*]

CLEMENCEAU [*on the threshold*]: I am beginning to regret 1918. It was idiotic, mad, but there was something . . . a little . . . magnificent about it. The times we are now living in are base.

# IX

## The Anniversary

On the 6th of November 1918, Vervins and Rethel were retaken from the enemy.

On the 8th the German delegates arrived at Foch's headquarters. The terms of the Armistice were read to them.

On the 9th William II abdicated. The English entered Maubeuge.

On the 11th Paris went mad! At 9 o'clock there was a terrific mob in front of the Chamber of Deputies. At 11 o'clock the guns of the Air Defence began to fire. France closed her eyes in an ecstasy of happiness.

At half-past two the Chamber began its session. Vague legal proposals were being discussed. At 3 o'clock a recess was taken. The sitting was resumed at four.

M. Deschanel suddenly recognized the President of the Council, and M. Clemenceau arose: a deafening uproar shook the room.

M. Clemenceau: I am going to read you the official text of the Armistice which was signed this morning at 5 o'clock by Marshal Foch, Admiral Wemyss and the German plenipotentiaries. This document runs as follows:

'Germany evacuates Belgium and all the invaded portions of France; she evacuates Alsace-Lorraine; she surrenders 5000 pieces of artillery, 25,000 machine guns, 1700 æroplanes; the Allies occupy Mainz, Cologne, Coblenz; Germany will give back all her prisoners of war without exchange; she will deliver up to the Allies all her submarines, six battleships, ten cruisers, fifty destroyers, etc., etc.'

Frenzied cheers !

He gets down slowly from the rostrum: he seems to be bowed down under the weight of events. They throw themselves on him. They fling their arms about one another's shoulders and yell through tears: 'Victory ! Victory !'

M. DESCHANEL: 'Here at last is the blessed hour for which we have lived for forty-seven years,' etc.

M. ALBERT THOMAS [1] cries out: 'We ask that the deputies from Alsace-Lorraine who are present in this room receive the honours of the session.' Everybody turns towards the rostra: the Abbé Wetterlé and Weil are there. They advance to the first row, and suddenly there sweeps upon them from left and right the Marseillaise ! . . . and whoever heard this Marseillaise has touched the heights of human grandeur.

On leaving the Chamber Clemenceau went to the senate. None of us dared to say a word to him.

Then he returned to the Rue Saint-Dominique.

People pressed into the courtyard and called out: 'Clemenceau ! Clemenceau !' He opened the window, looked at them for a moment and raised his arms, calling out 'Vive la France !'

He then shut the window and without seeing any of the ministers or generals who were waiting for a word from him he sat down on a little rep sofa and sank into meditation.

That evening he found this letter on his little table in the Rue Franklin:

[1] A Socialist Deputy.

ARMISTICE DAY, PARIS, 11 NOVEMBER 1918

*11th November* 1918

MR. PRESIDENT,

In your vast glory so well deserved, blessed as you are by our country and all the future ages of immortal France, please allow an enthusiastic heart which has always been faithful to your tremendous and inspired genius to convey to you its unutterable emotion.

France and the world acclaim you: the victory and your name are inseparable; you, so human, will be elevated to a place among the gods — I should not try to express to you on such a day my timid and boundless admiration if I did not remember very strongly the 2nd August 1914, when I saw you in your garden, by the side of the Tricolour, when your anxiety, your faith, the fire of those heights which burned in you always, caused us to burst into tears.

'I embraced you on that day, Mr. President, as a grateful France would like to do today. With the same impulse all my heart goes out to your modest and everlasting greatness.'

ANNA DE NOAILLES

AND NINE years later. . .

I take the Passy Métro. At the Pasteur station a couple of retired middle-class folk get in: they are M. and Mme. Pichon. M. Pichon carries on the lapel of his overcoat a little copper medal such as are being distributed in the streets nowadays to commemorate the Armistice. Mme. Pichon is wearing a similar medal on her dress. They take seats facing one another, he absent-mindedly looking out of the window, she erect, firmly planted on her seat, brushing away with the back of her hand the dust which has collected on her husband's clothes.

I arrive at the Rue Franklin just as a crowd of people are coming out exclaiming with amazement, 'What freshness!

What youth ! One would not put him at a day more than seventy !' It is the Society of Vendéens in Paris.

Albert shows me into the study. Clemenceau is with his former Prefect of Police, M. Raux. I tell him of the arrival of the Pichons and their little medals.

CLEMENCEAU: Poor Pichon ! Isn't that touching ! Have you no respect for anything ? [*I put three or four pamphlets on the table before him.*] What are these ?

MYSELF: I have brought you two numbers of the *Revue de la Société Préhistorique de France,* where you will find a whole collection of polishers.

CLEMENCEAU [*studying the pictures*]: So these are polishers ?

MYSELF: Yes, at least that is what they say.

CLEMENCEAU: Mine isn't at all like these. Nevertheless, I stick to my impression that it is a polisher. Leave them there. I will look at them later. I have just been receiving some people, amongst them two girls who brought me the flowers you see over there. [*Chrysanthemums. There existed a sort of tacit understanding that the flowers which suited him best were chrysanthemums.*] I said to them, 'Young ladies, it is a tradition that when a girl brings you flowers you kiss her,' and I kissed them both. Then they took my picture.

[*Albert enters and announces M. and Mme. Pichon.*]

CLEMENCEAU [*going to meet them*]: Well, here is Stéphen Pichon !² And how are you getting on ?

PICHON: Very quietly.

[*Mme. Pichon helps her husband to sit on the sofa. M. Raux and I start to leave the room.*]

MYSELF [*to Clemenceau*]: Please don't trouble to see us out.

CLEMENCEAU: Oh, yes, I will. I shan't have so much showing out to do today as usual.

---

² M. Pichon was a very old friend of Clemenceau.

*[M. Raux and I go out. We go to the Place du Trocadéro
and take a little walk for half an hour.]*

MYSELF: A great old fellow that, to have dominated this
thrusting age. . .

RAUX: Yes. . . A very great old fellow . . . and when one
thinks that there he is now with his polishers and his stories
of little girls from the Vendée who come to offer him their
cheeks . . . the day of the Armistice! Forgotten by the
whole country!

MYSELF: They will remember later. They will see him
grow into a legend.

RAUX: You and I will have seen it in our lifetime — to
have served him. . .

MYSELF: You and I don't see anyone whom we can serve
today.

RAUX: Good Lord! . . .

MYSELF: Moreover, I was recalling the other day that scene
which took place one evening in November 1917 in the Rue
Taitbout. . .

RAUX: In the office of *L'Homme Enchainé!*

MYSELF: When he announced to you that he was going
to take office and that he needed a man he could count on at
the Prefecture of Police. . .

RAUX: . . . and that he had thought of me. If I remember? My head was in a maze. Certainly they can't say that I
asked for the place.[3]

MYSELF: And that happened in front of me. I was at my
little table going through the post. You accepted with such
wan and dismal thanks that I was embarrassed. However,
Beauvais could not have been very pleasant just then.

RAUX: It was being bombarded day and night. But Prefect of Police under Clemenceau — in the midst of the Malvy
affair! — in the midst of the Caillaux affair! — and Turmel,

---

[3] M. Raux was then Prefect for the Oise.

Lenoir, Bolo [4] and all the rest ! You speak of having fun — I was for the moment a little king of France. And since the fall, eh. . . We have seen them all packed off, the little friends, haven't we ?

MYSELF: What a stampede — as if we had all had the plague ! All those chaps on whom I had ribbons pinned and rosettes and orders. It's very, very odd.

RAUX: All those fellows whom I pulled out of the gutter. Oh, well, let's laugh about it.

[4] These last two were shot. They were more or less traitors.

# X

## The Lonely Man

On the 23rd November 1927 the newspapers announce the death of Mlle. Adrienne Clemenceau, 'the sister of M. Georges Clemenceau, former President of the Council.' On the 5th December the death of M. Albert Clemenceau, his brother.

December 7th . . . At Père-Lachaise Cemetery. The obsequies of Albert Clemenceau.[1] The hearse appears, we follow it. We get out of breath climbing the slope. It is cold. At last we arrive, barely two steps from the twin tombs of La Fontaine and Molière.

There we find the last battalion of the last Clemencistes, both passionate and lukewarm. . . Alerme,[2] bitter, the lines of his face revealing his profound disillusion; Mordacq[3] with the lively eye and the steely limbs — he is wearing a little grey overcoat; Lallemand,[4] very grave . . . and others: M. Pichon, M. Lafferre.[5] . . . The family: Paul Clemenceau,[6] uncouth, his

---

[1] Albert Clemenceau was a lawyer. He played a part in the Dreyfus affair.

[2] Lieut.-Col. Alerme. Second in command of the Military Cabinet during Clemenceau's administration.

[3] General Mordacq. Head of the Military Cabinet.

[4] A former Prefect. Head of the Civil Cabinet during the ministry.

[5] Formerly Minister for Education.

[6] Clemenceau's younger brother. An engineer. Albert was the youngest of the three brothers.

skull and forehead as if modelled by blows of a fist; Michel Clemenceau, Mme. Jacquemaire,[7] René Jacquemaire,[8] etc.

Clemenceau arrived in his little Citroen driven by Brabant. He seemed today very old, very wan and bent. His head bare, his skull a waxen yellow. He walked up to the tomb, looked into the hole with distracted eyes, then went away again. . .

Alerme said to me, 'H'm, h'm. Fate does her job tidily. You will see that he will be left altogether alone —without even a dog.'

[7] Clemenceau had three children: a son, Michel, and two daughters, Mme. Jacquemaire and Mme. Yung.

[8] The son of Mme. Jacquemaire, a doctor.

# XI

## The Americans and the French

M. Clemenceau is sitting in his study with Mme. Albert
Clemenceau and Pournin, Albert Clemenceau's former secretary.

I wait in the dining-room. I have not seen this room since
the apartment was done up and, ye Gods ! how clean it is,
how resplendent ! All repainted and recarpeted, a grey Wilton carpet on the floor, a grey-blue paper on the walls — even
the shutters have been changed. The little sofa is now up-
holstered in pale blue rep. One would think a honeymoon
couple had just moved in for a lifelong stay.

The rest of the decorations have not been changed; I see
again the enormous antique bas-relief mouldings fastened to
the wall with thick iron staples; those yellowing photographs
of Greek temples, Greek statues — Praxiteles, Polycleitus. . .
I see once more the unfinished study by Monet; a view of
Venice: four monks coming out of some water where an incredible blue-green gondola is slumbering. Bits of pottery
brought from Egypt are piled up in a Japanese cabinet. On
the little table in front of the window are two books: *Culi-
nary Herbs* and an *Archæological Survey of India.*

[*Mme. Albert Clemenceau and Pournin leave. I hear*

*the front door close. The dining-room door opens and Clemenceau appears.*]

CLEMENCEAU: Hullo there, Martet! Are you evacuating the Rhine?

MYSELF: They're talking about it. . .

CLEMENCEAU: I hope they don't do anything more than talk about it. Be nice to the Boches, Martet! Give them back the Rhineland and, to prove beyond a doubt the purity of your intentions and the sincerity of your desire for peace, give them back Belgium, Alsace-Lorraine, Poland — the whole works!

[*We pass into his study. Clemenceau sits down. I wait for what he is going to say about his sister, his brother, his bereavements. He says:*]

CLEMENCEAU: I am just writing a little article for the Americans.

MYSELF: Oh, what about?

CLEMENCEAU: Well, several things. About themselves, what they are, what they are doing, what they've done that's beautiful, magnificent, grand; and also that's less beautiful, less magnificent and less grand. I want to speak to them as one speaks to grown men. Nobody has ever done that yet.

MYSELF: Will it be a book?

CLEMENCEAU: I don't want it to be as long as that. You know, people no longer read very much. They have cars, they eat — how they love eating! . . . there is a sort of renaissance of the kitchen. Nowadays people exchange cookery recipes where they used to exchange madrigals and jokes. I find that symptomatic. Petronius. . . This does not seem like a very good age. In short I am writing and scratching out; I shall see how it turns out.

I now have two secretaries, one of whom is making researches on the subject and discovering the most amazing

things. You can never speak too well of the Americans.
What an example of living, of will, of courage ! But why
must they be so pleased with themselves ? Their population
is made up of all the races of the world and yet the American
is thirty-six thousand times prouder of being American than
the Frenchman of being French. Oswald[1] — who from a
scientific point of view has a great name — said one day, 'The
United States is in advance of all other nations; not only is
she superior to them but she is the perfect example of a civilized state.' What ! Why do they say things like that ? Why
this intoxication ?

MYSELF: If we could only resemble them a little !

CLEMENCEAU: I understand. But the French have been
French for such a long time ! It comes so natural to them. . .
Hold on a moment. There's a man named J. Mark Baldwin
who once wanted to pay me a very nice compliment and wrote
me this [*he takes a sheet of paper and reads*]: 'We Americans, we people of action, are not mistaken in saying that
M. Clemenceau is cast in the same mould as ourselves. . .'
Are you wondering why ? Well, here is the answer: 'It is
because in his youth he lived in an American city where he
became impregnated with the spirit of American life. . .' It
is very nice of him, but one really should point out to J. Mark
Baldwin that there have been people gifted with a certain
will-power and a certain taste for action, such as Louis XI,
Richelieu and others, who did not go to America to become
'impregnated' in that way. At least history doesn't mention it.

As a mood it is a little disquieting. And not only because
of neighbouring countries, but for the sake of the people
amongst whom such things are thought and said. The Greeks
felt that: the supreme quality amongst nations, as amongst

[1] John Clyde Oswald, American editor, president of the International Benjamin
Franklin Society.—*Translator's note.*

individuals, in their opinion was modesty, which alone enabled both nations and individuals to keep their sense of proportion and to follow the right course to the end. Germany lacked modesty, and she cannot exactly congratulate herself on the result.

The Americans do very nice things: they are the youth and the hope of the world. And it is quite right that they should appreciate the fact. But peoples only arrive at complete self-expression by a constant striving towards perfection, and in order to arrive at this perfection they must realize that not everything they do is altogether admirable.

I want therefore to put all this together and try to tell them what I think of them, good as well as bad. I shall take advantage naturally of the opportunity to speak a few home truths to the French: they also have been somewhat lacking in understanding. Fate has decreed that I shall go on to the end of time repeating these little fables to people who won't listen. Everybody continues in his own way, for better or for worse — but at least it keeps me busy. What annoys me in the case of France is that all my life I have fought for what they call freedom of the press, freedom of speech, etc. Now I have come to believe that all these freedoms end in the worst form of slavery, namely degeneration. Before setting the French free it would have been better to have taught them what freedom was and how to make proper use of it. It seems to me that the preparation was insufficient.

[*Albert enters.*]

ALBERT [*announcing*]: M. Martin.

CLEMENCEAU: Which Martin ? I know a dozen.

ALBERT: The one from Champ-Saint-Père.

CLEMENCEAU: Oh, the little Martin ! Show him in.

[*Enter Martin. He was Clemenceau's former secretary whom I succeeded in 1915. Now he lives at Champ-Saint-Père (Vendée), growing wheat, keeping cattle, etc.*]

CLEMENCEAU: Well, Monsieur Martin! What's become of you?

MARTIN: Disgust with men has brought me to live in the society of pigs.

CLEMENCEAU: Splendid! And what have you come to Paris for? Are you getting married?

MARTIN: Certainly not, sir. The spectacle of the sort of hermaphrodites one meets in the streets, who have neither buttocks nor breasts and call themselves Parisiennes, has not given me the least desire to get married. I don't see myself having children with things like that.

CLEMENCEAU: They certainly are absurd. They wear skirts nowadays which come above their knees and change them four times a day. My poor mother probably had only two dresses and they fell to her feet — which did not prevent her from bringing up six children properly.

MARTIN: But what do you think of the way things are going, sir?

CLEMENCEAU: The same as you do yourself, Martin — except that I am in a very special situation: I don't care a damn about anything. It would be no good God giving me special attention — I have turned to marble.

MARTIN: How's your health?

CLEMENCEAU: I think I'm still in this world. That's as much as I can say. Oh, wait a minute, to pay you for having come as far as this I am going to show you something. [*He gets up.*] Where did I hide that thing? [*He looks about.*] It was a kind of paper. [*He finds it.*] Oh, here it is. These are the keys of the Bastille. I may give them to the Carnavalet Museum. . . Unfortunately I haven't the least idea who gave them to me. . . Of course that doesn't exactly help to establish their authenticity. [*He unrolls the piece of paper. Three large keys appear, very rusty, very light, with a bit of chain — like theatre keys.*]

MYSELF: They look like cardboard. But perhaps the Bastille was also made of cardboard.

MARTIN: It's another Glozel stunt ! What do you think about Glozel ?

CLEMENCEAU: What a very fine story that is ! They came to submit it to Boule.[2] A reindeer on a bit of flint. He said, 'Will you permit me to clean one end of your flint with a toothbrush ?' They answered, 'No.' 'Then take it away,' said Boule. Whereupon they told him, 'Then you can do what you like.' He took the stone, scrubbed it with a toothbrush, and at the bottom of the groove he found some strong glue. He said, 'The people of that age were not in the habit of putting glue on their flints.' Then he went to his bookshelves and brought back a volume in which there was an engraving: 'Wait a minute; ah ! here is the very reindeer they've copied.'

[*Albert announces Mme. Bensa. Martin and I rise.*]

CLEMENCEAU [*on the threshold*] : Martet, I had something to tell you — I don't remember what it was. Ah, here it is. Martet, you are not a very serious fellow.

MYSELF [*nonplussed*]: Why . . . no, I do what I can not to be.

CLEMENCEAU [*drily*]: You succeed very well indeed.

MYSELF: Why are you telling me this ?

CLEMENCEAU: You promised to come for me and take me to the Saint-Germain Museum.

MYSELF: I didn't want to at this particular time. . . with all your bereavements.

CLEMENCEAU: You might have come before or after.

MYSELF: I swear to you. . .

CLEMENCEAU: Don't swear and don't defend yourself. I'm not angry with you, and for an excellent reason — I like you.

---

[2] Marcellin Boule, a professor at the Museum.

MYSELF: But I object. I don't want to be liked under those conditions.

CLEMENCEAU: Well, that happens to be the way I like you. Do what you like about it. [*We have now arrived at the door.*] Au 'voir, M. Martet, au 'voir. [*And the door closes behind us.*]

# XII

## Concerning Positive Action and Several Other Matters

In Clemenceau's room. He is correcting certain typewritten papers.

CLEMENCEAU [*looking up*]: What can I do for you, Monsieur Martet?

MYSELF: Sir, the other day you said that you liked me, but that I didn't really deserve your friendship. Well, that annoys me.

CLEMENCEAU: I said that?

MYSELF: Perhaps not in those words, but that was the gist of your remarks.

CLEMENCEAU: If that isn't exactly what I said, it isn't exactly what I meant. Don't be a silly fool, Martet. Anyone who . . . but first there is that story of Saint-Germain. You promised to show it to me; you should have done so. A promise is a promise. You promised . . . and . . .

MYSELF: The trouble is I have too vivid an imagination. Once I've promised to do a thing, I think of it as already accomplished — it's already ancient history.

CLEMENCEAU: That is a terrible admission to make, for to-day all Frenchmen think and act just as you do. As soon as an idea has taken form in their minds they immediately

64

tire of it. They dreamed of the 'Victory.' But when it came they were no longer interested. The only time they're capable of positive action is when they haven't had time to think beforehand. In the second place, Martet — oh, don't think this is another sermon . . . after all, what's the difference — there is this to consider: after all, you are not really a fool.

MYSELF: I wouldn't go that far, sir. Yes, I mean it. I am a fool ! You've absolutely no idea how little interest I have in intellectual matters.

CLEMENCEAU: Martet, you are not without brains ! Now and then you manage to say things which are . . . well, true. Of course you understand I say they are 'true' because they agree with my own beliefs. After all, I can't tell whether your ideas would appeal to Briand or Poincaré. And in addition, you have several good points: you're unselfish.

MYSELF: I, sir ? Why, I'm worried to death because I'm not a millionaire !

CLEMENCEAU: If you're worried to death because you aren't one you will be one. There's nothing so silly as making money. But you are . . . well, what else are you ? You have a certain appreciation of the beautiful — for instance, you don't get Phidias mixed up with Bartholomé, or the Madeleine with the Parthenon. And yet you have a weakness, Martet, a very stupid weakness — you're lazy.

MYSELF: I? Good heavens ! I'm restless and can hardly live unless I have a pencil in my hand.

CLEMENCEAU: Martet, you haven't got enough will-power to stick in your eye.

MYSELF: What a pleasant description of me.

CLEMENCEAU: As a member of the present generation you're perfectly normal. It doesn't do any good to. . .

MYSELF: Sir, I think that I understand myself and that I. . .

CLEMENCEAU: Don't talk such nonsense ! How can you

possibly understand yourself ? You've never studied science.

MYSELF: And yet I can tell pretty well when machinery isn't functioning well. My trouble isn't any lack of will-power — it's my lack of confidence in the efficacy of action.

CLEMENCEAU: I realize that, dear fellow. A man who has to be convinced to act before he acts is what you describe — he's *not* a man of action. It's as if a tennis player before re-turning the ball began to question himself as to the physical and moral value of tennis. You must act just as you breathe.[1] How old are you ?

MYSELF: I'm forty.

CLEMENCEAU: Sapristi, when you're forty it's time to be doing something.

MYSELF: I'm writing a novel.

CLEMENCEAU: What ! a novel ! Confound all novels. You should be doing serious work. What ? Oh, anything !

MYSELF: For whom ?

CLEMENCEAU: For yourself ! Just tell me why it is that having seen what you have seen you've never written any-thing ? Not one line ! Don't you have anything to say of the period we're going through and of the men who are liv-ing in it ?

MYSELF: Why speak of that ? What difference would it make ? All effort is futile — you know it as well as I do. You've no more confidence than I have in the possibility of changing one fact into another.

CLEMENCEAU: Hold on, there ! I'll give you proof that I believe in the usefulness of certain acts and words: I'm in the midst of writing this paper for the Americans. I've got plenty to say — I've said it ! You see, I still preserve a certain faith.

[1] *'Pan rules us all. We must act. Action is the beginning, the means, the end. Determined action on the part of each man for the benefit of all, disinterested action (above childish vanity or dreams of reward in eternity or despair in lost battles or the fear of death), action leading toward an ideal—the moving force, the complete virtue. . .'*

This in an extract from Clemenceau's *Grand Pan*.

MYSELF: Well, I congratulate you. After all, your entire life and all your activities prove conclusively that nothing matters.

CLEMENCEAU: Nothing matters because all Frenchmen share your attitude, and because everyone shirks by saying: 'I still have sixty or eighty years to live; well, I'll try to while away the time in the most pleasant fashion possible sitting in my own little corner. . .' Do you have a conscience, Martet ? Doesn't it make some demands upon you ? Doesn't it make you want to move and strike out a bit ? Or does it say to you: 'There you are, sitting on the ground, your tail in the dust — You're well off, stay where you are ?' Martet, you're not an encouraging type.

MYSELF: Yet what can I do, sir ? I've already told you — ideas, ideas. . .

CLEMENCEAU: Nothing matters but ideas ! Granting that you don't have a brain in your head, you still can use your eyes. Put down what you see. Images are valuable. Moreover, aren't images ideas ? Speak, Martet, write, work !

MYSELF: Sir, if I made a book out of what I have seen and heard, you would say: 'Surely, you're not going to publish that ?'

CLEMENCEAU: Oh, I don't know. And at least, you would have done some writing. You mustn't confine yourself to what I think. It's annoying to find that you are dilatory.

MYSELF: But I'm not ! I look, I listen. . .

CLEMENCEAU: That's not enough. Reach a conclusion.

MYSELF: All right. I'll try.

CLEMENCEAU: Don't try — *do* things ! . . . You'll probably be lucky enough to have me with you for a few more months; bring me your observations and I'll tell you what I think of them. Are you willing ?

MYSELF: Agreed !

CLEMENCEAU: Splendid ! Monsieur Martet, I'd like to ask

you a question. A man has written to me saying that my style in *Démosthène* and in *Au Soir de la Pensée* is so obscure that it's necessary to read twice to get the meaning. Is that true ?

Myself: Yes, in certain passages. But I feel that if there is any justification to such criticism it's the fact that you wrote those books more for yourself than for others.

Clemenceau: I agree. What a shame that I don't have three or four more years to live — I might have rewritten those books for my cook ! Nevertheless, I ought not to have been obscure. I never correct or rewrite sentences. When something isn't satisfactory, I begin the chapter afresh. In my opinion — I don't know whether you feel the same way — the question of style is an arabesque; what difference do one, two, or ten words make ? It's merely a matter of the cumulative effect and the general construction. Once you've erected the framework of your building you cannot make additions without overweighting it, cannot withdraw anything without tumbling it to the ground. Looking at it from this point of view I have perhaps put too much detail into the *Au Soir de la Pensée*.

Myself: Oh, Monsieur, do not run down the *Au Soir de le Pensée*. What life it has — and vigor and honesty !

Clemenceau: Do you really think so ? I thank you. And yet I was eighty-five when I wrote it, racked by diabetes and scarcely able to stand up.

Myself: Ah, that was a real achievement of will-power. I wonder if it can be parallelled in all the history of the world.

Clemenceau: The trouble is, people have wrong ideas about old age. In the first place there is no such thing as old age — one is old only when he begins to act the part of an old man.

Myself: Sir, you speak like a young man.

Clemenceau: I speak as a man who does not anticipate fate. In business you see persons retiring at sixty. At sixty !

CLEMENCEAU ON THE LAWN BEHIND HIS RESIDENCE

What a shame! And what happens to them? They rot away. Of course they do — it's a law of nature. A man who's no longer good for anything must rot away. The truth is that all of you are just waiting for an excuse to twiddle your thumbs. And old age is one of the excuses — and nothing more.

The other day a man suggested that I start life over again. I answered: 'I beg your pardon, but there is no need for me to recommence life — I have only to continue it.' Then he said. 'Well, I can have you named Deputy from Colmar.' I stared at him aghast: 'Deputy?' I asked. 'Can you picture me in the Chamber? Why not in an asylum?'

MYSELF: Then do you feel, sir, that. . .

CLEMENCEAU: I feel that in my day things could still be accomplished in the Chamber; one could fight for some kind of ideal. Now that's all ended. Like everything else, it's had its day. It's no place for a young man.

MYSELF: And yet the Chamber in 1914 was never considered brilliant.

CLEMENCEAU: Damn it, no! It wasn't brilliant! I used to meet people there who. . . Oh, well, one wondered how a thousand or ten thousand persons could have voted for those freaks. But the present Chamber is even worse than the 1914 one. I said to that fellow: 'Can you show me what outlet there would be for my activity in the Chamber?' He shrugged his shoulders. Ask that same question of any of those men who are standing for election to the Chamber. They'll look at you in amazement. Not one of them has the slightest idea of going to the Chamber to defend anything or fight for anything. One is a deputy today just as one might be a registrar: it is one way to make a living.

MYSELF: And yet there are some persons of independent means who enter the Chamber.

CLEMENCEAU: So as to put it on their calling-card — although the word 'deputy' hasn't the prestige it used to have. If you're in a room and a deputy enters, there's a sudden constraint. Martet, I'm not going to be deputy from Colmar. I intend to remain young and active. The only thing that annoys me is that I can scarcely move. After walking twenty yards I'm exhausted. I loved to travel — I'll have to give it up.

MYSELF: I'm planning this summer to make a little trip — most inexpensively — around the Mediterranean — Cairo, Smyrna, Athens.

CLEMENCEAU: Lucky devil! Above all, see Greece. Ah, Greece — Greece, Martet! Greece is a glorious place. I remember one day in an out-of-the-way corner of the Peloponessus called Phigalia I had nothing to eat — oh, yes, I had two bits of chocolat. I saw a hen tied by its leg to a gate. I untied it and put it over a fire. Well, I couldn't dent it either with a knife or my teeth. It was like stone. But the temple is splendid. You know that it was built by Ictinus, the architect of the Parthenon? There are three temples that a man must see before he dies: the Parthenon, Phigalia, and Pæstum. You're going to Naples?

MYSELF: Yes.

CLEMENCEAU: Then see Pæstum. It's magnificent!

MYSELF: I'll try to see Pæstum. But I don't know whether I'll have enough money to see very much; I expect they'll treat me like an emigrant.

CLEMENCEAU: You're travelling on foot? That's the way! They now have steamboat companies and railways which allow you to see the Pyramids without getting out of bed. They bring them to you in the morning on a platter along with the mail.

MYSELF: Money is a terrible plague.

CLEMENCEAU: You can't mean that seriously. Look at my grandson Georges. He married a rather impressive collection of millions. Well, his father-in-law wanted him to become a jeweller, to sell diamonds. The other day he showed Georges a stone and said: 'What do you think of that stone ?' The youngster answered: 'Oh, what a beautiful emerald !' 'No,' replied Roseneau, 'it's the worst ruby I ever saw.' So you see what indignities fortune can impose. The youngster likes reading — which is a legitimate, even admirable occupation. Do you know what the father-in-law did ? He went to the Hotel des Ventes and bought a complete library for him. Would you want to read books under such conditions ?

MYSELF: You've just been reading, Monsieur ?

CLEMENCEAU: Yes, I'm reading a very amusing book — an old book of Alfred de Vigny's. Do you like de Vigny ? He's laborious and conscientious, which after all is something. But actually, if you examine carefully and look behind the words, you won't find much. He's a schoolboy philosopher. His love affair with the actress Dorval was stupid. He weeps and that's all there is to it. And yet about the same Dorval, in the case of a certain Gustavem who was later to become the famous actor Mélingue, the author says: 'He became her lover without having uttered one word.' Let that be a lesson, Martet. One always talks too much.

[*Albert enters.*]

ALBERT: M. Chichet [2] is here.

CLEMENCEAU: Oh pshaw, what does he want ? [*To me*] Come with me. I'll say a couple of words to him and then you're to take him away.

MYSELF: How has he offended you ? Chichet is very pleasant.

CLEMENCEAU: He reminds me of Napoleon III. [*To Albert.*] Show him into the study.

[*Albert leaves.*]

MYSELF: There's a sculptor who without even having seen you has made a bust that's a perfect likeness.

[2] Former editor of *L'Homme Libre*.

CLEMENCEAU:  What's his name ?

MYSELF:  Cogné.

CLEMENCEAU:  I've never had any luck with sculptors. Either they have genius and can't make a likeness, or else aren't geniuses but do make a likeness.  I don't know why it is but they make me look like an old fool.

[*Albert re-enters.*]

ALBERT:  Mme. Bensa is here.

CLEMENCEAU:  Into the dining-room.  I'm much sought after this morning.  I've always told you that I have lost none of my popularity.

[*We go into the study.  Chichet is there — very tall, with immense arms and legs.*]

CHICHET [*cordially*]:  How do you do, Mr. President.  Well, is your health good ?  I've been thinking of you constantly.

CLEMENCEAU:  Thank you, my friend.

CHICHET:  I must tell you something.  I am writing for two papers — the *Courrier du Centre* and the *Nouvelliste d'Alsace-Lorraine* — and every time that I can slip in a word about you and what you're doing, I do it.  Yes, on my word of honor.

CLEMENCEAU:  That's very, very kind of you.

CHICHET:  I've also interviewed Mordacq — just the other day; you'll hear of it soon . . . a rather curious incident.  And I was speaking of you to Albert Sarraut,[2] and Sarraut said: 'I'll certainly write to the President.'

CLEMENCEAU [*starting*]:  The devil !  And why ?

CHICHET:  Oh, well, just to assure you of his regard.  I mentioned the matter because you notice that to Sarraut you are still 'the President.'  It's an interesting point.

CLEMENCEAU [*drily*]:  Do you think so ?

CHICHET:  Don't you ?  [*A pause.*] And also I want to express to you my sincerest good wishes.

[3] Minister of the Interior.

CLEMENCEAU: What good are they?

CHICHET: Oh, not much. It's, uh, the thing to say . . . uh, like, oh well . . . I trust I have the pleasure of seeing you again.

CLEMENCEAU: Good-bye, my friend.

[Chichet departs.]

CLEMENCEAU: He looks more and more like Badinguet.[3]

[4] One of Napoleon III's surnames.

# XIII

## A HAPPY NEW YEAR

I GO into the dining-room, where M. Raux and Pournin are already waiting.

MYSELF [*to M. Raux*]: Monsieur le Préfect de Police, I wish you all happiness and prosperity.

RAUX: Glory and wealth to you, Monsieur Martet, and Paradise when your days are ended.

MYSELF: Did you go to the wedding of Mlle. Chiappe,[1] Monsieur le Préfect ? I hear that there were several pretty little children dressed as pages. . .

RAUX: Yes, I heard so. It must have been rather sweet. . . Oh, Monsieur Martet, if I had had the Cardinal Archbishop of Paris at the wedding of my daughter, to what position might I not have aspired! Clemenceau would never have forgiven me.

POURNIN: And Mandel ?

RAUX: They say that he is not going to have it all his own way at Lesparre.[2] How I should love to see him have a real contest !

MYSELF: But he will certainly be re-elected.

---

[1] Daughter of the present Prefect of Police.
[2] In the Gironde. Mandel's constituency.

RAUX: By Jove, he must be ! What should we do without Mandel ?

[*Clemenceau appears at the door of the dining-room.*]

CLEMENCEAU: It is Monsieur Martet's turn to speak.

MYSELF: How do you do ? I have not come to wish you a Happy New Year any more today than yesterday. I wish it to you every day.

CLEMENCEAU: It is a little formality which allows people to lead you to believe they have not entirely forgotten you. Come along. [*We go into the study.*] For a New Year's gift someone has sent me an article which says that the war was already half won when I took office and there was really nothing to do but carry on the good work which Messrs. Millerand, Viviani, Briand, Painlevé had so auspiciously begun. I daresay I shan't allow it to worry me.[3]

MYSELF: You seem to have a cold. . .

CLEMENCEAU: It is only a touch of laryngitis. It's tickling the back of my throat. But I don't think that my vital organs are affected.

MYSELF: I want to tell you that I have begun to work.[4] One of these days I shall bring you a manuscript. You will tell me to throw it in the fire. And I shall throw it in the fire.

CLEMENCEAU: It is quite possible, but I must read it first. I have already told you, Martet, you are not a man of action.

MYSELF: Tell me, sir, what do you mean by action ?

CLEMENCEAU: There you are ! When a man asks himself what is meant by action he proves that he isn't a man of

[3] This idea of the 'victory which was beginning to dawn' had been put forward several times. M. L. Dumont-Wilden answered: 'A critical situation. Russia, already disintegrated, had given up the struggle; American help still seemed a long way off: Italy had not yet recovered from the disaster of Caporetto, and Germany, freed by her victories in the East, was preparing to hurl the entire weight of her available divisions against our front. The Allies were crippled and alarmed. In France even, certain people, tired of the war, were already thinking of becoming reconciled to a defeat which appeared to them inevitable.'

[4] I had begun to write a history of the Clemenceau Ministry (1917–1920).

action. Action is a lack of balance. In order to act you must be somewhat insane. A reasonably sensible man is satisfied with thinking. Now, you are balanced. It is unfortunate for your sake, but there it is ! You were made for passing judgments. Well, good Lord, go ahead and pass them !

MYSELF: What a sentence !

CLEMENCEAU: And for what a crime ! But go ahead and judge, none the less. [*He gets up.*] I have had a visit from the Mother Superior of the Rue Bizet. I said to her: 'Mother, I respect you because you live for a single idea. I too live for a single idea. They are not the same, but it is possible that in a few billions of years they may end up by meeting.' Bring me your work. I will tell you what I think of it as if you were my son.

MYSELF: Thank you.

[*We are standing facing each other, and for one moment we look into each other's eyes without saying anything.*]

CLEMENCEAU: I hope you will be happy, Martet.

MYSELF: Sir, will you allow me to embrace you ?

CLEMENCEAU: With all my heart, my boy.

[*We embrace, and I go away with a beating heart.*]

# XIV

## Caillaux — The King of Afghanistan — A Word about England and the United States

*29th January* 1928

MYSELF: How are you, sir ?

CLEMENCEAU: All right, except that I'm coughing.

MYSELF: Still your diabetic bronchitis ?

CLEMENCEAU: Call it what you will, laryngitis, pleurisy, general decay. Words don't explain anything. All I can tell you is that I'm coughing. I am taking care of myself as well as I can and having my back cupped.[1] Is there any news ? Are you bringing me anything ?

MYSELF: Not yet. In a month or two. . .

CLEMENCEAU: I dreamed of Caillaux. What's become of him ? I am under the impression that the French people rather thought that Caillaux was a martyr to my well-known ferocity, but unquestionably not a saviour. . .

MYSELF: Do you remember the session of the Chamber on the 23rd December 1917 ?

CLEMENCEAU: No. What happened on the 23rd December 1917 ?

MYSELF: It was the occasion when Caillaux came for the last time to protest his innocence. . . I was on the little rostrum

[1] *Translator's note. — Ventouses.*

77

on the right which overlooks the Attachés' gangway, and
from there I was able to see the scene perfectly: Caillaux, in
profile, his abrupt movements, his hoarse voice, his purplish
skull; and you, sir, full face, on the Government bench, looking out from under knitted brows. . .

CLEMENCEAU: And what was Caillaux talking about ?

MYSELF: I must say he was certainly declaiming away !

CLEMENCEAU: H'm. That doesn't surprise me. He had
a sense of the dramatic. . .

MYSELF: He said: 'Do you remember, Mr. President, those
tragic sessions when you yourself were accused of treason, those
impassioned speeches by Déroulède, Millevoye. . . Is it your
desire that the injustice of those days be repeated in ours ?
Do you want another Dreyfus affair ? Then he added: 'You,
you, Monsieur Clemenceau, who today are all-powerful ! ' I
cast a glance in your direction. I thought that something start-
ling was going to happen.

CLEMENCEAU: What ?

MYSELF: I don't know. . . An unearthly electric disturbance. Caillaux had just conjured up those old struggles, had
appealed to your omnipotence, to your generosity. . . I wondered then what thoughts were going through your mind.

CLEMENCEAU: I was thinking there was France, that's all.[2]

MYSELF: You once rather liked him, didn't you ?

CLEMENCEAU: I didn't hate him. He impressed me as having at least a sort of go, a courage about him which I liked.
But if you ever want to take up politics as a career, Martet,
and want to get anywhere don't worry yourself with questions
of liking. Keep yourself always in readiness to break with
your friends. Otherwise you will be lost, lost. You will never
be able to carry through what you have decided to do. In
politics it is your friends who hold you back.

[2] *Translator's note.* — The phrase is: *Je pensais qu'il y avait la France, tout
simplement,* a sentiment which cannot, I think, be perfectly rendered into English.

Caillaux at the very height of the war with Germany kept pursuing his dream of an understanding with Germany, kept up intercourse with Germany; in my view that is a crime. If Caillaux before the war had the idea of maintaining the equilibrium of Europe by efforts at industrial and economic co-operation with the Boches he must already have been mad. For you only had to look at them in order to see that they had no other idea than to throw themselves on us and crush us. Perhaps in looking at the matter from a distance, in considering it in the seclusion of the study, one might hold dispassionately that the Entente with Germany, our perpetual enemy, was well worth the Entente we had with England — who is not our perpetual enemy. Up to 2nd August 1914, it was a little hobby with which to divert oneself if one wished; after the 2nd August 1914, one had to keep quiet about it.

As a matter of actual fact I did not trouble myself much about Caillaux.[3] I really didn't have as much to bother about as I had with Malvy; against him it was absolutely necessary to take up the cudgels. In Caillaux's case public opinion, the newspapers, the ordinary machinery of justice caught hold of him and balanced his account without my having to interfere. But if it had been necessary, I should have acted. I should not have rested until he was put out of the way. There is no room for thirty-six ideas in a country which is fighting for its life. There's only room for one.

[3] Clemenceau once said: 'It is probable that Caillaux is the only man with whom I have never had a controversy — it is strange but true — except perhaps a fortnight before I came into power. In my previous ministry I chose him for my Minister of Finance. And after I went out of office we met quite often; I have always spoken with him in a very friendly way. I never had any feeling of personal enmity towards him, and even in moments of extreme irritation you will find if you question him that he cannot say that I ever acted with hostility against him. To my knowledge he never did against me either. I am not asking that any measures be taken against him which could be called -- I do not say arbitrary, but which might indicate any feeling of animus towards him — I only ask that he should be treated as any ordinary citizen. If he was called John Smith there would not be a conference around a table to discuss the matter when four people had been proved beyond a doubt to have received money on behalf of Germany and a man was known to have had intimate relations with those four people.'

Malvy . . . you see, Malvy is the sort that lets things take their own course, go-as-you-please, with a handshake for everybody; while Caillaux is one of those gloomy ill-starred heroes such as you find only in Shakespearean drama. One should not despise them, for they bring into this world where everything is frayed, rubbed, worn, a sense of the picturesque. . . But for the sake of the public safety it is better to withdraw them from circulation.[4]

Do you know, I should very much like to have the opinion of the King of Afghanistan[5] on the subject. I should like to know how these things are settled among the Afghans. I think that there the Caillaux are hung up by the feet.

MYSELF: Afghanistan is a country which seems to have become very fashionable. The papers said the other day it is bigger than France.

CLEMENCEAU: I can believe it. But the same thing can be said about the Polar regions or the Sahara Desert.

MYSELF: What did you think of the King?

CLEMENCEAU: I found him very congenial. But there was one question which I put to myself. Can one be sure that this really is the King of Afghanistan? Have they asked to see his identity papers? Perhaps he is only a slightly brunette gentleman who is travelling for pleasure. One newspaper has a story that they took him to the Invalides and Doumergue showed him the flags captured from the enemy in 1870, and the King said, 'The enemy? which enemy?' There is in that question a valuable lesson in history and philosophy. He speaks French. The Queen is very nice. The son goes to the Janson de Sailly Academy.

---

[4] 'May I thank you for having spoken with me in so friendly a manner,' wrote Caillaux to Clemenceau in 1905, 'and tell you that I have been greatly touched by the kindly way in which you have talked about me and which I trust gives me the right to offer you, together with my sincere gratitude, my very deepest sympathy.'
[5] The King of Afghanistan was then in Paris.

It's all as it should be. A nice little ménage . . . Foucher [6] has invited me to go to a reception for them this evening at the Guimet Museum. I have accepted.

MYSELF: Everybody knows perfectly well what they have come to France for.

CLEMENCEAU: Of course; to buy arms.

MYSELF: Against whom?

CLEMENCEAU: Oh! against everybody who is annoying them. I am under the impression that since Locarno the manufacture of firearms has increased considerably. The tiresome thing about Afghanistan is that there is always a little too much assassination going on. Life there is perhaps more exciting, but death is tending to become monotonous. When I was in India and wanted to go to Afghanistan they told me, 'You will never come out of it alive.' In order to go as far as the Khyber Pass I had to have an escort of six hundred men with ammunition and baggage. But I did notice one striking thing: A caravan with magnificent camels, whose enormous mouths could break a head as easily as a nut. We saw them coming towards us in the distance. You should see a caravan from a distance. You would think it was a serpent uncoiling. We knew where the caravan was going and we attached ourselves to it. We arrived at a place they called a caravanserai. It is vedy entertaining, a caravanserai. . . All those people, all those shouts. . . People sit about, unpacking their merchandise, scratching themselves, delousing themselves . . . a stench of sweat, squalour. I noticed a very pretty little ewer, covered with smoke, in a corner. I asked the man, 'How much do you want for that?' He answered, 'Three francs. It's what I paid for it last year in a bazaar at Peshawar.'

Despite the restrictions, travelling in Afghanistan has been going on for some time. Scholars have been sent there. . . There is that poor — what do you call him — the man who

[6] The curator of the Guimet Museum.

7

went to Bactra.  He said to himself, 'It is impossible that there is nothing at all in that locality.'  Therefore he excavated, but found nothing.  He was furious.

When I went to the Khyber Pass they showed me a road; on the right of that road was English territory, on the left Afghan territory; and in the latter you can do anything you have a mind to.  It doesn't matter; you can kill your wife, your mother-in-law; no one would be so ill-bred as to pass any remark about it.

Well, one day a man was found murdered in English territory.  An investigation was held; the murderer was discovered and arrested.  He said 'You're quite right.  I did kill that fellow.  Only I killed him in Afghan territory.  But he was spiteful, extraordinarily spiteful.  In order to have me arrested for it he dragged himself into English territory, where he died.  Do you want proof of it ?  When I shot him from above he was sitting on that rock over there.  You can go over and look at it.  There are certain to be traces of blood on it.'

They went over and found that there was blood.  He was released with apologies.

MYSELF: Still another judicial error.

CLEMENCEAU:  To proceed to less cheerful matters, I have to announce that Aulard [7] has written me.  I have no idea what was going on in his brain.  He sent me a poppy from the Acropolis with these words: 'My dear friend, I am very fond of you.  I should like very much to see you again.'  I answered: 'My dear friend, for several years you have devoted the best part of your energies to supporting the men who are leading France directly to ruin.  We have nothing more to say to you.'  Whereupon Aulard took his revenge.

MYSELF:  No !

---

[7] The historian of the Revolution of 1789.  Formerly a close friend of Clemenceau's.  His too Pan-European ideas had separated them.

CLEMENCEAU: Yes, indeed. Aulard is the man to avenge himself behind those spectacles of his. There was a commission to examine proposed text books; Aulard and Lanson[8] were members of it. In the bosom of this commission they discussed my books and wanted to know if they were suitable for young people to read, and Aulard remarked: 'They are rubbish. I have never been able to read them myself.'

MYSELF: And what did Lanson have to say to that?

CLEMENCEAU: Well, Lanson did just this. . . He raised his hands in the air and then let them fall back again.

MYSELF: Did he say anything?

CLEMENCEAU: No, but that doesn't matter. I shall not withdraw my friendship from him. What happened will bother only him. We must begin with the principle that professors cannot be courageous spontaneously, without preparation. They don't have very rapid reflexes. When Lanson has time to see what is coming, to stir his pen reflectively in the inkwell, he is brave. That's about what it comes to.

MYSELF: You are still determined not to stand at the elections, sir?

CLEMENCEAU: No, there is nothing more for me to do in that way. Neither for me nor anyone else, for that matter. The mechanism has been destroyed. There are no longer any parties, neither majority nor opposition. . . Nothing whatever. The whole thing is like a kind of sponge. You squeeze it and muddy water runs out.

Altogether it reminds you of the last days of the Roman Empire. France has not Rome's conquests, but in the eyes of the nations she still cuts a good figure. They still turn to her like a great spiritual leader. . . But look about you now, Martet, at what is going on and tell me if it doesn't make you uneasy.

[8] The historian of French literature. Professor at the Sorbonne for several years. Clemenceau had a warm friendship for him.

MYSELF: But it is not only France which makes you uneasy. . .

CLEMENCEAU: No, that's true. England as well. She has been a very great lady, England, aloof, ruthless, but with an engaging quality about her. England alone is perhaps of all peoples the one whose will held on the longest. Unfortunately she has begun to show a kind of weakening, of lassitude. The conquest no longer serves to quicken the conqueror. What can you expect ? Their history goes back such a long way.

The English have three kinds of enemies to take into account: first, their natural enemies . . . and these are not the most formidable; next, their Dominions, their offshoots in Asia, Africa, and Australia, who are beginning to grow restive; and, lastly, the English themselves; the English of today are less enterprising than those of a hundred years ago. Some virtue is going out of them.

MYSELF: As for America. . .

CLEMENCEAU: America ! Just a minute. [*He shows me some sheets of paper spread out on the table.*] I am just engaged in surveying her at very close quarters and calling up my memories. One day in '66 or '67 I arrived at . . . I don't know where. . . I got out of the train with my bag. I got into a carriage; the coachman was a mulatto with barely a trace of colour. He said to me: 'I am very sorry, sir, I am only allowed to take a fare when all the white coachmen are engaged.'

MYSELF: Diagne[9] ought to hear of that.

CLEMENCEAU: They explained to me over there — very nice and intelligent Americans — that they were compelled to defend themselves against the negroes, that they were afraid of degenerating if they allowed the two races to mingle. I think there was something of that in it. But I also believe that that wasn't all. It's because the Americans are still too near their

[9] French deputy for Senegal, who is as black as ebony.

PERSHING, CLEMENCEAU AND POINCARÉ
*Arriving at the Place de la Concorde for a military review on the 4th of July* 1919

beginnings; they need a bit of past. It takes a country a thousand years to come to the point of understanding that a man is a man.

MYSELF: Do you think that one of these days America and England. . .

CLEMENCEAU: War? I shouldn't like it, for the sake of the United States. They have good ships and they are well manned, but the English have the sea in their blood. Pershing thought they could improvise generals and that it was enough just to raise millions of troops. He saw at Thiaucourt it was not as easy as all that.

MYSELF: What do you think of the American ideology?

CLEMENCEAU: I think it is a very nice little article for export. They say to poor old Europe: 'Now here is what you ought to do. Here are the fourteen points and the thirty-six points from which you should draw your inspiration.' If you say to them, 'Quite so. But we would like to know what you do at home and from what you draw your inspiration,' they answer you: 'That's easy. We draw our inspiration from the Monroe doctrine.' This business of reduction of armaments and outlawing war is just a colossal buffoonery. Poor Claudel gets so excited about it.

MYSELF: Have you ever read anything of Claudel's?

CLEMENCEAU: I used to think he was a carburettor, and then I read a few pages of him—no, he just didn't carburate. He has a kind of conscientious emptiness such as a Provençal would take on who was trying to attain an air of profundity. The Americans who read him between two halves of a football match must have a good laugh.

[*I get up. We pass into the vestibule.*]

CLEMENCEAU: [*taking a long-necked Japanese vase from the mantelpiece*]: Here, take this. It was Steenackers [10] who

[10] An old friend of M. Clemenceau. He is now dead. He had been French Consul General for Japan.

brought it to me from out there. . . [*He leads me out to the staircase and shows me odds and ends of pottery and stones spread out on a little round enamel table.*]

MYSELF: Have you been excavating ?

CLEMENCEAU: These are things that I dug up out of a drawer. They come from Greece. This thing here [*he hands me a little acorn-shaped cup of terra-cotta*] I picked up in a field at Delos. It was probably used to contain the oil for rubbing the bodies before the wrestling matches. . . [*He shows me a piece of reddish stone as heavy as iron.*] That was fixed in one of the seven gates of Thebes. . . You should see Thebes, Martet. And while I think of it, are you going to Athens ? If so, you should look up my friend, Philaretos.

MYSELF: He was not in Venizelos' Cabinet, was he ?

CLEMENCEAU: Something like that. He lives in the Villa Kallithea — which means Belle-Vue. A very nice chap, Philaretos. He wouldn't hurt a fly. I said to him one evening: 'I am going to leave you to work on the Acropolis.' It is true: the Acropolis in moonlight. . . It is stupendous ! You have those vast blue nights. I asked him what those pedestal affairs were at the foot of the Acropolis. He said: 'Those ? Aren't those tombs ?' Philaretos never suspected that once there had been another Greece.

MYSELF: So far I hardly know the Greece which I saw with you at the British. . .

CLEMENCEAU: H'm. There ! Yes, ah ! When you go into that hall and those Phidias's catch your eye ! The first time that I saw them I understood that all that I had ever thought about everything had to be revised. You cannot live without taking them into account.

MYSELF: The Parthenon brings order to the mind.

CLEMENCEAU: Did you hear that the Louvre has bought that head from the Parthenon which is called the Laborde head ? From the name of the man to whom it belonged. You know, the one of which I have a cast.

[*We go into the study.*]

CLEMENCEAU [*studying the head with a kind of rapt delight*]: There's something divine in that, isn't there ?

MYSELF: Yes; they achieve their goal.

CLEMENCEAU: And the Tegea head. Look at it. I can't ever walk by it without stopping. What do you expect to do after that ? The man who made that brow did it as if in a dream, with a caress of his hand. No effort, no study. How did those people conceive of an idea like that ? By what roads did they get there ?

MYSELF: There is in the sculptures of the sixth century. . .

CLEMENCEAU: No, that doesn't explain anything. On the contrary. Between archaic Greek art and the sculptures of the Parthenon there is . . . how much ? . . . a hundred years, a hundred and fifty years, several generations — and what a gulf ! I do indeed think that the marbles of Phidias derive from those awkward glum old idols . . . as man has descended from the monkey. For the very good reason that he couldn't descend from anything else. But I don't see the links. You might say that one fine day there was a spark and that it was made animate, human, divine. It's an extraordinary thing. The Laborde head is, with that of the Theseus,[11] the only one which remains from the pediment of the Parthenon.

When all that was in place under its own sun with that sea in the distance — it must have been something to look at. What do you think of Morosini who bombarded it with cannon-balls, and Elgin who carried away one of the caryatides from the Erechtheum and knocked the whole thing down with his hammer ?

[11] In the British Museum.

[*We retrace our steps down the corridor and return to the bedroom. Clemenceau sits down.*]

MYSELF: Am I keeping you from working?

CLEMENCEAU: Yes, but that's as it should be. If no one came to disturb me I should become stupid with working. [*Showing me the sheaves of paper laid out in front of him.*] Huh! Can you really believe that I could have had the luck to find all this to do? I need at least three more months to come to the end of it. Martet, give me three months.

MYSELF: Are you going to see the Revolutionary Exhibition at the Bibliothèque Nationale?

CLEMENCEAU: No, ought I to?

MYSELF: It's very good.

CLEMENCEAU: All right, I'll go. Is Aulard's portrait there?

MYSELF: There's a great deal of blood, a great deal?

CLEMENCEAU: What do you expect? The Revolution — its principles were excellent, but you always have men. . .

# XV

## GREECE

*19th February* 1928

CLEMENCEAU [*noticing the portfolio which I am carrying under my arm*]: Ah, at last ! [*I take the papers out of the portfolio and hand them to him.*]

MYSELF: I ask you only to look at them after I'm gone.

CLEMENCEAU: Oh ! Why ?

MYSELF: Because I say things which you will perhaps think I oughtn't to have said. But I shall be pleased to have your opinion of it all the same.

CLEMENCEAU: You'll have it all right. [*He begins to turn over the leaves.*] What's this ? M. Clemenceau ? You speak of M. Clemenceau. What's he ever done to you, that M. Clemenceau ?

MYSELF: I can only speak of what I've seen, and amongst the things I've seen the one which struck me most strongly was yourself. But don't read it, sir, don't read it.

CLEMENCEAU [*putting the manuscript down*]: What can you say about M. Clemenceau ? What indeed *is* there to say ?

MYSELF: How are you today, sir ?

CLEMENCEAU: I'm tired.

MYSELF: Spiritually ?

CLEMENCEAU: You put questions like Victor Cousin.

89

Physically, spiritually, it all comes from the same shop. Nevertheless I'm busy writing an article on the Debts. The trouble about writing is that you can never write all that you're thinking — you must use shifts and evasions. . . And you ? Have you had a visit from the King of Afghanistan ?

MYSELF: No. I don't associate with kings very much.

CLEMENCEAU: You're wrong — get firmly hold of the idea that most of the time kings think about exactly the same things as your tailor or your dentist. I've never known a king who had the soul of a king.

MYSELF: Did you meet the King ?

CLEMENCEAU: Yes, at the Guimet Museum. They asked me if I wanted to go to the reception they were planning for him. I said 'Yes.' So I turned up, and it all went off very pleasantly. They put me next to the Queen, who wanted to know who the old gentleman was whom they had seated next to her. She asked the King, who replied vaguely that it was some sort of fossil, now extinct. So, in order to fix this solemn moment in her memory, she took out her watch and looked at the time. I noticed that her watch was something quite extraordinary — like a crab-apple cut in two. In the centre of this instrument was a diamond — or thirty-six diamonds — I don't know the exact number. It seemed magical.

MYSELF: What did they show the King at the Guimet Museum ?

CLEMENCEAU: Well, fancy, they had the extremely bright idea of showing him photographs of Afghanistan. It was hardly worth the trouble to have him come so far for that.

MYSELF: What impression did he make on you ?

CLEMENCEAU: He came out of it not too badly.

MYSELF: Are you leaving for the Vendée soon ?

CLEMENCEAU: I don't dare to in this vile weather. And you — what are you doing ?

MYSELF: Preparing my trip to Athens. I'm absorbed in

the history of Greece. What a frightful thing it was, that catalogue of atrocities !

CLEMENCEAU: It had its great moments too, Martet !

MYSELF: The treacheries, the stupidities. When one thinks that the same people who fought the Marathon and Salamis. . .

CLEMENCEAU: Martet, I shall stop you right there ! In the first place, don't take Marathon, Salamis, Thermopylæ too seriously. All those yarns. . . I've visited the battlefield of Marathon. They pointed out to me the hillock where were buried the Athenians who died during the conflict. They totalled sixty-three. A battle in which the losses number sixty-three, some of whom probably died of sunstroke — we've seen better since then. . . After all, we only know Greek history through the Greek historians, and Herodotus is like a Marseillais. In speaking of Xerxes' army he says that they dried up the rivers by drinking them. The rest is in keeping. It's all been puffed out and distorted by people who write history like an exchange of fish-stories on the terrace of a café. Greek history is simply the history of three dozen individuals.

But, Martet, amongst those three dozen — and that's my second point — were some who did supremely great things.

MYSELF: Ah, but there isn't one of them who isn't under suspicion. Themistocles, Pausanias — all takers of bribes, perjurers. . .

CLEMENCEAU: There are others . . . Phocion. Don't you love Phocion ? Ah, there's a man I adore. I'd like to have been the friend of that fellow. The derider of the mob — 'What asininity could I have uttered that they applaud me this ?' He read the future, that man. And Socrates, Martet ?

MYSELF: Yes. There was Socrates.

CLEMENCEAU: Ah, Socrates ! Isn't he colossal, that man, against whom no reproach can be brought, who lived free, died free, pursued his way with that smile of his ? How many such do you find amongst us ?

MYSELF: But Plato, Plato, sir ?

CLEMENCEAU: What about him ?

MYSELF: Plato writing the *Symposium* when Greek strength and Greek thought were already being engulfed by catastrophe. Don't you find that joy in living and that serenity overwhelming ?

CLEMENCEAU: Yes, but — well, I'm not struck by Plato's philosophy. There is no man who has talked more nonsense and reasoned more absurdly — but when you've written the *Symposium*, Martet, and those paragraphs about the death of Socrates, you've well fulfilled your destiny. You're given a meaning to the prodigious adventure which is the history of the race. Another one I like very much is Xenophon. He isn't very shrewd, now and then. He narrates events without quite understanding them. But he is so decent, so balanced. What a splendid specimen of a man ! One day I happened to be in the village where he was born, at — oh ! this elusive memory of mine. In the morning I opened my window — I saw nothing but a swallow flying past [*he traces the curve of its flight with his hand*] — that was all that remained of Xenophon.

MYSELF: But the expedition to Sicily; Alcibiades.

CLEMENCEAU: Yes. Frightful. But. . .

MYSELF: And that avalanche which from year to year was on the point of falling — there never was a people who drew so little profit from experience. The Persians had outflanked them the first time at Thermopylæ by crossing the Oeta pass. Thermopylæ was flanked a second time, and by the same pass. The pass was no more guarded the second time than the first.

CLEMENCEAU: Quite so. But that's not the story of Greece only. Look at all those countries who are throwing themselves into the arms of the Boches just as if there had been no war, no Belgium violated, no ships torpedoed. It would seem that nothing can teach anything to anybody; people seem to grow new minds daily. They imagine that their age is exceptional because they live in it, that it's quite different from all others; they believe that they will live to see the beginning of a new era — then they forget to guard the pass. . . As if there ever were new eras.

MYSELF: And Greece in the hands of Rome!

CLEMENCEAU: I give you Rome. It's a degeneration. But Greece! There's a book on Greece by a man named Jardet which you should read. Jardet was a professor at the University of Lyons, and he conceived this history from the most enlightened point of view. He wrote his book, and died, after an illness of two or three months. Then it was learned that he hadn't left enough for his burial, and that his illness had exhausted all of his meagre savings. Not a penny was left for his wife. A collection was taken up — I contributed a trifle — and that, Martet, that's how you end up if you write a book on Greece.

MYSELF: I'm reading Æschylus at the moment.

CLEMENCEAU: It's beautiful, isn't it? What heights of grandeur!

MYSELF: It's beautiful because he believed in what he was doing. There is no more belief — one no longer even believes in the pen which one's holding.

CLEMENCEAU: That's it exactly. They opened their eyes wide on the world — they discovered it. The world was the world for them and not what it's become for us — words. . .

MYSELF: And Aristophanes.

CLEMENCEAU: That fellow — no. I can't see him in the picture — he spoils the composition. He understood nothing about anything whatever, took the great for the small, the small for the great, threw his venom, his rancour about promiscuously, broke everything, soiled everything. It's people like that who corrupt a country.

MYSELF: And Sparta.

CLEMENCEAU: When I arrived in Sparta I said 'Show me Sparta.' There wasn't any. The Eurotas rolled by, a pretty, limpid stream, but about as wide as this piece of furniture. In the museum, which is about as large as this room, there are a statue and a vase, both Attic. They're all that Sparta has left. I expected to find a countryside as dour as themselves, but no — great fertility, vines bearing enormous grapes. And I crossed the Taigeta, which is something of a mountain, I assure you, and arrived at a place called something like 'Coryza' — the women crossed themselves when they saw me and drunken priests kissed me on the mouth.

MYSELF: Did you go to Olympus ?

CLEMENCEAU: Twenty times ! Ah, Olympus. The Circus . . . you still have that before you. And if, on scraping away the earth with your foot and noticing the white line where the runners finished, you experience no sensation, it's because you're made of wood.

MYSELF: And the ancient cities — Argos, Mycenae ?

CLEMENCEAU: Magnificent ! All those huge piles — there's not one of those stone blocks which isn't too large to fit into this garden. They haven't the look of having been made for people like us. You begin to understand the buskin of the Tragedians. . .

MYSELF: I learned with surprise that the Asclepeion of Athena was quite small. . .

CLEMENCEAU: It is. But the temples of the Golden Age are miniscules, and the Asclepeion must be practically contemporary with the Acropolis. That's what constitutes the triumph of those people; they guessed that the key to the problem wasn't size but harmony. They were the only race who understood that. The Egyptians with their pyramids — what were they seeking ? They may pile stone upon stone, yet even by breaking their backs they cannot hope to scale the Heavens.

The Greeks did not look for their solution in space but in the mind.

And after the Asclepeion, which is so lovely in the evening by moonlight, with the children playing all round it, after the Parthenon, which has been so mistreated, which has inspired so much literature, you will see the Pnyx, Martet. The Pnyx reveals things. An old altar to Apollo — yes, that's all — made with artificial soil, so that the Athenian cobblers might determine the fate of Demosthenes.

MYSELF: And Crete ?

CLEMENCEAU: Crete ! Now and then, in the night, when I'm unable to sleep, I see Phaistos again. It's something that's fixed in my memory.

Ah, Greece, Martet. You must travel by way of Greece to get anywhere you're going. I believe that humanity reached its highest point there, easily, joyously. At Rheims, amongst all those Gothic sculptures, which are very fine and which one can't help admiring, there are two statues—copies of Roman things, probably, badly conceived, badly executed. Well, when you notice the folds of the draperies, which fall in that rhythm which the Romans stole from the Greeks, you're numbed, you can't see anything else — nothing but those two statues which are there as if in exile.

There's nothing beyond Æschylus, nothing beyond Plato, nothing beyond Socrates. It all ended in bloodshed and domesticity. Well, perhaps it's the history of all peoples, in all times. Baber, my friend Baber, the conqueror of Persia, used to have a pile of heads brought to him every morning, and when the pile was a little smaller than usual, he would say, 'It's pretty small, this pile. My men are getting slack.' Nevertheless, it was the same Baber who said, 'There are sighs which arouse the world to action.' Men are like that. And one may even wonder if all that blood and all that brutality were not necessary for the making of an Æschylus and the building of an Erectheium. Gentle and kindly men are pleasant to have about, but in general they don't create masterpieces. Soak yourself in Greece, Martet. It's something that's sustained me in trouble. When I was weary of all the imbecilities and the futilities of which politics is composed, I turned my spirit towards Greece. Others went fishing. To each his own way.

## XVI

## Rue Saint-Dominique — The Trip to London

I toss my notes into a drawer. They help me neither to remember nor to muse. I have only to open my memory at this or that page — the proof-sheets it contains are not yet yellowing. . .

What street is this? The Rue Saint-Dominique! The old mansion in which the Republic houses its Ministers for War. Who is that man in the middle of the courtyard? Commandant Crepet, commander of this fortress, who exercises supreme authority over its guard, its dozen rifles and its drum. And this? Brum, brum! Mordacq! And that? . . . Thin and whistling like the winter wind in the keyholes. Mandel! . . . And that great gesticulating devil? Ignace. . . And that charming, so charming man? 'I am your friend. Use me and abuse me!'[1] Sabini! Dear Sabini![2] And that thickset man like a horse trainer? Derby! This one is Pétain, that one Mangin!

I behold the shade of that great devil of a National Guardsman coming into view. Very blond, very erect, his eyes as blue as faience ware, and sublimely devoid of all expression,

[1] The original is in dialect. — *Translator's note.*
[2] Commercial attaché to the Italian Embassy. M. Clemenceau liked him. Sabini began by overwhelming me with cases of oranges. Then the orange season came to an end. After that he made me a Commander of the Order of the Couronne Royale.

who bowls me over with a salute of his enormous open hand. Whilst I rush up the stairs every morning, four at a time, in a horrible panic at the thought of being late. I can see the people who brought up my post — those letters, those hampers of letters! How men love to write! What an idiot the chap was who invented writing! There is not a country under the sun which has escaped that folly. Here is a letter from MM. Gianoulopoulo and Patras and M. Benito Villanueva of Buenos Aires. What do they want? Four, eight, a dozen pages. All languages: 'Dearest old friend, . . .' writes Margot Asquith. 'The game is hard,' writes Capel. . . 'But you shall (*sic*) win it.' I turn these letters over and over. Shall I speak to him about this? Yes — no — if I do speak to him about it . . . but if I don't. . .

I go into Clemenceau's office. Mandel is there.

'And then?' Clemenceau asks him.

'You must read Capus's article, chiefly those words which cannot fail to surprise. . .'

The 'surprising' words read and noted.

Mandel with a gesture of his hands as if he were making the orb of the world turn round and round, with a twist of his back as if he were trying to roll over in a gutter — Mandel conveys that that's all, although nevertheless . . . but we might say all . . . all . . . and yet not altogether all.

Clemenceau turns to me.

'At your service.'

At my service, but not for long. Just time to say to him:

'A letter from Sir Francis Bertie.'

'What does he want?'

'He is leaving for London.'

'Next?'

'A letter from. . .'

The door opens. . . Herscher,[3] Alby,[4] Mordacq enter. The

---

[3] Colonel Herscher. Head of the Military Secretariat.
[4] General Alby.

front, tanks, trenches, spies, G.H.Q., the war. I go back to my room. The office which I share with Mandel[5] is full of people. There is Colonel Edmond Théry, 'the European economist,' in the uniform in which he dresses himself up on holidays and other occasions of public and private rejoicings, with the badge of the Legion of Honour pinned on his stomach — the pot-bellied apparition which symbolizes in this sort of establishment some vague mysterious science in a perpetual state of bankruptcy. There is Alerme — undeceived, disillusioned. 'What? It surprises you? But it's always that way. The more stupid it is, the more chance it has of sticking.'

My old friend Wormser[6] . . . Cassé-Barthe[7] . . . 'Er . . . er . . . I stutter . . .,' Fontin,[8] smiling and silent, his hands in the hip pockets of his trousers.

The bell! It's the 'boss.' I take a writing-pad and pencil and go in. He is alone, lowering. He looks towards the window and says:

'A telegram for Barrère:[9] I HAVE NOT YET RECEIVED M. ORLANDO'S REPLY AND CANNOT WAIT ANY LONGER. PLEASE REMIND HIM THAT EVEN TODAY THE WORD "PROMISE" HAS SOME MEANING. . .'

Then follow ten pages of my writing-pad. Not a pause. Never a request for a repetition. His thoughts unfold themselves lucidly and straightforwardly. When he has finished:

'Read it over,' he says.

I do not know how I succeeded in reading it back, for he dictated it at breakneck speed. Not a word to change. The flow was perfect.

'Have it typed.'

I go out, and return ten minutes later. He is with Foch.

[5] M. Painlevé's old office. Clemenceau installed himself in the former office of the head of the Cabinet.
[6] Head of the Cabinet later, when Mandel was elected to the Chamber.
[7] Second in command of the Civil Cabinet. He became prefect. He would make several starts before he could express any idea.
[8] 'In command of a mission,' and I could never find out what mission.
[9] French Ambassador at Rome.

'What is it ?'

'Your signature. . .'

He takes up his formidable goose quill, dips it in the ink, scratches the point on the edge of the inkwell, signs. I go out again.

People are waiting about for me in the billiard-room. Who ?  Generals who are asking for decorations and whom Mordacq has sent for a little walk.  Colonels who want the rosette or a general's stars.  Priests, nuns, old gentlemen with troubled faces who have something 'very interesting and important' to communicate to Clemenceau. . . Women who need coal for their stoves. . . Emirs who wish to assert their loyalty. . . Manufacturers of trench mortars. . . Journalists. . . Old cronies whom I have not seen for fifteen years and who look as if they had just crawled out from under the furniture ! 'Hullo !  you haven't changed a bit.'

I receive them.  Between two doors in a beautiful draught, without even listening very closely to what they tell me.  I am thinking that I have a paper on my table which I must show to Clemenceau. . . Every three minutes I ask the door-keeper: 'Isn't he alone yet ?'

'No, there is M. Boudenoot [10] with him.  Or there is the Greek Minister.  Or there is Colonel Repington.'

The poor wretch who has just come up to seek my aid and protection tells me his little story:

'You understand: if before the end of the war I am not nominated a veterinary surgeon of the second class. . .'

Suddenly the door-keeper dashes out:

'The President is putting on his hat.'

I leave the vet, rooted to the spot.

'What else ?' Clemenceau asks me.

'A letter which a Dane has sent you. . . It seems that your friend, Brandes. . .'

[10] A Senator.  President of the Army Commission.

AT THE FRONT, WATCHING AN AIR FIGHT

*Marshal Foch is seen to the right with his stick under his chin*

'The dirty dog! What has he done now?' [*I read the letter.*] 'Nothing could surprise me about that fellow.'

The morning passes. Afternoon comes. All day I hear the hum of the hive where the fate of nations is at stake. The great machine for making war is in action. What about the Italians? Herscher declares: 'They are getting themselves together and establishing a front.' What about Russia? She has collapsed. The Ukraine and the Caucasus are pulling apart. The English? They are fighting around Saint Quentin and Cambrai. . . Our troops? The traitors? Alby reports: 'No. 34 has met No. 122 at Geneva.' . . .

The soldiers melt away, giving place to the civilians. . . Here's Klotz: How does the Loan stand? Boret:[11] And the wheat? Bread? Milk? Nail . . . Malvy? . . . Ignace . . . Vincennes?[12]

Delysia! Delysia! The journey to London. A voice whispers to me: delve in your memory for that beautiful girl. . . it was in. . .

In March 1918 we left Paris on Wednesday the 13th via the Gare du Nord. At Calais there was a cold drizzle. We went aboard an old boat called the *Pas-de-Calais* whose captain seemed quite indifferent to the possibility of being torpedoed. 'A Boche submarine? Oh! Do you think so? It would surprise me.'

The voyage was pleasantly sad. A fairly strong sea, greenish-yellow in colour, a cold, biting wind; and, once we were out in the open sea, a mist. We went on, rolling and pitching. Even the least timid amongst us looked askance at that dirty water whence so many periscopes might suddenly appear. We were escorted by I don't know how many destroyers, who circled around us like watchdogs. Suddenly everyone was on

---

[11] Minister for Agriculture and Food.
[12] It was at Vincennes that traitors and spies were shot.

the alert. A destroyer had darted away towards the open sea. 'There they are !' someone cried. 'Submarines !' It was only an empty bottle.

I can see ourselves on the boat, Clemenceau in a black over-coat and black bowler hat which, when we had left port, he replaced with a little house cap. He paced up and down the deck from prow to stern and from port to starboard, amongst windlasses and coils of rope.

'Well, so you have gone and left your little wife ?'

'Yes.'

'I don't need you. You might just as well have stayed behind.'

'I know that, sir. You never do need me.'

'But I prefer to take you along. Primarily to take you away from your little wife. You are too much under the thumb of women, Martet.'

'Well, sir, it's a very gentle thumb.'

'And besides, you should see London. London in war time is a strange sight.'

I see Foch again — with his cap at an angle, his long-skirted coat, his little stick under his arm, a kindly, dreamy light in his eye; Weygand, dark and sturdily ugly, withdrawn from the world; Pichon, the good Pichon. He was wearing a cattle merchant's cap. I see Spiers again, a happy man, thirty years old and a general. He is thin, lithe and charming.[13] Who else ? That round, peaceable fellow: it's Orlando. There is General Giardino. . . there is Barbier. . .

They handed out to all of us enormous cork belts enveloped in white canvas, and we wrapped them round our stomachs. Orlando looked as if he were wearing the kind of harness they put on children to support their first toddling steps. Pichon was girdled with a dozen large white sausages.

[13] He was the liaison officer between the British War Office and our Ministry for War.

When they brought one to Clemenceau he said:

'What are you bothering about me for ?'

I ask Barbier:

'Why haven't the Boches the nerve to turn up here ? What a scene for history !'

At last we are at Dover. The great cliffs of Shakespeare . . . Then the neat little English countryside. And then London . . . London. Clemenceau was quite right. It is a strange and sinister place. Everybody is disguised as a soldier, men, women, kids . . . and everybody is dancing everywhere. . . Upstairs, downstairs, in the drawing-room, in the cellar . . . tangoes, Bostons, and all soberly, so soberly. The English dance the way other people pray. Fagalde and Charles de Noailles [14] took me to a kind of grillroom — until the early hours of the morning I saw couples in military uniform, male and female, passing back and forth by my table as if possessed, all ages and colours, looking at the infinite with their blue eyes, advancing, retreating — one, two; they seemed on the point of bursting with homesickness. It was melancholy, sad. And what is that over there ? A wounded chap, whose poor head is wrapped in gauze and gives forth the horrible perfumes of the chemist's shop. The hospital dance, the operating-table dance.

I say to Noailles:

'Don't they make the skeletons dance, too ?'

I had just arrived from Paris, where scarcely anyone danced and where the nights were torn asunder by bombardments and the shrieks of sirens. But Paris had kept her laughter. People laughed even as they tumbled down into their cellars. . . London where the nights were peaceful and where everybody Bostoned and tangoed, was funereal, even on gala nights.

I asked Fagalde to introduce me to some French people. He took me to call on Delysia. Delysia is French, she should

[14] He was working under Fagalde's orders.

be called Dupont or Durand. She happened to prefer Delysia: she was wrong. There is no prettier name than Dupont, unless it is Durand. She offered us dinner, and immediately after the last course said:

'Listen ! Listen !'

She sang — the most stupid of French songs . . . but with what a voice and what spirit ! You would have taken her for a bugle. Brave Delysia !

'Well,' Clemenceau asked me, 'have you seen Westminster ?'

'I have seen Delysia, sir. . .'

On the 17th we returned to Paris. On the 18th the newspapers published this paragraph: 'During his stay M. Clemenceau has participated in London at Conferences at which the Italian Prime Minister and other Italian ministers were present. M. Clemenceau appeared very satisfied with the conferences which he had had with the English and Italian ministers, and states that the most complete understanding was reached with the minimum of effort.'

With the minimum of effort ! He should have seen the English dancing !

They would not have understood one another so easily.

# XVII

## THE DARK DAYS

ON THE 17th March 1918, Clemenceau returned from London. The German offensive began on the 21st, five days later. On the 23rd the English resistance gave way. On the morning of the 24th the British communiqué announced that 'powerful attacks launched by massed infantry and artillery have broken our line to the west of Saint-Quentin.' It was a fact. The English front was broken.

The dark days began. . .

CLEMENCEAU left at dawn, wrapped in his thick brown woollen overcoat, wearing his grey drooping hat, colossal, savage, his dynamic will desperate but unbreakable. Brabant was on the driver's seat.

On the 23rd he is at Compiègne waiting for Pétain. On the 24th and 25th he is at the front; he goes back there the next day and the next. He is drawn by that infernal cauldron where the fate of nations is being determined. He goes to the very edge of the battle, breathes it in. The fearful need there is to establish cohesion between all those men, all those spirits, all those races ! Some, disheartened, pore over their maps and have too much sense of reality not to despair. He raises them up with 'Come on, let's get on with it.' The others, the hot-heads, no longer see anything as impossible in the smoke and frenzy of action, and would like to throw in everything, grab victory by the throat. He calms them with 'Patience !'

He returns to Paris, exhausted, covered with dung and mud to his knees, but with the inspiration of Salamis still before his eyes. There is not only the front . . . there is also the rear gasping and burning in fever. There is the Chamber of Deputies. On the 23rd, the day when the English front broke under the German pressure, he hastened into the corridor of the Chamber.

'What's happening ?' asked the deputies.

'Don't make those faces. They are sending reinforcements. Nothing to fear. . .'

On the 27th — Noyon had just been abandoned, they were getting ready to evacuate Montdidier — he comes to the Chamber. 'The situation has appreciably improved. The German onslaught is weakening.'

There are the ministries. There is the Elysée. On the morning of the 25th, while the French troops in the Noyon sector were engaged in the 'terrific struggle' of which the communiqué spoke, there was a meeting of the Cabinet: the military, diplomatic, and economic situation was gone into. . . For it was not only a question of fighting. It was a question of eating.

There was Paris, which now lived only on its nerves, bombarded and racked at night by the Boche 'planes and the scream of the sirens, in the daytime by Big Bertha. On the morning of the 24th, before leaving for the front, Clemenceau went to make the round of the ruins: houses with gaping walls, looking as if they had been sliced off by a razor and snatched from the adjacent walls. . . The round also of the wounded and the dead.

Then there was the group which was already wavering and

vacillating, which was looking to us; and Clemenceau tele-graphed to Lloyd George on the 28th, just as we had evacu-ated Montdidier, 'We are firm and confident of tomorrow.'

There he is, the man of seventy-seven who has seen every-thing, lived through everything, experienced everything, and to whom only this one last horror was lacking — the devasta-tion of his country. M. Claveille [1] wrote to him on November 19th, 'Perhaps you may remember the momentous confidences you made to me on the 15th August 1918, at Marseille-en-Beauvaisis, and which I had the honour to receive from you on one of the most anxious days of the war. My thoughts are carried back at this moment inevitably to those confidences: they recall to me with complete fidelity the courage and tenacity of my illustrious chief, who is so prominently asso-ciated with our country's triumph. . . It was the greatest honour that I could have wished for in my modest career to have been summoned to serve under your orders.' General Guillaumat wrote to him, 'The army of the East is following with anxiety the fluctuations of the struggle which has been going on for the past fortnight and of which it knows that you are the guiding spirit. It is for that reason that it asserts its confidence and dares to hope.'

So FEW years have passed since then and already it is all so far away. How quickly horror is forgotten !

[1] Minister for Public Works and Transport in the Clemenceau Cabinet.

## XVIII

## The Elections — One Evening in December — The Vendée

*1st April* 1928

CLEMENCEAU: How do you do, Monsieur Martet ? Delighted to make your acquaintance.

MYSELF: How do you do, sir ? Delighted to have made yours thirteen years ago. How are you ?

CLEMENCEAU: Like a man in the last stages of decay, thank you.

MYSELF: Albert tells me that you are leaving for the Vendée.

CLEMENCEAU: Yes; oughtn't I to ?

MYSELF: Certainly, but you didn't tell me about it.

CLEMENCEAU: Oh, reproaches ! I beg your pardon, Monsieur Martet. I'll take you if you like. . .

MYSELF: Thank you. Because of my littleness I think I had better stay close to the shore.

CLEMENCEAU: So much the worse for you ! I should have shown you something that is rarely seen in these parts of the world: a sky — with passing clouds. . . What are they saying about the elections ? Just think ! I am having a most unpleasant experience — I am wondering if I ought to vote. Do you believe in voting, Martet ?

MYSELF: Sir, whoever it was that fought for universal suffrage it certainly wasn't I.

CLEMENCEAU: Who is there to vote for ? Poincaré or the Communists ? I don't like the Communists very much — and Poincaré . . . Poincaré . . . well, you know the affection I have always had for him. In my constituency there is a man called La Roch-Thulon [1]. . . Obviously I cannot vote for a La Roch-Thulon. One just doesn't vote for a La Roch-Thulon. Pacaud ? [2] He said to me when he presented himself for election to the Senate, 'If you were nice, you would write a sweet little letter to tell all the good that you know about me.' I wrote the sweet little letter, and then what did Pacaud do ? He deserted me. I don't know if you have ever noticed it, but I seem to have a talent for being deserted.

MYSELF: Men do not like being loyal. It makes them feel that they are losing their personalities.

CLEMENCEAU: They express themselves better by betrayal. Then who is there to vote for, Martet ?

MYSELF: It's a question which a number of people are putting to themselves. There have never been so many people who are wondering whom to vote for. To make things even there have never been so many candidates. Yesterday evening there were five hundred and ten for the Seine alone.[3]

CLEMENCEAU: Five hundred and ten ! It's terrifying. But it's understandable. When politics was a matter of ideas, that discouraged and frightened off a few. Today it's quite the opposite. . . I begin to believe that Mandel will be elected. I see that a certain journalist has referred to him as a species of *microbe*. . . There is no better single word for depicting him. He has a life. . .

MYSELF: Have you heard from him ?

CLEMENCEAU: He telephones me now and then and asks

[1] A reactionary candidate.
[2] Another candidate, a radical.
[3] There were 921 on the day of the election, for 59 seats.

me if he can come and see me.  I answer neither yes nor
no. . . So he comes.  He tells me things.  He has an idea,
though only one, but he holds on to it firmly: he wants to
be elected and enter the Chamber in order to scold people. . .
Haven't you ever wanted to be a deputy ?

MYSELF:  I prefer to watch men of action act ! . . . act !
. . . act !

CLEMENCEAU:  Quite so.  And you find that. . .

MYSELF:  Lovely !  There are such marvellous results !  I
bought myself a pair of shoes yesterday.  I paid 175 francs
for them.

CLEMENCEAU:  Well, you get the point all the same !  Have
you read Jouffroy, Martet ?

MYSELF:  No, sir.

CLEMENCEAU:  That's a mistake.  In the first place he is a
man who knows how to write.  I should almost incline to
accuse him of writing too well.  His sentences are too well
turned: they are like too beautiful women — they don't excite
you.  You admire them and haven't the least desire to. . .
Every now and then it happens that I write things with subjects, predicates, objects . . . they unroll like carpets.  I have
to recall them in order to rewrite them badly, because life
itself is imperfect.  And it is life that matters before all else.
This granted, there is nevertheless a page of Jouffroy about a
certain December night which is very good.  I will read it to
you.  I had a book . . . I don't know what possesses my
books: they hide themselves somewhere, insinuate themselves
into corners . . . there is no way of getting them back again.
I borrowed this one from the Bibliothèque Nationale.  Practically all of the Bibliothèque Nationale books are round here
somewhere.  [*He reads.*]  'I shall never forget that December evening when the veil which had obscured my natural
skepticism was torn.  I still hear my footsteps in that narrow
bare chamber where, long after the hour of sleep, I was ac-

customed to stride up and down. . .' [*And the reading went on, the beautiful sentences unrolling like carpets.*] And here at the end, 'Frightened by the empty unknown into which I felt myself being drawn, I turned my thoughts in vain for the last time towards my childhood, my family, my country, all that was sacred and dear to me; the inflexible tide of my thoughts was too strong; parents, family, memories, beliefs, it was compelling me to leave them all.' Eh ! What do you think of that ?

MYSELF: It's well said.

CLEMENCEAU: Because it is well thought. There's a man who at least has questioned himself. How many people are there who question themselves ? It's that way because it's that way, and it will still be that way tomorrow. . . There you have the entire content of their spirits. While Jouffroy took his little lamp, turned its rays on his soul and said, 'Let's have a look ! What is there there ?' And he realized that there was nothing there.

MYSELF: How did the idea of reading Jouffroy occur to you ?

CLEMENCEAU: Because Jouffroy, as you see, had an idea. I once had it . . . I have found it again in him. Jouffroy asked himself if the human race will suffer the fate of the other animal species which have disappeared, and, if so, whether it will disappear through inadequacy of numbers or because it is preparing its own death with its own hands. I am going to take that up again. I want to express the idea that the law which governs humanity — the law which it cannot avoid, which it hasn't the right to avoid — is the law of progress, and it is progress that kills humanity. We get excited, we agitate ourselves, we expend our energies, we enunciate our ideas each time that we extract something from chaos it is only a new poison, which leads us a little further on the road to extinction. While speaking of this I might say two or three words about liberty, government, democracy and so forth.

MYSELF: It isn't a very cheerful subject.

CLEMENCEAU: Don't take me for a cheerful author.

MYSELF: It is obvious that the genius of man up to now has reached its highest point in the manufacture of poison gas . . . but. . .

CLEMENCEAU: But what ? Oughtn't it to be said ? . . . Truth should always be stated, and as unmistakably as possible. Then I shall leave on Tuesday at 4 o'clock in the morning. I shall be at Tours at eight, and lunch at home.

MYSELF: I see that in the Vendée the sea has broken the dykes and that there are dozens of acres under water.

CLEMENCEAU: Yes, between Aiguillon and La Tranche. At that point the land is protected from the sea by a little mud dyke about as high as this. You can imagine that the sea would have some fun with it . . . there is one man who tells how he had to go into the water up to his neck to find his cart horses. It seems that there's going to be a high tide on the 21st. I shall be there.

MYSELF: Have you any news of your house ?

CLEMENCEAU: Yes. It's still standing. The flowers are growing. I shall enjoy myself . . . take it easy, relax, and await the end with a smile. I shall have two guests, Martin and one other, the son of one of my old school friends — a chap without a very wide outlook, but he doesn't need that. What would he do with it ? The son has a nice little fortune; he doesn't do anything but read . . . that's all he does. He has read *Au Soir de la Pensée* three times and sends me a chit from time to time.

MYSELF: Have you noticed that your old friend Linyer [4] has just been elected senator for the Loire-Inférieure ?

CLEMENCEAU: What pleased me was that he was put up

[4] A barrister at Nantes, the owner of a fine property by the sea.

against Briand's candidate.  Linyer is a nice fellow.  Do you remember his forest of evergreen oaks ?  He has three or four hundred hectares in which I love to walk.  What a bore that the Linyers are Catholics !  They believe that God comes in the night to make their little oaks grow.  It's quite a harmless idea.  Linyer once said to me, 'The Church imposes its discipline on me and I submit to it.'  I only regret that he can't find that discipline in himself but is compelled to go and borrow it from the Pope. . . Let's talk about something else.

MYSELF:  And the landlord of your house at Bel-Ebat ?

CLEMENCEAU:  Oh, he's a character, that fellow !  He lives in a kind of château [5] full of furniture and knick-knacks and a lot of things which would rejoice the heart of an antiquary. You can't imagine what a mess it's in.  Clocks on top of one another, buffets without tops or bottoms !  He lives there like a kind of lunatic and breeds horses.  His bedroom is three times as big as this room.  When you go into it you see a bed that would hold four people, and old saddles and odd boots strewn about everywhere.  He eats at one corner of the table and says, 'I am a Bohemian.'  He has something like twenty or twenty-five millions.  No fool . . . he travels, with another specimen of humanity that must be his wife.  Every now and then you hear that he is in Java . . . or China.  And he reads — and how !  He reads whatever falls into his hands. One day he said to me, 'Please explain Pascal's doubts. . .' His name is Comte Luce de Tremont, but he says, 'My father called himself Luce for short.'  He also says, 'In the Vendée I go to Mass: it is the tradition.  But in Paris it would never enter my head.'

MYSELF:  What are you taking away to read ?

CLEMENCEAU:  Plutarch, my friend; I am going to reread Plutarch.  I should like to try to understand why there were

[5] La Guignardière, near Avrillé.

once so many great men and why today there are so few.

MYSELF: Have there ever been so many as all that?

CLEMENCEAU: Yes, there have been. . . The ancients were able to make whatever they wanted of the facts. They magnified everything; they made a great battle out of a broil between porters and donkey drivers. Now we have the men themselves; we have their spirit, their outline; we know what they said, what they thought. Socrates is great painted by Plato, who saw him in one way, and he is great painted by Xenophon, who saw him in another. I only wanted three words of Socrates in order to know what there was in the fellow — intellect, light, courage, grandeur. Amongst the Romans there were fewer characters; nevertheless, there was Lucretius, whose sayings were a little inflexible, Cicero. . . He wasn't too bad, Cicero. . .

MYSELF: And how all that ended!

CLEMENCEAU: Yes, Rome because of Byzantium, which was an appalling phenomenon. . . Athens, as you know . . . Ægos-Potami — and the rest! It's sinister. When nations die abruptly it's all right, but when they just drag along and are enticed into debauchery. . . They are like those old fellows who go balmy and end up by marrying their nurses. Hold on, though! There is still one man who isn't balmy and who seems to me to be worthy of Plutarch. I mean Cristal.[6] He is in his ninety-ninth year: he is just about to die, and he writes me this letter. [*Clemenceau hands me a letter from 'Père' Cristal. It is written on cheap ruled paper but in a neat and firm handwriting.*]

MYSELF [*reading*]: 'I shall be very glad to see you during your journey. . .'

CLEMENCEAU: I wrote that I would call and see him on my way to the Vendée.

MYSELF: 'But I shall not be able to ask you to dinner — a

---

[6] The large wine-grower in Anjou.

thing I never do for anybody. For I am no longer of this world; I am getting ready to die. But before going away it would give me great happiness to shake your hand. . .' Yes, yes, it's a charming letter. Cristal is as good as his wine.

CLEMENCEAU: I shall go to see him. They wanted to marry him off recently . . . at ninety-eight! People haven't any pity. And the person who wanted to change her name to Madame Cristal, knowing that I was on good terms with him, wanted to get on good terms with me. She therefore sent me a copy of *Démosthène* and asked me to write an inscription in it. Only she spelled it *inscripshun*.[7] Poor Père Cristal! I trust that he'll remain a bachelor. If he gets married at ninety-eight he's practically precluded by time from ever getting a divorce. . . He was once asked what his father did, and he answered, 'He's a chimney-sweep.' I don't know if he's very rich. He has twelve hectares of vines which he no longer cultivates as he says there is a shortage of labour. But he has the nature of a dog and it is quite likely that he did everything possible to chase his hands away.

MYSELF: Where does he live?

CLEMENCEAU: At Parney, near to Saumur. A striking spot. I follow the Loire on the embankment: the road runs along the river. The banks are of sand and there are magnificent poplars. . . There is no better air than that country's, and no corner of France which is more French. I cross the river at Montsoreau: gardens, châteaux everywhere — it's heavenly, and that bewitching language! Have you ever drunk Père Cristal's wine?

MYSELF: Yes, every time I've had a chance.

CLEMENCEAU: There is scarcely need to say that a country which has that is a great country, because there cannot be good wine without a great history and a great civilization. So I shall go to see Cristal; I shall exchange a number of pro-

---

[7] *Dédicasse.—Translator's note.*

foundly philosophical thoughts with him, especially about death. . . He seems to have some very well-worked-out, definite ideas on the subject, and I believe he could clear up a number of obscure points for me. Four hours later I shall be at Saint-Vincent with my feet in the sand.

MYSELF: They tell me that a café has been opened next door to you at Saint-Vincent.

CLEMENCEAU: Quite true. The Ocean Café. I hope that it'll go broke. All those poor people who go to the seaside get so bored. Someone tells them, 'Why not go to Saint-Vincent-sur-Jard ? You can see the house belonging to that fellow . . . you know . . . Clementel . . . who did something or other during the war . . . some name like Clementel . . . Clemenceau. . .' So they turn up with their tennis racquets and their cameras. Sometimes there are five or six worthy folk lying in ambush waiting for me to show myself. . . Some idiot thought that he could make his fortune by selling them glasses of red wine. I'm only waiting till he calls it 'Clemenceau's Bar,' and then I shall go and ask him to take me on as page boy. Martet, I love the Vendée. Why ? Because I passed my youth there: I know every field, every farm, every village. I have ridden on horseback through all those sunken roads. Sometimes you'll ride two or three miles without seeing the sun. Where are you from ?

MYSELF: I was born in Angers of a Parisian father whose mother came from Tours and whose father from Carpentras.

CLEMENCEAU: I see. It's very complicated. At bottom you really have no country. My people have always lived in the Vendée. And it's odd: I love the Vendéens. They are respectable people. I am just rereading the memoirs of Madame de la Rochejacquelin. They are good. They have an ideal. And to defend that ideal they have something obstinate, limited, and savage in them — which I like. It wasn't

CLEMENCEAU'S COTTAGE IN THE VENDÉE OVERLOOKING
THE GARDEN

CLEMENCEAU WALKING IN HIS GARDEN

the nobles who made the wars in the Vendée; it was the peasants who sought them out and said, 'Lead us !'

MYSELF: Yes, they took up arms because they didn't want to be soldiers.

CLEMENCEAU: But you must see people as they are and against the background of their own age. What meaning could the Rhine have for a Mouchamps[8] peasant in 1792 ? What did even France mean to him ? Who had spoken to them about it ? They were happy, those people. They cultivated their bit of ground; they had their rosaries and their crucifixes, which were the answer to everything. But one day somebody came and said to them, 'That isn't everything. Let's go and learn about liberty and fraternity from our brothers in Italy and Prussia.' They answered, 'Thanks ! Go yourself, if it amuses you !' When they learned what 'my country' meant, you see what they were capable of doing. There were no better soldiers. Furthermore, the wars of the Vendée would not have amounted to anything — just little skirmishes. They only became serious because of the bankruptcy of the government; when there was a strong government, nothing ever happened.

You will say that it's stupid, but I'm happy at the thought that I shall be buried at Colombier.[9] There is a little wood there which was planted by my father. I have a little arrangement with the local authorities whereby they have a man to keep an eye on it — a slightly absent-minded eye. One day I went there. I saw a lovely pile of refuse at the foot of a tree. I said to the man, 'You oughtn't to let cows walk round here.' He came closer, bent over, looked at it. 'That, sir ? That isn't a cow, that's a Christian !' So you see: everybody has some use of it. We are all one big family. The wood is

[8] The birthplace of the Clemenceau family.
[9] The château of the Clemenceau family. It is situated in the commune of Mouchamps.

part of a property which was left to my sisters. They sold the château. I took a walk through it with my grandfather, a silly dried up old fellow in a high hat and not an idea under it. I wonder how he produced my father. He used to read the *Book of Facts*. Isn't that very Second-Empire! There have been all sorts in my family: peasants, bourgeois. Yes, I'm satisfied to be buried amongst them all. . .

MYSELF: Extraordinary! I really don't understand. . .

CLEMENCEAU: What don't you really understand?

MYSELF: This anxiety about what's going to happen after your death. You have got Sicard[10] to make a stele to put on your grave. . . Do you think that once you're dead you will get any pleasure out of your tomb?

CLEMENCEAU: I don't think anything. It amuses me. And I must tell you: no one is to go to my burial — except myself. I'm just to be left in peace.

MYSELF: But, once more, what difference can that make to you?

CLEMENCEAU: And, once more, it's silly, it has neither rhyme nor reason; it's anything you like — but that's the way I want it.

MYSELF: And if, despite your injunction, I want to go to your burial?

CLEMENCEAU: Martet, you won't do that! I forbid it. Oh, there is something I wanted to tell you. Near Saumur there is a kind of megalithic remain on which I should be happy to have your opinion. It is a sort of château with enormous stones. Go and see it. You can then tell me what to make of it.[11]

MYSELF: If it's megalithic it's certainly not in my department.

CLEMENCEAU: If it were in your department I should not be

---

[10] A sculptor.
[11] It is mentioned in *Au Soir de la Pensée*.

talking to you about it. You would only tell me a lot of non-sense. [*I get up. He shows me out. In the hall he says:*] Perhaps you are right not to produce children. This life is decidedly not a very handsome gift.

MYSELF: I haven't had any children, but I've adopted one.

CLEMENCEAU: Oh, is that so! What? A boy?

MYSELF: A girl. . .

CLEMENCEAU: So you've found one already made. Therefore I can't say that that makes one poor unfortunate the more. But it doesn't make one poor unfortunate the less, for you are satisfied merely to change the form of its misery.

MYSELF: That's all there ever is.

CLEMENCEAU: You're right: that's all there ever is. *Au 'voir, mon vieux.*

# XIX

## 'My Crimes'

*11th May* 1928

PIÉTRI telephones me, 'Clemenceau wants to see us both to-morrow at two o'clock.'

'Oh, what's going on?'

'Can't tell you over the telephone. . . He's making some plans.'

*12th May*

I say to Albert, 'Then you've come back from the Vendée?'

'Yes, the weather there was frightful. We came back before the elections.'

I go into the study. The radiator gives out an infernal heat. Piétri arrives and then Clemenceau comes in, very alert. He is wearing enormous bedroom slippers lined with fur.

MYSELF: But how does it happen that you're here? I didn't know of your return. . .

CLEMENCEAU: In the Vendée I was worse than here, and I had a number of things to do which I am going to tell you about.

MYSELF: Then you didn't vote down there?

CLEMENCEAU: No. I voted here in the first ward of the 16th arrondissement for a man called Pierre Dupuy,[1] who

---

[1] Director of the *Petit Parisien*.

has one thing to his credit — he published verbatim my remarks on America, which my warmest partisans carefully
refrained from doing. He was my first choice on the ballot;
my servant asked me to make him my second also, but I
answered, 'Oh, no, once is enough.'

MYSELF: Is that all you have done for universal suffrage ?

CLEMENCEAU: That's all. Universal suffrage is a toy with
which people are beginning to get bored. One should not
say that, however, because the people must have a religion.
But that's how it is . . . sadly and with the expression of
my regrets. . . M. Piétri, M. Martet, sit down.

[*We sit down. Clemenceau at his large Louis XV. desk,
Piétri and I opposite him in two armchairs.*]

CLEMENCEAU: Well, then, I am in the midst of preparing
for my disappearance.

MYSELF: Charming idea !

CLEMENCEAU: Oh, it's not so bad ! It's an event that can
be considered without boredom, provided you carry it out in
an orderly and dispassionate manner. I am ill, you see; my
hands burn as if they were on fire. I have this racking cough
again — and then I am going through a very bad period. I
have finished writing my article on the Debts. At present
I am writing a kind of monograph on Monet. Yes, indeed;
does that surprise you ? Well, I have felt for a long time it
was my duty to write it. And so I am now at it. I write, I
erase, I add — it won't go. I no longer have my old accuracy
and rapidity. It's something that's leaving me. In short, I
have summoned you. I want to arrange certain papers, to
say certain things. After which I shall feel easier in my
mind. I thought of you two . . . of Piétri who is the most
upright and most devoted man I have ever met, who has made
these last years so much easier in a way that I cannot express . . . and without him it is certain that I should never
have been able to write *Au Soir de la Pensée.* For *Au Soir*

*de la Pensée* is for me the end, the ultimate achievement; if I had never written that, I should feel myself uncomfortable in Eternity.

And I thought of you, Monsieur Martet. You have faults — a great many faults: you don't believe in anything, you doubt yourself, you doubt everything; you regard the world with that skeptical smile. And to shake you out of that rôle — which has nevertheless enabled me to know what you were thinking and saying — I have had to scold you. However, from the point of view of dependability and judgment you'll do.[2] I have two friends — yourselves. That is why you are here.

MYSELF: Thank you, sir.

CLEMENCEAU: Now let us see how we are going to arrange things. [*He shows me a bundle of papers on his desk.*] First, I give you this: it is an article on Alcibiades which Cavalotti gave me a short while before his death. You can do what you like with it. You can publish it, edit. . .

MYSELF: ? ? ?

CLEMENCEAU: Cavalotti is not of the highest class. He stupidly died just when he might have done great things or at least respectable things. In a few days I shall give you two other articles by Cavalotti. They tell me that one of them is very good. Next, here is an envelope which I found in a corner which has your name on it. I do not know what is in it: bills, drafts of letters — probably nothing of any interest. . .

MYSELF: I'll look them over at home.

CLEMENCEAU: That out of the way, and before coming to the examination of the other papers which I have here, there is a little talk I should like to have with you — it's purpose is not to soothe my conscience, as you might think. I merely

---

[2] I apologize for this testimonial to my dependability and judgment. I am more embarrassed than pleased about it.

want to clarify certain of your ideas in view of various contingencies which may arise. When I fell from power in 1920 I thought that it would be sufficient to withdraw into the ranks in order to be left at peace. I even thought that in order to find refuge from all controversy the best thing would be for me to dash off to the other end of the world. If I am absent, I thought in my simplicity, people won't dare to say anything. Hardly had I set foot on the boat when an illustrious Marshal of France began to cast aspersions upon me . . . as you know.[3] It is what made me think that when I am no longer here, people will suddenly find their courage again and hurl themselves on my corpse with little wriggles of joy. That is the way things go, and I do not care a hoot except that if I have tried to accomplish anything it is right that something at least of this accomplishment should survive, even if it is only the thought that inspired it. That is why I am going to speak to you of my crimes.

MYSELF: Your crimes ?

CLEMENCEAU: Yes. I have committed three crimes in my life.

MYSELF: That's not very many.

CLEMENCEAU: The first crime of which I am accused is that I had Lecomte and Clément Thomas assassinated. That was the affair of the 18th March 1871. I have a complete file on the subject somewhere which I shall hand over to you: do with it what you like. In '72 I undertook an investigation of the subject in order to assemble all possible evidence. You will see that there are about a hundred letters, among which are those of Méline and Schoelcher. In addition I had begun to write a statement of all the facts, including those which preceded and those which followed the 18th March: I spoke of my trips to Bordeaux, M. Thiers'[4] promises. I wrote an ac-

[3] Clemenceau had left for India. This was the moment which Marshal Foch chose to reproach him with having given France a 'bad' peace.
[4] For all this see later, Chapter XXV.

count of how I passed every minute of that day of the 18th March. You will find the manuscript somewhere about. . . It shows exactly how the thing happened: the truth is that if I had arrived a minute sooner they would have shot me at the same time as the generals. It gave me at thirty an excellent insight into the stupidity of public life to find myself between two parties, both of whom sought my death. Even that did not cure me. . .

MYSELF: But do you believe that they still blame you for Lecomte and Clément Thomas ?

CLEMENCEAU: I can tell you that I have a very peculiar memory. I can remember distinctly that such and such a thing has happened, but I only remember vaguely if it took place before or after another event. I can still hear the shouts of Baudry d'Asson [5] and other such freaks demanding my explanation of that business. But whether it happened yesterday or twenty years ago I don't know. . . Store that batch of papers away and do whatever may be required with them in future. My second crime is this. . . Do you know that we have lost Leblois [6] ?

MYSELF: I have heard it mentioned.

CLEMENCEAU: Yes . . . he hardly gave the impression of having been a blazing comet. Well, I was told several times that Leblois was a fellow whom it was well to be suspicious of. I must tell you that I have been accused of taking part in some rather strange conspiracies. . . You know that I was charged with taking payment for defending Dreyfus. Every time I have ever done anything in my life they accuse me of having taken money for it. I was accused simultaneously of taking English and German money: a kind of Treason Trust. As far as the amounts which are supposed to have brought me to Dreyfus's support are concerned, there is a let-

[5] A deputy.
[6] The barrister. Brother of the general. He played an important part in the Dreyfus affair.

ter from me to Leblois where I say in substance, 'My dear
Leblois, thanks for having allowed me to pay the debts of
*Justice*.'[7]  Was it that letter, I wonder, which gave people
the idea of accusing me of having taken the money ?  It's
possible.  But in the first place it won't escape your attention
that in writing that paper — in writing and signing it both —
I wasn't hiding very much.  Secondly, Leblois had looked me
up and said, 'Will you let me do now for *Justice* what I
wasn't able to do sooner ?'  He had brought I don't know
how many thousand francs. . .[8]

My third crime. . . How stupid of me, I've completely forgotten my third crime !  Oh, yes, it's Cornélius Herz.  I must
say that Cornélius Herz was a thoroughly bad lot.  Unfortunately it wasn't written all over his face.  He had been
introduced to me by Hébrard,[9] which was not a bad sponsor-
ship.  Fate decreed that at that particular moment I should
be on bad terms with my wife.  When the cholera broke
out at Marseilles I left with two or three deputies.  We were
going to visit the cholera patients.  There was a possible chance
that I might not come back.  I therefore wrote on a piece of
paper, 'In the event of my death I should like my two children
brought up under the supervision of M. Cornélius Herz.'  As
you see, I was very lucky in my choice of a teacher.

MYSELF:  He could at least have taught them arithmetic. . .

CLEMENCEAU:  Here then are my three crimes.  I will tell
you the facts about them and give you documents on certain
of their aspects.  It will be your task to see what is the best

---

[7] *Justice* had ceased publication because of lack of funds.

[8] Bernier told me (in September 1928) that *Justice* was a limited company but
that nevertheless Clemenceau had assumed all its debts personally—a not very common practice in the world of journalism.  He paid these debts by monthly instalments, and these instalments were crushing him.  Bernier knew Leblois: he had
said to him, 'Nevertheless it is unfortunate that a man like Clemenceau has to
flounder about in the midst of such difficulties !'

Bernier also told me that the good X — an old friend of Clemenceau's — had lent
him 10,000 francs to wipe out these debts.  He only asked him 12 per cent interest.
Bernier used to call him 'the 12 per cent friend.'

[9] A director of the *Temps*.

use to make of them. The only thing that worries me is whether you ought to keep the papers. After my death they will search my house, obviously, and they know that you have been my secretary, so probably they will also come to yours.

MYSELF: They will come, but it won't do them any good. These aren't State papers.

CLEMENCEAU: No. I have made a pile of the State papers: we'll look them over together and then I shall perhaps ask you to take them to the Foreign Office — or wherever else they belong.

MYSELF: All I ask of you — and that is only so that I shall not have any difficulties with any of them later on — is to give me a paper saying, 'I give you this and that, etc.'

CLEMENCEAU: Agreed. You shall have that paper. It is a good solution. When will you come back to fix all this up?

MYSELF: When you wish. As soon as possible. Beginning on Monday if you like.

CLEMENCEAU: I take my gymnastic lesson at eight o'clock. At 8:45 I shall have finished. Will you come on Monday at nine?

MYSELF: Yes.

CLEMENCEAU: And you, Piétri?

PIÉTRI: It suits me perfectly.

CLEMENCEAU: Once that's done, I shall be satisfied. In the past fortnight I have burnt thousands of letters. When you have taken charge of the rest I shall be glad to leave this happy world.

PIÉTRI [*handing him a sheet of paper*]: In the meantime please sign this for me.

CLEMENCEAU: Anything you wish, Piétri. Even if it's my death warrant. Especially if it's my death warrant.

PIÉTRI [*to me*]: I am proposing that M. Clemenceau buy some 6 per cent Loan. He has made a fantastic amount of money with his books. I have even been compelled to say to him, 'Here is some money: it should be spent. Why be stingy ?'

CLEMENCEAU: I'm no longer stingy, Piétri. I have launched out into cyclones of expenditure. I was very keen the other day to subsidise Mandel. He came to see me. It appears that all the forces of the Government have turned against him.

MYSELF: He won't think any the less of himself because of it.

CLEMENCEAU: That's what he said, through his nose. What do you think of the punches and kicks that the *Action Française* and the priests are exchanging ? It is one of the most side-splitting farces of our times. There is only the *Action Française* to take the Pope seriously and only the *Action Française* to take him to task. One fact is certain: that wherever the priests and the communists can do it, they will help one another out. In Alsace it was they who put the autonomists out of business. But the government is going to act. . . Have you ever read, 'Tomorrow the Government will act !' And when the Government acts, you know there will be action . . . or at least activity.

# XX

## The Avalanche of Hatred

Cornélius Herz. . . Clemenceau may well remember him. There was not a moment in all his life when so many enemies were reaching for his throat. I reread *Leurs Figures:* it is in Barrès that this monster should be studied.

On the 21st November 1892, M. Jules Delahaye ascended the rostrum of the Chamber and denounced the Panama scandal: 'Three millions were distributed amongst a hundred and fifty members of Parliament. . .'

'Their names ! Their names !'

Barrès wrote, 'Constant in his policy Delahaye named no one.'

François Sturel, the hero of *Leurs Figures,* some time later sought out Jules Delahaye at his house and said to him: 'Go into the rostrum again: declare that the Commission of Enquiry declines to investigate; then, when they revile you, as they are sure to do, announce that you refuse to name these grafters to this worthless and suspected Chamber, and that you will only go to the country, and so forth.'

Jules Delahaye answered: 'If I name the grafters they will go out of the house with their reputations rehabilitated and me under more prison sentences than Latude. . .'

Then Barrès notes cries of disappointment and also of approval.

There you have the whole of the book.

*Without any proof whatever* Barrès accuses Clemenceau then of having sold himself to Cornélius Herz. *Without any proof* he accuses Clemenceau of being 'Cornélius Herz's man'; he accuses Clemenceau 'of silences and contradictions which arouse alarm'; he accuses him of having given his assistance to Cornélius Herz by consent and having deserted him through fear. A book which had but one purpose — to drive his antagonist to prison or to suicide.

On the 20th December 1892, Déroulède ascended the rostrum, and Barrès reproduces his speech with warmth: 'Who was it after all who introduced, vouched for, nationalized this foreigner[1] little by little, yet in so short a time ? For you must realize that he did not introduce himself, that it was not even another foreigner who took him by the hand and made him at home in our midst; for that a Frenchman was necessary, a Frenchman of position, influential and audacious, who was at the same time his patron and his protégé, his sponsor and his support. And this agreeable, this loyal, this tireless intermediary, so active and so dangerous, you all know him, his name is on all your lips; but not one of you would dare to name him: for there are three things about him which terrify you — his sword, his pistol, and his tongue. Well, then, I shall defy all three and name him: it is M. Clemenceau !'

A speech which Barrès calls 'an oration of unheard-of violence wildly applauded — it must be called sublime. . .'

And Déroulède continues:

'M. Herz admits having given M. Clemenceau two millions. What were these payments for ?  Since the editor of *Justice* affirms that his paper has never done anything for Cornélius

---

[1] Cornélius Herz was an American citizen of German origin.

Herz, why has this experienced financier, this more rapacious than fastidious man of affairs, put so much money into a hopeless investment ?  This deduction seems to be unanswerable: since it is averred that the editor of *Justice* has never sold anything publicly to Cornélius Herz, what did he sell him secretly ?  What really occurred between this foreigner and this politician that no trace was left of any exchange of service ?  Is it possible that the one should have given everything and the other nothing ?  That this German would have been content to pile up these sums without any interest, any purpose, without profit to himself ?'

Then Déroulède made the direct charge:  'We cannot help wondering if what he expected was not precisely all those overthrows of ministries, all those attacks against men in power, all the trouble which you and your great talent have caused to all the business of the country and of Parliament !'

Applause from Barrès.

The war came and M. Clemenceau was in power.  On the 11th July 1918, Barrès delivered a speech before the League of Patriots.[2]  He exclaimed, 'We have now at the head of our Government a man who is celebrated for his power to stimulate and elevate the morale of the French people. . . We have not always loved him, perhaps: well, today we do love him, all of us, with all our hearts, for the one reason that he is necessary to France.'

What did Déroulède think about it ?

Well, when Clemenceau left for the United States after the war, 'Mr. President,' Barrès wrote to him, 'On the eve of your departure the League of Patriots wishes to send with you their homage and good wishes.  We salute the tireless chief who is going alone, his pilgrim's staff in hand, on a long journey to serve France and Truth by the power of his words and the inspiration of his presence.  May God protect you,

---

[2] Of which Maurice Barrès was President.

President Clemenceau, you who remain the spiritual force of a kind unique in the world, the heart of France who would not let her die in those tragic days when she sank bleeding under her wounds.'

And now ? Did not Clemenceau sell himself to Germany after all ? What becomes of *Leurs Figures* ? Bernier told me that Barrès said to him one day at Buré, 'It is the great regret of my life that I wrote that book. . .'

But he did not go so far as to disavow it publicly.

# XXI

## THE MINISTERIAL DECLARATION

ON RETURNING home I tried to get to the bottom of the documents which Clemenceau had given me. I found the original of the Ministerial Declaration of the Clemenceau Cabinet. It has been said of this Declaration that it was 'a page to preserve in the History of France.' I hereby put it at the disposal of History.

Five sheets. . . Clemenceau drew it up on the little table in his bedroom, between two piles of old papers, on the back of five large sheets whose front bore the heading of the Senate in the top left-hand corner. He jotted down on the first page 'Gentlemen,' . . . and without an erasure, with a steady pen which never wavered or hesitated, he indited the first phrase: 'We have taken up the reins of Government in order to carry on the War with redoubled efforts and employ our every energy with the maximum efficiency.'[1]

He attacks the second sentence: 'We present ourselves to you with the single thought of a united defence (he crosses out *defence* and writes *war*). We should like the vote of confidence which we are asking of you to be an act of confidence in yourselves, an appeal to the historic virtues which have made France in the hour when France. . .' The last

[1] 'With a view to greater efficiency, says *l'Officiel*.

words had become involved.  He crossed them out . . . 'which has made us Frenchmen.  Never has France felt more clearly. . . '

So he went on to the end — one might say in the same key and in the same manner, limiting himself to the substitution of a word here and there, or to the suppression of certain phrases which sounded too harsh and were too characteristic of their Clemenceau.[2]

The celebrated theme of this famous Declaration will still be remembered: 'Justice shall take her course.  The country will know that it is defended.'  One might say that the entire Declaration revolves about these tragically ominous words. . . At the bottom of the third page he had just written: 'We shall show neither weakness nor vindictiveness.'  He adds, 'Justice shall take her course.  The country will know that it is defended.'  But he was in too great haste, and before ending his programme with the evocation of this spectre he has several things yet to say.  He therefore rubs out 'Justice. . .,' etc., and writes above it: 'All matters pertaining to the public safety[3] . . . all accused persons before courts-martial.  The soldier of the law making common cause with the soldier of battle.'  And the terrible words reappear.  He writes again: 'Justice shall take her course.  The country. . .,' etc., and again he rubs it out and finally carries it over to the following page.

The Declaration was read on the 20th November 1917, by M. Nail in the Senate and Clemenceau in the Chamber.  I was in the Chamber on that day, and for the first time in my life I came into contact with that curious assembly. Clemenceau always read rather badly, looking for the words and failing to give that impression of strong and unbending will-power which the Chamber expected of and feared in him.

[2] He had written: 'Crimes against France which call for prompt and implacable punishment.'  *Implacable* is crossed out.
[3] This phrase was suppressed by *l'Officiel*.

But there were interpellations — they gave him time to recover himself.

M. Varenne [4] wanted to say that 'To criticize and to govern are two different things,' and 'that nevertheless they were quite willing to try, on condition that at all times . . . that it was understood. . .' M. Compère-Morel asked for an explanation of the Government's views on economic matters. M. Jean Hennessy proposed that an inter-Allied general staff be created. M. Forgeot finally spoke for the purpose of expressing his doubts and his fears and articulating his reservations. While everyone was in consequence expecting him to say, 'Let us not vote for Clemenceau,' his exhortation was 'Let us support him unanimously !'

After M. Forgeot it was M. Ossola, and after M. Ossola it was Clemenceau. He had listened to all this without saying a word and left the orators to have their say in their own way. Again he ascended the rostrum, grave, bowed. . . And once there he did not make a speech . . . rather he questioned himself. He was in power. Had he sought it ? No, but there he was, and tremendous things were expected of him . . . would they be realized ?

The Chamber was full to bursting. In the aisles, where we were packed together to the very foot of the speaker's platform, people were sitting, standing, suffocated, nearly torn to bits, and looking round them in a kind of silent stupor. They looked at this man of nearly eighty, to whom had just been given something like the two hemispheres of the globe — for it was a question of far more than the fate of one nation — taking the globe in his hands, turning it over and weighing it, with an air of saying to himself, 'Shall I try ?'

Then Clemenceau looked in the direction of M. Varenne, who was buried behind his great black beard: 'M. Varenne,' he said, 'whom I should have thought more familiar with the

[4] A Socialist Deputy. Afterwards Governor of Indo-China.

# RÉPUBLIQUE FRANCAISE
## LIBERTÉ — ÉGALITÉ — FRATERNITÉ

# DÉCLARATION
## DU
# GOUVERNEMENT

### LUE, LE 20 NOVEMBRE 1917, AU SÉNAT

### par M. LOUIS NAIL, Garde des Sceaux, Ministre de la Justice

#### ET A LA CHAMBRE DES DÉPUTÉS

### par M. GEORGES CLEMENCEAU, Président du Conseil, Ministre de la Guerre

MESSIEURS,

Nous avons accepté d'être au Gouvernement pour conduire la Guerre avec un redoublement d'efforts en vue du meilleur rendement de toutes les énergies

Nous nous présentons devant vous dans l'unique pensée d'une guerre intégrale. Nous voudrions que la confiance dont nous vous demandons le témoignage fût un acte de confiance en vous-mêmes, un appel aux vertus historiques qui nous ont faits Français. Jamais la France ne sentit si clairement le besoin de vivre et de grandir dans l'idéal d'une force mise au service de la conscience humaine, dans la résolution de fixer toujours plus de droit entre les citoyens comme entre les peuples, capables de se libérer. Vaincre pour être justes, voilà le mot d'ordre de tous nos Gouvernements depuis le début de la Guerre. Ce programme à ciel ouvert, nous le maintiendrons.

Nous avons de grands soldats d'une grande histoire, sous des chefs trempés dans les épreuves, animés aux suprêmes dévouements qui firent le beau renom de leurs aînés. Par eux, par nous tous, l'immortelle Patrie des hommes, maîtresse de l'orgueil des victoires, poursuivra dans les plus nobles ambitions de la paix le cours de ses destinées.

Ces Français que nous fûmes contraints de jeter dans la bataille, ils ont des droits sur nous Ils veulent qu'aucune de nos pensées ne se détourne d'eux, qu'aucun de nos actes ne leur soit étranger. Nous leur devons tout, sans aucune réserve. Tout pour la France saignante dans sa gloire, tout pour l'apothéose du Droit triomphant. Un seul devoir, et simple : demeurer avec le soldat, vivre, souffrir, combattre avec lui. Abdiquer tout ce qui n'est pas de la Patrie L'heure nous est venue d'être uniquement Français, avec la fierté de nous dire que cela suffit.

Droits du front et devoirs de l'arrière, qu'aujourd'hui tout soit donc confondu. Que toute zone soit de l'armée. S'il doit y avoir des hommes pour retrouver dans leurs âmes de vieilles semences de haines, écartons-les.

Toutes les nations civilisées sont engagées dans la même bataille contre les formations modernes des vieilles barbaries. Avec tous nos bons alliés, nous sommes le roc inébranlable d'une barrière qui ne sera pas franchie. Au front de l'usine à toute heure et partout, rien que la solidarité fraternelle, le plus sûr fondement du monde à venir.

Champ clos des idéals, notre France a souffert pour tout ce qui est de l'homme. Ferme dans les espérances puisées aux sources de l'humanité la plus pure, elle accepte de souffrir encore, pour la défense du sol des grands ancêtres, avec l'espoir d'ouvrir, toujours plus grandes, aux hommes comme aux peuples toutes les portes de la vie. La force de l'âme française est la C'est ce qui meut nôtre peuple au travail comme à l'action de guerre. Ces silencieux soldats de l'usine, sourds aux suggestions mauvaises, ces vieux paysans courbés sur leur terre, ces robustes femmes au labour, ces enfants qui leur apportent l'aide d'une faiblesse grave : voilà de nos poilus. De nos poilus qui, plus tard, songeant à la grande victoire, pourront dire comme ceux des tranchées : J'en étais. Avec ceux là aussi, nous devons demeurer, faire que, pour la Patrie, dépouillant des misères, un jour, nous-nous soyons aimés.

S'aimer, ce n'est pas se le dire, c'est se le prouver. Cette preuve nous voulons essayer de la faire. Cette preuve nous demandons de nous aider. Peut-il être un plus beau programme de Gouvernement?

Il y a eu des fautes. N'y songeons plus que pour les réparer.

Hélas! il y a eu aussi des crimes, des crimes contre la France, qui appellent un prompt châtiment. Nous prenons devant vous, devant le pays qui demande justice, l'engagement que justice sera faite selon la rigueur des lois. Ni considérations de personnes, ni entraînements de passions politiques ne nous détourneront du devoir ni ne nous le feront dépasser. Trop d'attentats se sont déjà soldés sur notre front de bataille, par un surplus de sang français Faiblesse serait complicité. Nous serons sans faiblesse, comme sans violence. Tous les inculpés en conseil de guerre. Le soldat au prétoire, solidaire du soldat au combat. Plus de campagnes pacifistes, plus de menées allemandes Ni trahison, ni demi-trahison : la guerre. Rien que la guerre. Nos armées ne seront pas prises entre deux feux La Justice passe. Le pays connaîtra qu'il est défendu.

Et cela, dans la France libre, toujours. Nous avons payé nos libertés d'un trop grand prix pour en céder quelque chose au-delà du soin de prévenir les divulgations, les excitations dont pourrait profiter l'ennemi Une censure sera maintenue des informations diplomatiques et militaires aussi bien que de celles qui seraient susceptibles de troubler la paix civile, cela jusqu'aux limites du respect des opinions Un bureau de presse fournira des avis — rien que des avis — à qui le sollicitera. En temps de guerre, comme en temps de paix, la liberté s'exerce sous la responsabilité personnelle de l'écrivain En dehors de cette règle il n'y a qu'oppression anarchie

Messieurs, pour marquer le caractère de ce Gouvernement, dans les circonstances présentes, il ne nous a pas paru nécessaire d'en dire davantage. Les jours suivront les jours. Les problèmes succéderont aux problèmes. Nous marcherons du même pas, avec vous, aux réalisations dont la nécessité s'impose Nous sommes sûrs de votre contrôle. La question de confiance sera toujours posée

Nous allons entrer dans la voie des restrictions alimentaires, à la suite de l'Angleterre, de l'Italie, de l'Amérique même admirable d'élan. Nous demanderons à chaque citoyen de prendre toute sa part de la défense commune, de donner plus, et de consentir à recevoir moins. L'abnégation est aux armées. Que l'abnégation soit dans tout le pays. Nous ne forgerons pas une plus grande France sans y mettre de notre vie

Et voici qu'à la même heure, quelque chose de notre épargne, par surcroît, nous est demandé Si le vote qui couronne cette séance nous est favorable, nous en attendons la consécration par le succès complet de notre emprunt de guerre — suprême attestation de la confiance que la France se doit à elle-même quand on lui demande pour la victoire, après l'aide du sang, l'aide pécuniaire dont la victoire sera la garantie.

Messieurs, cette victoire, qu'il nous soit permis, à cette heure, de la vivre par avance dans la communion de nos cœurs à mesure que nous y puisons plus et plus d'un désintéressement inépuisable qui doit s'achever dans le sublime essor de la France libérée, de tous les plus hauts espoirs.

Un jour, de Paris au plus humble village, des rafales d'acclamations accueilleront nos étendards vainqueurs, tordus dans le sang, dans les larmes, déchirés des obus, sublime évocation de nos grands morts. Ce jour, le plus beau de notre race, après tant d'autres, il est en notre pouvoir de le faire. Pour les résolutions sans retour, nous vous demandons, Messieurs, le sceau de votre volonté

*Pour copie conforme :*

*Le Président du Conseil, Ministre de la Guerre,*

### GEORGES CLEMENCEAU.

Paris. — Imprimerie des Journaux officiels, 31, quai Voltaire.

## PROCLAMATION OF 20 NOVEMBER 1917
*Clemenceau forms a New Government*

common facts of everyday politics, has accused me of having shown myself unfavourable to arbitration. M. Varenne, do you really mean that ? It was I who sent M. Léon Bourgeois as France's delegate to a pleasant conference at the Hague. This conference formulated a mass of principles of international law which Germany is engaged in violating at this moment. . .'

As for M. Forgeot: 'M. Forgeot wants us to consider the question of peace whilst we are making war. And he asks me what are my war aims. My war aims ? Victory !'

The room bursts into a frenzy. M. Pierre,[5] in his long frock coat, up there where he seems to be final arbiter of the laws and traditions of this assembly, M. Pierre himself thrills — and then it's over. After several words by M. Albert Thomas, who tries to explain why the members of his party have thrown their support against Clemenceau, and how in surveying Clemenceau from the corner of his (Thomas's) eye, and spying and peering and prying, he descried all the turns and twists in his road, the Socialists have nevertheless decided that they 'will co-operate fully in all efforts for the national defence. . .' the vote is taken.

The vote of confidence is carried by 418 to 65 — the 65 votes of M. Albert Thomas and the members of his party, who could not wait any longer for the occasion to attest their unshakable intention of 'co-operating fully,' etc. !

MM. Malvy and Caillaux refrained from voting.

[5] Secretary-General to the Chamber of Deputies.

# XXII

## Old Papers

IN THE study.

CLEMENCEAU [*seeing me come in*]: Well, Monsieur Martet !

MYSELF: I've arranged my papers and I'm bringing you a certain number which seem to me of somewhat too confidential a character to be left in my drawer: they ought not, moreover, to be left in yours. I brought them away when we left the Ministry. Here they are.

CLEMENCEAU: Good. I'll look at them. Come this way. [*We go into the bedroom. Clemenceau leads me to a little secrétaire which stands beside his bed. He opens a drawer and says, 'Take it.' I put the drawer on the desk and, as Piétri arrives, Clemenceau says:*] Well. Tell me what's in it. . .

MYSELF: Papers, sir, more papers.

CLEMENCEAU: What sort of papers ?

MYSELF: First there is Joffre's despatch of the 27th December 1915 on the battle in Champagne, a despatch which begins with the words, 'The causes of our initial success were that the Command knew how to plan and prepare the operation. . .'

CLEMENCEAU: Noble words !

MYSELF: Then there is a second copy of this despatch: it

136

has been annotated in pencil by I don't know whom. Then three other copies, not annotated. Then here is a criticism of this despatch. . .

CLEMENCEAU: Oh! By whom?

MYSELF: It isn't signed. The author of this document says, '*The Command knew how to plan and prepare,* asserts General Joffre. That is a mistake and it was precisely the lack of sufficient preparation which caused the plan to miscarry.' Otherwise it is quite a free and easy review of Joffre's despatch.

CLEMENCEAU [*showing me other papers*]: And these?

MYSELF: This is still another anonymous examination of Joffre's despatch. Thirty-four typewritten pages. But it seems to me to be more carefully, more closely written. The argument goes deeper into various matters: Tahure, Ripont, La Butte du Musnil, the Trou Bricot. . . 'It was the advance beyond the first zone which marked the critical instant for the offensive. And it was precisely the beginning of this step which the High Command had neither foreseen nor prepared against. . .'

CLEMENCEAU: Who could have written that?

MYSELF: Mangin? Ferry?

CLEMENCEAU: What a string of generals has filed through these doors!

MYSELF: A despatch from a commander on the attack which took place on December 14th: 'The day cost us seventeen officers and an as yet undetermined number of men which will probably exceed six hundred.'

CLEMENCEAU: Naturally for nothing. For the *communiqué.* I took a stand against that sort of thing, so they accused me of undermining the morale of the country.

MYSELF: Documents on the Sarre. A copy of a very interesting letter from Paul Cambon to Delcassé.

CLEMENCEAU: Of what date?

MYSELF: The 22nd December 1914. It is about the entry of England into the war. 'To fix the dates and thereby establish certain facts of which it is advisable to keep a record.'

CLEMENCEAU: Paul Cambon was a good man. A bit inclined to lord it and also, to be quite frank, a bit of a bore. . . But he didn't fly into tempers and saw clearly enough. Nor is Fleuriau at all a bad sort. He would be even nicer if he didn't wear those silly riding stocks round his neck. . .

MYSELF: And a document of twenty-eight typewritten pages signed by M. Meunier-Surcouf, deputy, and dated May 1916.

CLEMENCEAU: What does he want ?

MYSELF: He declares that 'a head is required for the French army.'

CLEMENCEAU: By Jove ! That's Foch's man !

MYSELF: A letter of no great interest from M. Jonnart, who says. . .

CLEMENCEAU: Oh, don't tell me what he says. I don't care a hang. He's a man who spent all his life in resigning. I appointed him Minister of the Blockade. A week later he resigned.[1]

MYSELF: Documents about Malvy, Leymarie,[2] Caillaux. A note from a general on 'the situation at Verdun.' A report on the use of artillery. A despatch from Pétain on the Champagne offensive. This ends with the words: 'An enormous expenditure of effort and money is necessary. We ought not to fear to look the difficulties in the face. We shall not succeed in overcoming them by denying them.'

CLEMENCEAU: Yes. Everything he said and everything he wrote was always full of good sense. Too full of good sense. He wanted a grain of madness in him.

---

[1] November 23rd, 1917.
[2] Head of M. Malvy's Cabinet.

MYSELF: Documents about pacifist propaganda, about Merrheim,[3] Almereyda [4] . . .

CLEMENCEAU: What do they say about Almereyda ?

MYSELF: 'After having been in an indefinite way an apprentice to a photographer he arrived in Paris in October 1899 at the age of seventeen, coming from Mont-Dore-les-Bains (Puy-de-Dôme). In 1900, on the 28th May, he was sentenced to two months' imprisonment at the Correctional Tribunal of the Seine for complicity in a robbery.'

CLEMENCEAU: It must have been in consequence of that that he felt himself ripe to guide the consciences of his contemporaries.

MYSELF: Telegrams from Lallemand to the Minister of the Interior. He was then Prefect of the Loire. It is about the pacifist-defeatists. These telegrams are a little wild. He was always seeing revolution the next day.

CLEMENCEAU: Yes, he was a gallant fellow. Next ?

MYSELF: A letter relating to the Norton affair. There's a man who writes you, 'Several days ago I had an opportunity of speaking with some of the "patriots" who had resolved to save France by forging papers to prove that you and several others had sold it to England. . .' and told you all the details of the conspiracy.

CLEMENCEAU: Keep it. It may be useful.[5] Is that all ?

---

[3] A notorious syndicalist and pacifist.

[4] Director of a pacifist paper called the *Bonnet Rouge*. He was accused of treason and was found hanged in his cell.

[5] Apropos of the Norton affair it would be profitable to reread *Leurs Figures*.

A poor negro, Norton, had brought to Millevoye documents to prove that Clemenceau had sold himself to England. His treason was said to have brought him £20,000. While writing his book Barrès knew perfectly well that Millevoye had been the victim of a devilish hoax. 'But,' says Barrès, 'it must be admitted that Millevoye fell into this classic trap because of a forgery supplied by the very people whom the hoax inculpated in order that they might be able to cry out that they had been calumniated.' It was Clemenceau who had invented the mythical Norton! On the 22nd June 1893 Millevoye told his story from the rostrum: 'I can vouch that M. Clemenceau committed treason. I accept the responsibility for the authenticity of the papers on which I rest my charge. . .' And then Millevoye

MYSELF: That's all.

CLEMENCEAU: Now here is what I'd like you to do. Take all these papers home with you, look them over, and arrange them. Then tell me whether they ought to be given back to the Government or merely burnt. When will you be back ?

MYSELF: Tomorrow morning. I believe it would be better also to take home the papers which I brought you this morning. I'll examine them in the same way.

CLEMENCEAU: Right !

MYSELF: But there is one thing I hope, and that is that I shan't be burgled today or tonight. . .

CLEMENCEAU: Piétri, tell your friend Chiappe [6] not to let Martet be burgled today. Tell him to wait till next week.

*[Piétri and I leave. My portfolio is stuffed with papers capable of starting a grand conflagration. I return home. I look through these terrible papers. In one there is an envelope on which is written in Clemenceau's hand: "Beware !" and which I did not open that morning. I find others . . . still others. . . I find the minutes drawn up by M. Jeanneney of a sitting of the Cabinet where the question of the left bank of the Rhine was vigorously discussed; a letter from Clemenceau to M. Tardieu of the 24th November 1923 on*

went to pieces under ridicule. 'Oh, Clemenceau's laughter,' wrote Barrès, 'the laughter of an overstrained man who can no longer contain himself !'

But let us leave Barrès.

I find amongst my papers this letter from Millevoye addressed to Clemenceau on the 3rd May 1916: 'My dear Mr. President: Will you please name a day and an hour in the near future when you can grant me an audience. I have a most important and urgent message to convey to you. . .' And the note finishes with these words: 'Very sincerely yours, Your most devoted L. Millevoye.' I find another letter from the same Millevoye to the same Clemenceau. It is dated November 1, 1917: 'My dear Mr. President. . . Your ever devoted. . .' Well?

We owe to the Norton affair the fine plea which Clemenceau uttered to the jury before whom he had brought his accusers; to it we owe the magnificent Salernes speech of the 8th August 1893. But because of it Clemenceau was beaten in the legislative elections of '93. The clericals and the socialists made every effort to put his opponent in.

From 1893 to 1902 Clemenceau was out of the Chamber. In 1902 he was elected senator for the Var.

[6] Prefect of Police.

*the same subject; letters from M. Poincaré, Mangin, etc.*
*A veritable powder magazine.*]

MYSELF [*to my wife*]: Were we planning to go out this evening ?

MY WIFE: Yes. We were going to the moving pictures.

MYSELF: I think it would be better to stay. . .

MY WIFE: Oh, why ?

MYSELF: Sh ! . . . Sh ! I'll whisper something to you. . . Come here. . . [*I tell her. She exclaims 'Oh !' and hurries to the door to see if the bolt is firm.*]

## XXIII

### The Armistice — The Left Bank of the Rhine — Mangin

15th May 1928

CLEMENCEAU: Hullo! Are you working?

MYSELF: Yes. I've arranged all the papers and put them in two convenient piles: papers to be burnt and papers to be sent back. I want to speak to you about them presently.

CLEMENCEAU [*showing me two letter-books on his desk*]: Next, take a look at these. They're things that I dug up yesterday evening.

[*I run through the first book and then the other.*]

MYSELF: Do you realize what is in these two books, sir?

CLEMENCEAU: What?

MYSELF: The telegrams you sent in '18 and '19! Telegrams to Cambon, Barrère, Jusserand! All your cablegrams to Wilson, House, Orlando, Lloyd George! All your code telegrams. All the secrets of the two years of your ministry. How do you happen to have them here?

CLEMENCEAU: How should I know?

MYSELF: Weren't you ever asked to give them back?

CLEMENCEAU: I wonder if anyone even knew that they existed. Perhaps they don't even know I did any writing during my ministry.

MYSELF: But suppose you had been burgled?

CLEMENCEAU: Well?

MYSELF: All our secret codes would have been discovered, including the military and foreign affairs ciphers!

CLEMENCEAU: Well, what of it? It couldn't have been helped!

MYSELF [*continuing to turn over the books*]: Yes . . . yes . . . I recognize them. . . These are the telegrams which you used to dictate to me and I then had typed. You were telegraphing to the English to ask them to extend their front, to the Americans to ask them to send more men, always more men; to the Italians to ask them to get on with the fighting. The correspondence for November and December '17 and that for January '20 is missing. Might you not have put it away in some corner or other?

CLEMENCEAU: No! I've nothing else left!

MYSELF: I didn't expect to find even this!

CLEMENCEAU: Well, you see, fate wanted to arrange this surprise for you. Presently we shall see what we ought to do with these volumes. Tell me first about the papers which you've gone through.

MYSELF: I should like first to talk to you about two or three things.

CLEMENCEAU: Go ahead.

MYSELF: Well, you spoke to me on Saturday about three 'crimes' of which you might have been accused: (1) 18th March 1871; (2) Cornélius Herz; (3) the money which you were supposed to have taken for defending Dreyfus. . .

CLEMENCEAU: Yes. I've never added up all the sums which they accuse me of having accepted for one thing or another, but they would make an impressive total. The truth — as far as it concerns the debts of *Justice* — is that when my father died I did not receive a legacy of a penny.

MYSELF: As for the 18th March '71 and Cornélius Herz, I

have that clear. Where I need further explanations is on the third point. You told me: 'Leblois was a man to be distrusted.'

CLEMENCEAU: It was Mathieu Dreyfus [1] who passed that remark on to me. And Mathieu Dreyfus is a good, straightforward fellow.

MYSELF: But did Leblois say specifically: 'I have a paper proving that Clemenceau accepted some money'?

CLEMENCEAU: I can match that with this little remark of Anatole France's. . .

[*Piétri comes in: we shake hands. He notices the two letter-books.*]

PIÉTRI: What's that?

MYSELF: Nothing of any importance! Only the secret correspondence of M. Clemenceau in '18 and '19 with his ambassadors, with Lloyd George, Woodrow Wilson. . .

PIÉTRI: The devil! How did it turn up here?

CLEMENCEAU: That's just what we were wondering.

PIÉTRI: There is enough there to hang all three of us! What are you going to do with it?

CLEMENCEAU: We shall see presently. Let me go on with my story. I countered the phrase of Mathieu Dreyfus with another which Anatole France flung me. In his last years Anatole France, as you know, was in a pretty bad way spiritually. I never used to see him any more — there was nothing more to see him for — it was dreadful.[2] Anatole France said one day: 'I myself have seen a document which proves that Clemenceau took money to defend Dreyfus.' And since I only remember a letter I wrote to Leblois. . . Leblois had come to see me at the time of the downfall of *Justice;* he had taken a certain number of shares. . . I wrote him that letter to thank him. Is that clear?

---

[1] The brother of Alfred Dreyfus.
[2] Clemenceau never forgave Anatole France for his skeptical attitude towards certain things like the army, his own country, etc.

MYSELF: Quite. But what is equally clear is that if people
do one day reproach you with anything it won't be with
things which are now ancient history. . .

CLEMENCEAU: Ah ! Then what will it be ?

MYSELF: They already charge you with certain things which
you did or didn't do during the war and the peace negotiations.

CLEMENCEAU: For instance ?

MYSELF: First of all, the Armistice.

CLEMENCEAU: Why the Armistice ?

MYSELF: They object that you signed the Armistice too
soon and prevented our troops from entering Germany.[3]

CLEMENCEAU: Oh ! That, Martet ! How can you talk
like that ! In the first place the Armistice is a military question and only soldiers have the right to say whether or not
the order to cease fire shall be given. And what did Foch
say ? He repeated over and over again: 'The Germans are
asking for an Armistice. We can and ought to give it
them.[4] There were three reasons for this: because our men
were completely worn out; because, if it had been necessary
to continue the war, it would have cost us another hundred
thousand men — and a hundred thousand men are a hundred
thousand men, whichever way you look at it — and because
the Germans gave up everything, handed over their artillery,
their rifles, their prisoners, evacuated France and Belgium.

[3] M. Emmanuel Bourcier went specially to interview General Mordacq.
'I could have wished that they had awaited the result of the strategic operations
against the rear of the German army in Lorraine. But my voice would not have
been heard.' And later:
'The march on Berlin ? It was planned and it was possible. I can prove it
whenever one likes.'
See *Paris-Midi* for November 24th, 1927.
[4] See the *Petit Journal* for January 3rd, 1928.
'Is it true,' an editor of the paper asked Marshal Foch, 'that it was your intention to launch a formidable attack in the direction of Metz on November 12th,
1918, and that it was only the Armistice which prevented you ?'
'Do not let us have any exaggeration ! In the first place it would not have
been on the 12th but on the 14th. Next, such an attack would have extended
my front, which already covered 300 kilometres, to 340. Another 40 kilometres,
if not more. . . Moreover, were not the Germans completely defeated ? We must
not have any regrets.'

Would you have liked to go on ? Why ? For the pleasure of seeing more blood flow ?

And secondly, you know that it had been agreed — we had given the most formal undertakings on this point, and it was on the basis of these undertakings that the United States entered the war — that, once President Wilson's Fourteen Points were granted, we would lay down our arms. The Boches accepted these points. Would you have had us then, in spite of that, in spite of everything, go on with the war ? We should have had against us in that case not only Germany but America, England. . . It would have been madness !

MYSELF: Then the question of the left bank of the Rhine. I find in your papers a copy of a letter from you to M. Tardieu, dated 1923, a letter which M. Tardieu has not to my knowledge made public, and in which you say particularly. . .

CLEMENCEAU: Read it to me. I forget what I said to him.

MYSELF: First there is a note accompanying the letter:

*Paris, 25th November* 1923

The enclosed letter was written by me on the evening of November 24th, after a visit from M. Tardieu, to give a precise form to any amendments which my Cabinet Ministers present at the session [5] might care to make.

G. CLEMENCEAU.

[5] The sitting of the Chamber of Deputies on 23rd November 1923, to consider the foreign policy of M. Poincaré's Government. It was during this sitting that M. André Tardieu made one of his most effective speeches: in it he magnificently defended the peace treaty and recalled all the attempts at 'sabotage' which had disfigured it during the previous four years. His famous apostrophe to the Chamber is still remembered: 'It is an odd fact that this Chamber, which is always and on all questions split in two, is only able to achieve enormous majorities on those divisions which vote away some right from France !'

M. Poincaré on his side declared that he had signed the treaty very reluctantly.

THE BIG FOUR

*Left to right: Orlando, Lloyd George, Clemenceau, and Wilson*

Here is the letter:

*Paris, 24th November* 1923

MY DEAR FRIEND,

You know that I have made it a rule never to answer criticisms which have been belied by subsequent events. After yesterday's session, however, it would perhaps be better to nail down certain 'facts.'

There has *never* been any dispute between the President of the Republic and myself on the question of the Rhine frontier. When the proposals for a guarantee were made to me by the English Prime Minister and the President of the United States I placed the question before M. Poincaré without delay. The upshot of my letter was as follows:

'I cannot see myself saying to the French people: we have won the war with the assistance of our good friends and allies. We are now about to break with them and make a separate peace at the instant when they offer to reinforce the political and military agreement by a formal undertaking.'

The President of the Republic answered me that it was impossible to pursue this discussion.

Two or three days passed without M. Poincaré making the slightest allusion to the subject. Surprised, I reminded him of his previous assent. He answered me quite briefly, without labouring the point, that he had not *understood* me very well. I ought to have been used to this style of language by now! It was not easy to give two meanings to my words. The matter called for an explanation which was not forthcoming.

Later, Marshal Foch spoke to me of a military pact to intervene in case of aggression. It was my opinion that this pact would be a necessary consequence of the engagements undertaken by the various governments after ratification by their parliaments, but that one could not put this result on the same plane as the cause which brought it about. Without previous military alliance, England and America entered the war on our side and employed their resources to such good effect that Germany will have to pause and reflect when confronted by such a formal engagement on the part of these two powers.

I informed the President of the Republic of my point of view, and there was no response on his part.

Finally, on the occasion of a debate in the Cabinet, the proposal was voted unanimously *without the President of the Republic saying a single word*. All the ministers can bear witness to this fact.

Today M. Poincaré states that there were several 'conferences' on this subject with the President of the two Chambers and Marshal Foch. It was indisputably his right, but in my opinion he should have notified his Prime Minister, since it was the latter's opinion which led to the rupture. Finally, from the constitutional point of view these 'conferences' between the President of the Republic and Marshal Foch, my subordinate, should obviously not have taken place unknown to me. Why then were they held in this manner?

And then again, the question of the Rhine implied such changes in our future policy with regard to the peace that neither Marshal Foch nor the Presidents of the Chambers were in a position to decide it. There was only one authority to convoke — the Cabinet. The President of the Republic, who was empowered by the constitution to convoke it, did not do so.

His vague threats to resign[6] moreover were not submitted to me. How can they be reconciled with his attitude of silence

[6] M. Alexandre Varenne had just said, 'There always remains to the President the right to resign.' M. Poincaré answered: 'In fact it is the one right that remains to him, that of resigning. And for him it certainly would have been a deliverance. If he did not resign it was because after having weighed the pros and cons, after having conferred with the Presidents of the two Chambers and Marshal Foch himself, he considered it his duty to remain in office.' (Sitting of the Chamber, 23rd November 1923.)

towards the Council, before whom no such suggestion had ever been breathed ? On the other hand, when I proposed to him several times during the war that I should resign, M. Poincaré always answered that if I resigned he would go into retirement also.

As for the question of military control, which still remains unfortunately very much to the fore, I do not know what better could have been done by those who consider the present arrangement inadequate. At the moment we see it overborne on the insistence of England, who found her own guarantees in the destruction of the German navy at Scapa Flow, whilst on land the German menace could by no possibility be directed against anyone but us. We therefore find that we have given way on the one issue where it was essential that we should stand firm. We shall see the consequences.

CLEMENCEAU: There is not a word in it that we can change. It is correct, every bit of it. Poincaré never wanted to conduct himself like a President of the Republic nor Foch like a soldier. One day Foch said to me:

'You know, I suppose, that, constitutionally, I am not under your orders.'[7]

I answered:

'I feel very friendly towards you, but if there is one bit of advice I can give you it is not to try that game on me.'

He was satisfied that I meant what I said.

MYSELF: But do you really think that Marshal Foch's and Poincaré's policy is one which cannot in any event be upheld ?

CLEMENCEAU: I might answer you, my dear boy, that what grated on me in this business was not the policy, but the way in which it was upheld behind my back, before my eyes, at the very time when I was having to struggle with Wilson and Lloyd George to conduct the war and negotiate the peace. But no, I shan't say that. Foch's and Poincaré's policy was a

[7] It was on October 1st, 1918, that Marshal Foch made this statement.

bad one in itself. It is a policy which a Frenchman, a French Republican, can only adopt as his own momentarily in the hope of obtaining compensating benefits as part of the bargain. That sort of thing is best left to Bismarck, the famous man of iron.

MYSELF: You believe nevertheless that it was right — and you think it all the more since it was at your insistence that it was done — to take possession of the Rhineland for fifteen years ?

CLEMENCEAU: That is not the question. We are only in the Rhineland to ensure the execution of the Treaty. If the Boches fulfil their contract we leave. If they do not fulfil it we remain. We shall remain beyond the fifteen years, we shall remain a hundred years if necessary, until they have paid whatever they owe us — and we shall do it by virtue of Articles 428, 429, and 430 of the Treaty, whose existence no one seems to suspect. But who has read the Treaty ? And if, once we have evacuated, the Boches violate their contract, what then ? We shall reoccupy the territory, still by virtue of these Articles. Well, we have the Rhine, haven't we ? What more does anyone want ? That we keep it permanently ? In that case let's speak candidly. Let us say annexation. I wonder if it has struck you that that is a word Foch and Poincaré avoid pronouncing. They are bound to recognize that that word no longer exists in our time. Annex the Rhineland ? It would be the same as renouncing all that we fought for. After having won with the help of the English and Americans it would be equivalent to saying to them at the moment that the job is finished — and well finished, thanks to them — 'and now we shall take this, we shall take that. . .' 'I beg your pardon,' the English and Americans could properly answer, 'you will take, *you* will take ! But what you are going to take doesn't belong to you alone. There are three of us who helped bring the wild beast down.' And what would be their opinion then of this war for the freedom of mankind ? That there were still oppressed peoples but that this time it was the Boches who were the oppressed. Can you see me putting my signature to a scheme like that ? Our country has no other interest than to uphold a principle. What principle do you see in that ?

MYSELF: Then there is the Mangin affair.

CLEMENCEAU: He's another, still another, who added to my troubles.

MYSELF: I want to speak to you about it because a great many people accuse you of not having backed him up properly and of having taken his command away from him.

CLEMENCEAU: Well, I should have liked to see *them* try to disentangle themselves from him.

MYSELF: I find in your papers a certain number of documents regarding Mangin. First a letter which Mangin wrote to you personally, an intimate, familiar letter in which he thanks you for what you have done for him, for the support which you gave him. . .

CLEMENCEAU: The one who disliked him most was Pétain. I had the devil of a time to pacify Pétain. He couldn't even hear his name mentioned.

MYSELF: . . . and assures you of his gratitude and devotion. In his letter Mangin reveals himself completely: full of fire, of life, effervescent and excitable — also full of bitterness and rancour. He speaks of a 'poison' which has been cast over him.

CLEMENCEAU: He was intolerable. In August 1918 Foch had to get rid of him because he had made I don't know how many communications to the press. I alone behaved with a certain leniency towards him. Foch himself took on that dry little tone of his, 'You are not going to begin again, are you ?' which did not prevent Mangin from beginning again every time he had a chance. Mangin was a great soldier and a great commander, but he did not think that obedience was made for him.

MYSELF: Next there are all the documents of the Dorten affair and the question of Rhine separatism; your letters to Mangin recommending caution, your telegrams to Jeanneney, whom you instructed to look into the subject.

CLEMENCEAU: The Dorten affair! Separatism! H'm. They were angry with him because of that too. At Pirmasens, a little German village occupied by the French troops, the Boches besieged the separatists in the Mairie, entered finally by breaking in, and cut their throats in cold blood. This, if you please, under Poincaré's ministry. And in a village — you grasp that — which we were occupying. That should tell you what sort of future separatism — Mangin's great idea — had before it.

MYSELF: These, then, were your three 'crimes' of which I was speaking. When I am able to recall some others I will talk to you about them.

CLEMENCEAU: That's right. Now let's arrange these papers.

MYSELF: First, here are the papers which I think should be burnt.

CLEMENCEAU: Why?

MYSELF Because they ought not to be in your hands — and there is no occasion to send them back to the Government.

CLEMENCEAU: Why not?

MYSELF: Because they are only copies.

CLEMENCEAU: What are they about?

MYSELF: Well, you have, for example, this report by Joffre on the Champagne offensive of 1916, and this report of Pétain's on the same operation. In my opinion the best place for them is the fire.

CLEMENCEAU: I am greatly prejudiced in favour of the fire. People never burn enough !

MYSELF: Next to those papers there are others which you ought perhaps to keep.

CLEMENCEAU: For example ?

MYSELF: For example, this letter from Millerand, who, with a few restrictions on certain features of the Peace Treaty, declares that the treaty is 'worthy of our victory.'

CLEMENCEAU: Yes, let's keep that. Even if Millerand is of no great importance in the history of France. I never saw anyone more bewildered than Millerand at the War Office. They would say to him, 'Damn it, man, order some guns !' and he would answer: 'Oh, do you think that they are really necessary ?'

MYSELF: Here's a file of letters which Poincaré wrote you during your ministry.

CLEMENCEAU: Oh, how he could write ! Every time I saw his dainty little handwriting it threw me into a fury.

[*Etc., etc. Burn, keep, send back. . . When we had finished Piétri and I left. In the taxi Piétri said to me:*]

PIÉTRI: Apropos of these letters about the paper *Justice* . . . Do you know this story ? One day during the war Clemenceau learnt that a woman who was then living at Arcachon had in her possession a note signed by him in acknowledgment of a debt of twenty thousand francs lent to Clemenceau by the woman's husband.

Clemenceau jumped into a car and arrived at Arcachon. The woman said to him, 'Yes, I really have the note, but I wonder if you owe me anything whatever.'

'Oh,' said Clemenceau, 'why ?'

'Because,' she said, 'you wrote in this note that you recognized a debt to my husband of twenty thousand francs, and that you would give this back out of the profits accruing from *Justice*. Did you make any profits ?

'Profits ! My dear lady, profits with a newspaper that called itself *Justice* !'

'Then you don't owe me anything.'

'All right, then here are your twenty thousand francs.'

He climbed back into the car and returned to Paris.

# XXIV

## 'IT MUST NOT BE SAID'

16th May 1928

PIÉTRI is already there.

CLEMENCEAU [*to me*]: Well, have you looked for those two volumes yet?

MYSELF: Yes, sir, and I have thought about them, too. They are exclusively about the war and the peace from January 1918 to December 1919, all of which, at least your telegrams to Cambon, Barrère, etc., were collected by your private secretariat. It is probable that amongst the telegrams which you sent there are others which you dictated to Mordacq, Herscher, Lallemand, etc.

CLEMENCEAU: Sure to be.

MYSELF: Those aren't here. Nevertheless there is enough here to precipitate a catastrophe if they fall into other hands.

CLEMENCEAU: And — ?

MYSELF: And so they should be given back to the Government. Or else they should be burnt.

CLEMENCEAU: Beyond a doubt it is better to burn them. They must be burnt. Don't you realize that if I gave these papers back to Poincaré I should provoke arguments and questions which would simply never come to an end. Poincaré would write and ask me for explanations. That would be too tiresome.

PIÉTRI: On the other hand, it is provoking to suppress a document which represents an extraordinary page of history.

CLEMENCEAU: The pages of history! You know, I myself haven't at all the soul of a historian. I have only the soul of a man who wishes to God the world would leave him in peace.

MYSELF: Would you like me, after I have run my eye over these papers for the last time, to run over them yet once more — which would be the last of the last — to see if there is anything amongst them which might provoke from the Government a demand for explanations? If I see anything which might disturb your peace, I'll tell you.

CLEMENCEAU: Right. Secondly: Piétri and I have just been having a little chat. Piétri was telling me that I ought to leave a paper explaining what I did at the Peace Conference and why I was not able to do more.

PIÉTRI: I do think that there are certain points which you would be able to clear up.

CLEMENCEAU: It is extremely simple, you understand. All the disappointed failures of politics and journalism are here to say, 'You might have done this, you might have done that.' I should have liked to see Briand, Painlevé, Renaudel, Franklin-Bouillon and the others confront Germany, confront England, confront the United States, the whole world. It is eight years since I left office. For eight years now Briand and Poincaré have been passing their time sitting around little green baize-top tables to make a lot of other little peace treaties with our former friends and enemies. Every time they get up it is noticed that they haven't obtained anything. Not only that, but they have let go of a little more, of boats, of millions, billions. Millerand! What he alone gave up! It's mad!

I did what I did and I did it alone, and I ask you to whom

I might have turned for advice — to those same Briands, Poincarés, Millerands ?   Because for three years they had been making war and weren't able to bring it to an end.  Was that a sufficient reason ?

They say to me now: 'You didn't obtain anything,' and I claim that I did, that I obtained everything that I could reasonably have been expected to obtain.  But there you are ! The only value of a treaty is in its application.  You must go on and see it through.  What have they done ?  Nothing ! Speeches !  Oh, good Lord, those speeches !  What speeches !

They say to me, 'You should have broken with our Allies.' I nearly did.  Forty-eight hours before the ratification of the treaty I nearly broke off relations: Lloyd George wanted two years of occupation or nothing.  Wilson arranged that matter . . . fortunately !  Do you see me saying to Parliament, 'I have broken it off' ?  I should have had the whole world against me.  And with perfectly good reason.  It would have meant the loss of everything.

The treaty was not so grand, I am quite willing to admit that, but how about the war ?  Was *it* so very grand ?  It took four years and I don't know how many nations to bring Germany to her knees.  It was necessary to go looking for allies all over the face of the globe and recruit troops even amongst negroes . . . twenty times during the war it was believed that everything was at an end.  We touched the bottom of the abyss, but France came out of it alive, her territory recovered, her colonial empire increased, while Germany was broken and disarmed under the threat of our guns.  And now . . . M. Marin isn't satisfied.  All those chaps shrieking blue murder, throwing out their chests, become suddenly arrogant and uncompromising to the point of imbecility as if we alone, without help or support or a supreme effort, had broken Germany's neck !

They would like one of those merciless peaces such as Napoleon used to impose when he overthrew an empire in three cavalry charges. I wonder if they can be serious.

PIÉTRI: Exactly what they are, and all that you have been saying ought to be said publicly. . .

CLEMENCEAU: Well, what do you think about Piétri's idea, Martet? Ought I to write something? If you want to know what I really feel, I much prefer a quiet life. If they attacked me on a particular phase of the Treaty — but they haven't!

MYSELF: My advice is that you ought not to write anything.

CLEMENCEAU: Why?

MYSELF: For several reasons. Firstly, because you have remained silent for eight years, and your attitude only has a meaning — as you've said yourself — if you maintain it to the end.

Then you want to be left in peace, and if you undertake to answer you will have it less than ever: every answer will call forth another answer; and finally, because by answering you would give the impression that you doubt yourself and your own work, that you have put the question to yourself and have found arguments and apologies, recognizing that the Treaty wasn't able to defend itself.

CLEMENCEAU [delighted, makes a gesture as if he were sweeping everything away]: There! He's said the right thing. It's decided![1]

PIÉTRI: I agree in principle, but nevertheless there are two or three points which remain obscure. . .

CLEMENCEAU: Well, Martet will clear them up. If I undertook to speak now they would say, 'Ah ha! He feels the criticism. He must be wrong.' [To me] And are you going to study these two volumes for the last time?

MYSELF: Yes.

CLEMENCEAU: Are you going to take them away?

[1] Clemenceau followed my advice, as it turned out, until April 1929.

MYSELF: I should prefer not to. I can do it here.

CLEMENCEAU: Right! When?

MYSELF: Immediately.

CLEMENCEAU: I will arrange a place for you. We should never talk; there is always too much talking going on.

PIÉTRI leaves. Clemenceau goes into his room. I make myself comfortable at the horseshoe table, and attack the two volumes. There are two kinds of letter-books, whose pages are of the flimsiest tissue paper. On each page there is pasted a sheet of the pad on which I took down in a sort of semi-shorthand the telegrams which Clemenceau dictated to me, or — most frequently — the typed transcript of the notes.

I read all these pages over — what a marvellous book! How clearly, freshly, tidily and straightforwardly the chief and master organizer of this great machine thought! How splendidly active he was! When it is published how it will increase his stature!

At eleven o'clock I have finished.

Clemenceau returns.

CLEMENCEAU: Done?

MYSELF: Yes, sir.

CLEMENCEAU: And?

MYSELF: It must be given back to the Government.

CLEMENCEAU [*depressed*]: Very well. I will give them back. I'll say, 'Here are some papers which I've found; I'm sending them back to you. Don't ask me for any explanations about them. I don't remember a thing, and anyway, I'm dead!'

MYSELF: I want to point out to you that each of these pages is numbered, but that there are several on which nothing was pasted.

CLEMENCEAU: That's nothing to do with me. Have you

thought this over carefully ?  Knowing Poincaré as you do, do you think that it is wise to take him all that ?  Aren't you afraid that. . .

MYSELF:  I'm not afraid of anything.  Your work here shows up very well; there is no mystery about it, and I don't see what questions they could ask you.  Furthermore they're only copies, and duplicates undoubtedly exist at the Quai d'Orsay or the War Office.  Poincaré therefore is acquainted with those duplicates, and if anything has seemed mysterious to him. . .

CLEMENCEAU:  He would have taken it up. . . But hold on !  Are you telling me that there are duplicates at the two Ministries ? . . . Then these haven't any value !

MYSELF:  I said 'undoubtedly.'  I believe so, but I'm not sure.  In any event I don't know where or how they are filed.  There is probably one telegram in one folder, and another in another folder a mile away.  Whilst these books enable one to trace your every effort and every thought day by day: you can follow their development.

CLEMENCEAU:  Good !  You may go and take them to Poincaré, but you're very annoying.  Now come along and I will give you various documents on old affairs, the Commune. . .

[*We go into the hall.  Clemenceau shows me two large parcels tied up with cord which are waiting for me in a corner.*]

CLEMENCEAU:  There !  They are yours.  Do with them what you want.  Probably three-quarters of them should be burnt. . . Burn them.  I myself have burnt thousands and thousands of old papers.  But there are records which I have prepared myself with a view to a possible emergency.  I am handing on to you these trenchant weapons in case the struggle should be resumed when I am at the right hand of God.  [*Calling*] Albert !  [*Albert appears.*]  Find a taxi and put these things into it.

CLEMENCEAU AT WORK IN THE STUDY OF HIS RESIDENCE IN THE RUE FRANKLIN

[*Albert goes to look for a taxi. Clemenceau and I remain without moving or speaking in the opening of the doorway which leads out into the garden.*]

CLEMENCEAU [*dreaming*]: The flowers are here. . .

# XXV

## 18TH MARCH 1871

IN ONE of the two parcels of old papers which Clemenceau had given me I found — and I ran through it at once with deep emotion — the account dictated to his secretary and corrected with his own hand, in which he had thought it necessary to set forth all the tragic days of March 1871 as he saw them and as he lived them.

Clemenceau had a long life and passed through many bitter hours; but no memory ever haunted him with such persistence as the memory of those terrible times and all the madness that, as a young mayor of thirty, he perceived at the bottom of civilian insurrection, during which he wondered so many times if his own life's adventure were not going to end there in futility.

Later there will appear these two hundred pages which he dictated or wrote without preparation or reflection. Actually they constitute the only memoirs which Clemenceau has left and they represent beyond a doubt the saddest moment of his life.

For the moment I shall merely reproduce the chapter which he devotes to the 18th March. It is an excellent picture and even more: one recognizes the man of science, the man of the *Génération des Eléments Anatomiques*[1] who leaned over his laboratory table to study the birth of a revolution and 'observe' it with curiosity stronger even than distaste.

Certain facts are rapidly recalled: since the 4th September 1870, the day of the proclamation of the Republic, Clemenceau had been mayor of Montmartre; Paris had surrendered, and by the 27th January the Prussians were on the point of entering the capital. On the 26th some of the National Guard had taken possession of forty guns assembled in the parks of Passy and Wagram, and in order to get them away from the Prussians hoisted them to the very top of Montmartre and Belleville. Nearly two months passed, and M. Thiers' Government, hearing the angry muttering of the Parisians due to their frequent deceptions, determined to disarm them. Clemenceau intervened, pointing out the dangers which would arise from putting this scheme into effect; M. Thiers promised to wait. Unfortunately the promise was not kept.

It was the failure to carry out such undertakings which led to the shocking tragedy of the Commune.

I now yield the stage to Clemenceau.

ON THE 18th March, at six o'clock in the morning, I was awakened by M. Dereure, my colleague, who told me that the Buttes of Montmartre had just been occupied by the troops, and the guns retaken. He added that it was only with the greatest difficulty that he had been able to come to me, the streets being barred by the military, who allowed no one to pass.

While speaking I saw that he was studying my face and the meaning of my words carefully in order to find some indication as to whether I was warned of the Government's undertaking. As I condemned the conduct of the Govern-

[1] The title of the medical thesis which Clemenceau wrote.

ment in this matter with strong indignation Dereure took my side. For his part he did not then appear to believe in the possibility of even an attempt at resistance. He considered the guns already definitely seized and did not conceive that a counter-offensive on the part of the National Guard would even be attempted.

I drew this conclusion only from his attitude and the general sense of his words, for this question was not even raised between us in our interview. He told me further that General Lecomte was commanding the military, that some of the National Guard had been wounded, and that a certain number of prisoners had been taken.

I advised him to return immediately to the Mairie, where his presence was necessary, and told him that I was going to the Buttes to see the General and to take stock of the situation.

He left. As I had been dressing while we were talking I shortly followed him.

I went directly to the Buttes. I had to parley several times with soldiers who barred the way. The Outer Boulevard and the streets which I traversed were either deserted or practically so. The news of the coup was just beginning to spread. On the doorsteps and in front of all the still closed shops men in shirt sleeves were chatting and preserving a completely calm attitude. Of National Guard, uniforms or arms, not a sign. The nearer I came to the top of the Buttes, the more relaxed seemed to be the attitude of the soldiers. Up there, there were a great many civilians. They chatted with the soldiers, several of whom had laid their rifles down on the pavement to go into the bakers' shops.

A detachment of constabulary and police were guarding the house at No. 6 Rue des Rosiers.

I arrived on the upper plateau, where I found General Lecomte in the midst of several officers who were walking about between pieces of artillery, with no apparent occupation.

I went up to him and informed him of my position. I reminded him that I had seen him at the Ministry of Public Instruction on the 22nd January and expressed my extreme surprise and disappointment at the Government's decision to use force without having warned us of its intention.

The General answered that it was not his place to enter into any discussions, that he had merely received his orders and was executing them. He told me that he had been waiting for quite a long time for transport which had not arrived.

I then said to him that the population seemed quite calm in the district through which I had just come; I considered it extremely important that the artillery should be removed with the least possible delay.[2]

After leaving the General I proceeded to the house at No. 6 Rue des Rosiers, where the chief of the constabulary, Piquot, allowed me to enter. About a hundred prisoners were assembled in the courtyard and several more could be seen at the windows.

They told me that there was a wounded man in one of the rooms. I went in. I found a National Guardsman belonging to the Engineers Auxiliary Corps lying on a mattress on the floor. Two women were lavishing attention on him. One was the canteen keeper of a battalion of the Arrondissement and the other was Louise Michel.[3]

The room, a tiny one, looked onto the garden.

I observed that the wounded man had received a bullet in his side: it had perforated the peritoneum. He still had a little hæmorrhage; a sheet covered the wound. No attempt at a dressing had been made. I devised a first-aid dressing as well as I was able. The wound was obviously mortal.

Since he appeared to be suffering terribly and was, further-more, extremely badly accommodated there, I announced my

[2] Compare all these facts with the various statements made before the court martial, including my own statement. — *Note by Clemenceau.*
[3] The celebrated revolutionary. — *Note by the author.*

intention of having him taken to the Lariboisière hospital. I believe, without being able to swear to it, that Captain Piquot was present and was informed of my intention, but raised no objection, at least at the moment.

I returned to the Mairie immediately in order to get a stretcher. On the way it seemed to me that the attitude of the crowd had not changed appreciably. There were undoubtedly more people in the streets, but they did not seem excited.

I returned to the Rue des Rosiers with the stretcher carried by two National Guardsmen whom I had requisitioned from the detachment at the Mairie.

The demeanor of the crowd during this second journey did not yet appear in the least threatening.

I went into the house, had the wounded man placed on the stretcher and had it carried into the courtyard through the window of the ground floor. While he was there and the policeman was taking his name and address, Captain Piquot came up and warned me that General Lecomte was opposed to the wounded man being removed to the hospital.

I went back to General Lecomte, who said that he was opposed on the grounds of prudence to the transfer of the wounded man, that the sight of him might rouse the mob, that he could be taken care of and would be moved to hospital after the military operations had been terminated.

I replied that the district, as I had previously said, was quite tranquil and that I did not believe personally that the transfer presented the objections set forth by the General. Nevertheless, I could do nothing but yield, and I withdrew without further argument.[4]

---

[4] The indictment against the assassins of Generals Lecomte and Clément Thomas states that I wanted to incite insurrection by carrying out the manœuvre known as 'parading the corpse.'

It goes on to say that I wanted to move a wounded man who had already received all possible care from a military surgeon. I countered by the demand that they produce this military surgeon, that they ask him to state where and when he examined the wounded man, what was the nature of the wound, and what

I noticed on my way that the crowd in the streets was swelling; at the same time I saw a large number of soldiers who had laid their rifles on the pavement and were chatting familiarly with the people of the neighborhood. I have heard it said that the troops had had nothing to eat all the morning. I myself saw people give victuals to the soldiers; I saw quite a number of soldiers at the bakers and the wine sellers. In the Rue du Mont-Cenis two young officers were taking a stroll in the most casual fashion, chatting away with no appearance of alarm. Nevertheless, I noticed a National Guardsman reproaching in lively fashion a soldier for having taken part in this expedition, and I was surprised at the piteous expression on the face of the soldier, who was accepting the abuse without protest.

When approaching the Mairie I met in the Rue de Vieux Chemin a National Guardsman who, when he recognized me, abused me roundly. He was in a great state of excitement. He, no more than the others, was thinking of venturing upon resistance. He did not call upon any group whatever to start resistance, but he proclaimed that he wanted to go and get his rifle in order to fire on any soldiers who might attempt to remove the guns.

I made a very strong effort to dissuade him, but he talked on without stopping and would not listen to me. Finally, he became a little calmer and promised me that he would go home.

---

dressing he had prepared for it. I affirmed that there was no doctor, no dressing, and that I had given first aid myself.

Captain Piquot announced triumphantly that a military surgeon had come before me, but that he had limited himself to looking at the wound and had prepared no dressing. Captain Piquot, who was present at my two interviews with the wounded man, still declares that no one had spoken to me of this surgeon. It is permissible to regret that the Judge-Advocate did not require Captain Piquot to give his explanation on this point before drawing up his indictment. There remains therefore solely the testimony that I merely wanted to have the wounded man, who had had no care, transferred to hospital at a time when there was no sign of insurrection and when there were no indications anywhere of any preparation for armed conflict. — *Note by Clemenceau.*

When I arrived at the Mairie Square I saw a group of twenty people, most of whom I knew. I was aware of their influence on the National Guard of the arrondissement and had even negotiated with them for the restoration of the guns. My colleague, M. Dereure, was amongst them.

On my arrival there was a hush. I understood that they were suspicious of me and believed that I was working on behalf of the Government. I repeated to them the conversation which I had just had with the General on the Buttes. They declared that they were betrayed, but though extremely incensed said not a word about the possibility of resistance; nor did they seem to be thinking about it, for, having returned to the Mairie shortly after, I saw them from the window of my office disperse in different directions. They seemed discouraged and not as if about to make an appeal to arms.

A few moments later I saw a member of my Armament Committee, M. Sabourdy, arrive. It was about half-past seven. He told me that he had been wakened by firing and that he had seen soldiers fraternizing with the National Guard.[5]

I described my two journeys to the Buttes. It is evident that at that moment the situation did not seem to me to be critical. For, although I was alone at the Mairie, I sent M. Sabourdy with his colleague, M. Huet, to the Rue Lepic to settle some dispute or other with a landlord. It is obvious that if I had thought at that juncture that the situation might suddenly become worse, I should have kept him with me. For, I repeat, I was alone at the Mairie.

M. Sabourdy was away quite a long time.[6]

The Mairie Square was practically deserted. After a short interval several National Guardsmen passed by unarmed, and other groups appeared a little later. Several of them seemed very excited.

---

[5] Ask him where, when, and in what circumstances. — *Note by Clemenceau.*

[6] Ask him how long and exactly what he was doing during this period. — *Note by Clemenceau.*

At some time which I cannot state exactly, but which must have been between eight and half-past, I heard the call to arms for the first time. The sound came to me faintly; it must have been at some distance from the Mairie.

A moment later a National Guardsman, alone and unarmed, posted himself at the corner of the Rue des Abbesses opposite the Post Office and sounded his bugle. While I was wondering if it would not be better to stop him, and thinking of the consequences of a possible refusal by the National Guardsmen of this post if I ordered them to do so, armed groups (the first) appeared in the Mairie Square.

Within the space of a few minutes the whole aspect of the Square was changed. Armed National Guards were running about in all directions and in the greatest confusion. These fellows seemed to be obeying no orders coming down the street and not even to have thought of forming themselves into companies or battalions: they called out, they were shouting; it was all a perfect bedlam.

Later, however, properly formed companies spread out into the Square by way of the Rue Marie-Antoinette, a drummer at their head. They seemed animated by great enthusiasm and kept crying out, 'Vive la République !' not even pausing when passing in front of the Mairie.

I noticed amongst the troops officers whose opinions I well knew and who I assumed were going against their will. I suspected that their men had compelled them to come with them and to take part in what looked much more like a popular demonstration than preparations for a battle.

All this lasted for a little while, up to the moment when I noticed to my great surprise soldiers of the line[7] mingled with the National Guards.

Then suddenly cannons, dragged by hand, arrived in the Mairie Square. I learned at the same time that the precious

[7] Soldiers of the Government.

transport had finally turned up, that the National Guards had recaptured in the Rue Lepic[8] the guns which were being taken away, and that the military had fraternized with the people. This had been effected, moreover, quite in a friendly manner and without a shot being fired.

During this interval M. Sabourdy returned;[9] he told me what he had seen, and it was he, I believe, who apprised me of what had taken place at the Buttes.

A few moments later several very excited National Guardsmen presented themselves in my office and confirmed his story. General Lecomte was a prisoner, as well as a certain number of the police and constabulary.

A little later I saw a detachment of these last two bodies arrive at the Mairie and detained as prisoners at the Guardhouse which had formerly been occupied by the National Guard and had now been evacuated by them.

Captain Piquot was with these men. I went up and spoke to him. He was thoroughly calm. I apologized for not having been able to house him and his men in more comfortable fashion. He answered that a soldier is used to putting up with anything. I advised him to go home, remain there, and not to call attention to himself. I forbade his men to leave the Guardhouse. The exasperation against the military constabulary was already considerable, and especially against the police; I was afraid that the sight of them might arouse angry memories in several of the more feverish spirits.

I returned quickly to my office, which was filled and all kinds of people were turning up armed with the most contradictory and incredible versions of what had happened.

I should mention the visit of M. J.,[10] a member of the Central Committee, who was one of the people with whom

[8] M. Deschamps saw them take the Rue Lepic again with the aid of women and children. — *Note by Clemenceau.*

[9] What had he witnessed on his journey ? —*Note by Clemenceau.*

[10] Josselin.

I had negotiated most consistently for the return of the guns. During the siege he had been in charge of one of the branches of the food supply. His task was still going on since he had not yet rendered his accounts. He told me that since it was impossible to foretell what was going to happen he was going to turn over to me the money which was in his possession. The secretary of the Mairie inspected our books and settled up his accounts.

I observed his attitude of extreme distrust of myself and pretended not to notice it.

Finally he could no longer contain himself and said:

'Well, you've cheated us.' And when I made a gesture: 'Yes, yes, you continue to negotiate with us merely to lull us to sleep, and you cannot expect me to believe you were not hand in glove with the Government.'

I was so dumbfounded by his tone of deep conviction that I could not find a word to answer. I was bewildered, astounded; nevertheless, my attitude was such that, seeing a tear of rage on my cheek, without my having said a word he begged my pardon for having insulted me and swore that he would never again believe what he had just said.

Unfortunately the attitude of the majority of the National Guard who appeared in my office had caused me to understand how generally this conviction was held. In this lay so great a danger that I felt compelled to take every possible precaution to protect at all costs the prisoners I was holding and who were so detested by the people.

At about ten o'clock Captain Mayer of the 1st Company of the 169th Battalion [of the National Guard] arrived.

He came to tell me that General Lecomte and a number of his officers were prisoners in the Château-Rouge.[11] He told me that these gentlemen were asking for their lunch and since he had no funds available was wondering whether I

[11] A hall in the Rue de Clignancourt where public dances were held.

would supply the necessary money. I authorized him to have the lunch brought from a neighbouring restaurant and questioned him about the attitude of the people.

I had known Captain Mayer during the siege. He was a blunderer and easily influenced, but I had always found him quite well disposed. I had no reason to suspect him of the desire to harm anyone. He had an urbane manner and a kindly disposition, which did not allow me to doubt his benevolent intentions towards the prisoners. Moreover his language was reassuring. He told me that the General and his officers were comfortably housed, and promised to see that they did not want for anything.

I asked about the behaviour of the people. He said that it was good: the guns had been retaken without striking a blow,[12] the troops had been fraternizing with the people, there was no feeling of hatred in their hearts and that no sign of hostility towards the General and his officers was visible.

I asked Mayer which battalion was guarding the prisoners. He answered that it was his own, that his men were there, that he could count on them, and that there was no danger of any kind. I said to him: 'Pay close attention. I have entrusted the care of the prisoners to you. You will be answerable for them to me, won't you?'

He answered: 'Quite. That's all right.'

This remark was repeated at least twice. Sabourdy heard it. Mayer had [denied it] at the beginning of the trial, but later went back on his assertion. Furthermore, Chicandard stated a moment afterwards that he had met Mayer, who told him that I had just entrusted him with the care of the prisoners.

---

[12] That was only true in the 18th arrondissement (Montmartre) where not a shot was fired to recapture the guns. A little later, however, there were collisions in the Place Pigalle between National Guards and Chasseurs. One officer was killed. I believe that his men refused to fire. Ask Sabourdy. An hour later the officer's horse, which had also been killed, had been completely cut up for food by the crowd. Not a trace of it was left. A characteristic detail.—*Note by Clemenceau.*

I [declared] quite formally during the trial that the scope of my words should not be exaggerated at a moment like that, and that they did not then justify so grave a significance as subsequent events would seem to have given them; that, although my actual words were those which I had repeated, it should not be lost sight of that at that moment the General and his officers did not seem to be in any danger [13] and that what I had in mind at the moment was 'if anything happens which we do not now foresee, come and warn me.' It is obviously what Mayer should and could have understood. Nothing more. I could not ask him to do anything more in so much as he had no more authority than his men were willing to recognize. I could only insist that he alone should ward off the danger which did not yet exist and which was unforeseeable.

I should add that I considered myself fortunate to have had to deal with Captain Mayer, whose intentions I could not suspect, as I said above, and who had the advantage of a very considerable influence over his men because of the important part he had played in the matter of the guns. At this juncture he had held his command for some time and seemed to possess considerable authority on the Buttes. I could not therefore but congratulate myself on seeing the prisoners in the Château-Rouge under his protection.

A few minutes after the departure of Captain Mayer, Captain Chicandard came in. My office was not getting any emptier. There also arrived various people from the centre of Paris who came to obtain information on the state of affairs. I only had a very short interview with Captain Chicandard. This officer, who belonged to the same battalion as Mayer, also had a detachment in the Château-Rouge.

[13] This is so true that they themselves, who could see the crowd from the windows, thought that they were perfectly safe, and the proof is that when Captain Beugnot renewed his acquaintance with Mayer, whom he had previously met at Villemessant's (Villemessant was the founder of *Figaro*), they began to talk about women and Villemessant. — *Note by Clemenceau.*

As he was explaining the facts I said to him:

'I have already seen Mayer and entrusted the prisoners to his care. Go and help him. I entrust them to you the same as to him. Watch over them and do whatever may be necessary.[14]

I had lunch in my office after making out the necessary requisition to assure provisions for the prisoners.

My assistant Jaclard had gone to the Mairie at about ten o'clock, when everything was practically over, so far as he remembers.[15] He then remained at the Batignolles and was not informed of what was happening until much later.

We exchanged our impressions on the events of the day and as we were wondering what was going to come of all this mess which we were witnessing, we agreed that the struggle could only be ended — as everyone about us seemed to believe — by another, and probably another conflict was going on whilst we were speaking in some other quarter of Paris. The idea that the aggressor might escape by flight from the results of the conflict which he had provoked could not have occurred to anyone.

I expressed strong indignation at the conduct of the Government with respect to myself. I complained of the false position in which they had put me by having recourse to force without warning me, after they had made me run backwards and forwards so long as they had thought it possible to negotiate. But I told him clearly that I did not believe that it was a time to hesitate as to which line of conduct to take.

'Whatever point of view one takes,' I said to him, 'there is one conclusion which is unmistakable; the Prussians are infesting Paris. If the Government is overthrown this evening or tomorrow and the new Government does not give them

---

[14] Ask Chicandard at what time he met Mayer and when Mayer told him that I had entrusted the prisoners to his care. Did he come to see me before or after ? —*Note by Clemenceau.*
[15] Ask Sabourdy what time Jaclard came. — *Ibid.*

satisfactory guarantees they will beyond a doubt occupy the city. I cannot believe that any party is strong enough to saddle itself with such a responsibility. Whatever our feelings with regard to the Government, it is our duty to act in such a way that the grave error which it has just committed shall have the least unfortunate consequences possible. 'Moreover,' I added at the end, 'it seems impossible to me that the troops will not resume the offensive and the Government remain masters of the ground.'

Jaclard [16] told me that in principle he shared my opinion, and that he understood as well as I the dangers of the movement which had commenced, but that his friends were in the movement and that he could not without dishonour refuse to go along with them, at least during the fighting. Moreover he added, 'I shall try to prevent them from doing too many foolish things. Obviously I shall have a great deal to do.'

As to my predictions on the outcome of the struggle he did not endorse them without reserve. He believed that the Government would sustain a serious reverse and be reduced to accepting some form of compromise after having lost or practically lost the struggle.

We said very little about the imprisoned officers. Since no danger seemed to menace them their imprisonment was no more than a minor incident in a struggle whose distressing consequences were troubling us above everything else. I told him what I had done. He approved and said further that he would personally keep watch at the Château-Rouge and would without fail have himself informed of everything that might happen. I repeat that we did not press this question because at that moment it did not seem to have the importance which it acquired later. The causes, the outcome, and the conse-

[16] Whilst Jaclard [was] present we learned that the same things had happened at Belleville as at Montmartre, and that in consequence the insurrection was of far wider extent than we had at first thought. — *Note by Clemenceau.*

quences of the conflict now going on occupied our attention almost exclusively.

He left me with the promise to return and give me news if things took a fresh turn.

My assistant Dereure did not reappear at the Mairie during the entire day, or if he came he could only have remained a very short time, and I think that I can swear he did not set foot inside my office.  In any case I have no recollection of his being at the Mairie during that day,[17] nor during the night.  The next morning when I went to the conference of the mayors at the bank I left the Mairie absolutely empty; he had quite openly thrown himself into the movement with the strongest illusions about its outcome, and as he had always distrusted me he took care not to establish a centre of his operations in the Mairie.  His conduct with reference to me lacked the frankness which marked Jaclard's.  It was a question of temperament as well as intelligence.

At about eleven o'clock M. Stupuy arrived.  Having learnt what had happened and supposing that I might be in need of help, he had come voluntarily to offer me his services.[18]

I told him he could render me a great service by going out to find a few of my colleagues or assistants who would be able to lend me the aid of their authority.

He left.[19]

At about 12:30 or one o'clock MM. Lockroy and Langlois appeared, the latter having been advised by Tolain.[20]

I repeated the events of the morning to them.  When they

---

[17] There was certainly a witness who during the course of the trial declared that Dereure came to the Mairie several times that day, but this witness only came to the Mairie at night.  He is the same man who saw me with a red sash.  There is no occasion to discuss this man's statements.—*Note by Clemenceau.*

[18] Ask him to give evidence on what he saw that day. — *Ibid.*

[19] I think it was Tolain whom he went to find first.  Ask him to whom he went, what he saw, what he said, what he did.  Ask Tolain what he did and saw. — *Ibid.*

[20] Ask Lockroy who had summoned him, and get his statement. — *Note by Clemenceau.*

spoke about the captured officers I told them that they were at the Château-Rouge, where they were quite out of danger.

It may be said that if I had had any reason whatever to suspect danger it would have been easy for me to send my two colleagues to the Château-Rouge: I should in this way have shifted a heavy responsibility to their shoulders. I did not do so because I thought that the National Guardsmen, who suspected that I was working on behalf of the Government, would probably have had similar suspicions of them, and that the effect of such precautionary measures would be the reverse of what might have been expected. It might have brought the prisoners into peril if any indication was given that fears were entertained for their safety.

I said to Langlois and Lockroy that it was necessary for our colleagues to come to the Mairie, that there we were at the centre of the movement, that some turn might take place which would allow them to take hold of things and direct them to a more or less happy conclusion, that in any case we ought to deliberate on what was to be done.

They left to hunt up our colleagues.

During this time this is how the Mairie Square looked: battalions camped round their guns, parties of National Guardsmen as well as soldiers of the line preceded by bands.

Towards two o'clock my friend M. Lioret, Sub-prefect of Issoudun, who had been in Paris for the last twenty-four hours, thinking that I might be in difficulties, came to offer me his services.

As far as he can remember, the Mairie was practically deserted when he arrived. Everybody had left to see what was going on outside. Sabourdy had remained in the room next to mine.

I answered M. Lioret, that the best service which he could render me would be to stay with me so that I might have someone whom I could trust at hand in case of need.

A moment later M. Stupuy returned.  He reported on how he had fulfilled the mission with which I had entrusted him.

At about three o'clock Jaclard came in.  We exchanged a few words and he went on into the room used by the Committee of Armament.

A moment later I heard a noise in this room and, opening the door, found myself face to face with about fifteen people who were deliberating.  Amongst these were Paschal Grousset, Gerré, J——.  I requested Jaclard to come into my room and asked him what these men wanted.  He answered with an embarrassed air that it was the Committee which had taken up its quarters there in order to deliberate and expedite orders.  I told him in the presence of Stupuy and Lioret that there could not be two authorities in the Mairie, that so long as I was there I was the sole head, and that I would not permit any committee to take possession of the place surreptitiously.[21]

Confronted with my definite decision Jaclard said that he would go and prevail upon the Committee to withdraw.  I waited a quarter of an hour or twenty minutes in extreme anxiety, wondering what the National Guard would do if I summoned it to expel the Committee, which did not seem to want to leave.  Danger of a conflict.

I recalled Jaclard and declared that I gave him another ten minutes and that if after that time the Committee had not left I should call upon the National Guard — whatever the risk involved — to expel the Committee.

Jaclard only required five minutes.  At the end of that time the Committee had in fact left.

After its departure I received a visit from several of the National Guard, most of whom were unknown to me and who had come from the arrondissements in the centre of Paris

[21] I think that a moment earlier the members of the Committee had come to ask me for a room and I had refused them.  Ask Stupuy and Lioret. — *Note by Clemenceau.*

to find out what had happened at Montmartre since the morning. They brought conflicting news of what was going on in the centre of the city.

At about half-past four Captain Mayer, followed by Captain Garcin, came into my office. Mayer, greatly troubled, told me that if I did not come as quickly as possible they were going to shoot Generals Lecomte and Clément Thomas.

I remarked that that was impossible: the newspapers had announced that Clément Thomas had left a little while before for America.

Mayer answered: 'If it is not Clément Thomas it is someone whom they take for him. In any case come as quickly as you can because they are talking of shooting him.'

The expressions which Mayer was using, although indicating that the situation was serious, allowed me to suppose that the crisis had not yet reached as acute a stage as one might have feared.

I took my sash from my drawer and hurried out into the streets, followed by the two captains and M. Sabourdy, who were in the adjacent room and whom I told in passing to follow me, without saying what it was about.

MM. Lioret and Stupuy offered to follow me. Convinced that I was running into grave danger I refused their assistance. I instructed them to watch at the Mairie, to protect the prisoners, and to ward off as best they could any emergencies which might arise.

I put on my sash in the street while running.

I had understood by Mayer's remarks that the affair was not going on at the Château-Rouge, but I did not yet know where it was happening.

Mayer told me that we ought to proceed towards the Buttes. We were too agitated to attempt to clear up in our minds how the situation which we had to remedy had arisen. Furthermore one moves less quickly while talking. We ran and walked as fast as we could, practically without saying a word.[22]

Considerably out of breath we climbed straight up the Buttes, practically along the wall of the church. Captain Garcin twice expressed his intention of leaving us, saying that his lungs could not stand it any longer. I insisted on his following us, foreseeing that we might have a struggle ahead of us and that his uniform would give us some authority over the mob.

Hardly had we turned the corner of the wall when a man dashed up and told us that the Generals had just been shot. We did not stop to answer him but hurried along even faster. He did not seem to be perfectly sure of his facts but appeared rather to be repeating a rumour than something which he himself had witnessed.

The Buttes were covered with armed National Guardsmen. We were caught up in the mob. My sash called everybody's attention to me and I at once became the object of the most hostile demonstrations. They accused me of having conspired with the Government to have the guns taken away, of having betrayed the National Guard, and insults were hurled at me on all sides.

Placing myself between Mayer and Sabourdy, who were both well known in the arrondissement and were my only protection, I continued on my way without answering.

Whilst we went on I heard such things as:

'It's all over ! Justice has been done ! The traitors are punished ! If anyone isn't satisfied we'll do the same to him ! It's too late !'

I crossed the upper plateau, where I had met the General in the morning, and arrived in the Rue des Rosiers with Mayer and Sabourdy, having lost Garcin on the way. As we arrived opposite No. 6 a detachment of National Guards came out,

---

[22] Route followed. Look it up. — *Note by Clemenceau.*

THE BATTLE OF THE 18TH MARCH 1871

*From an engraving in L'Illustration, 25 March 1871*

in the midst of whom were several officers of the line. It was no longer possible to doubt the assassination of the Generals since everyone was now repeating the news with great enthusiasm.

The detachment of Guards having taken a route to the left, I cut across their path and asked where they were taking these officers.

M. Beugnot,[23] who states that I had a tricolour sash — and it is quite possible — declares that I was very pale. I do not doubt it, for I was under the pressure of extreme emotion. As for him, he was livid and so changed that seeing him later during the trial of the assassins of the Generals, I could scarcely recognize him.

The officer who led the detachment, Lieutenant Meyer,[24] told me that he was going to save the officers and that he was leading them to the Vigilance Committee for safety. I still hesitated a few seconds, because after the blow of the frightful news I feared that they were trying to deceive me and wanted to shoot the officers.

Captain Beugnot spoke a few words to me, of which I understood nothing, either because I was too overwhelmed to grasp their meaning or because he was not in a condition to express himself clearly. I understood, however, more from his attitude than anything else, that he approved of what Lieutenant Meyer was doing. I therefore stepped out of the way and the detachment proceeded.[25]

Momentarily there was a sensation of emptiness in the street. I crossed the ground which the departing Guardsmen had just occupied and went up to J., the same member of the Central Committee who had that morning accused me of having

[23] Aide de Camp to the Minister for War. He was amongst the prisoners. He afterwards accused M. Clemenceau of doing nothing to save the Generals.

[24] Not to be confused with Captain Mayer.

[25] The indictment at the trial of the Generals' assassins states most categorically that I did not go to the Rue des Rosiers. What a pity that Captain Beugnot saw me in it ! — *Note by Clemenceau.*

betrayed them. I expressed to him my horror of the crime which had just been committed. M. Sabourdy, cutting me short, expressed himself to the same effect in extremely strong language. J., who seemed on the verge of collapse and was staggering in profound bewilderment, simply repeated vaguely, 'It's frightful !'

Suddenly a terrific noise broke out and the mob which filled the courtyard of No. 6 burst into the street in the grip of some kind of frenzy.

Amongst them were chasseurs, soldiers of the line, National Guardsmen, women, and children. All were shrieking like wild beasts without realizing what they were doing. I observed then that pathological phenomenon which might be called blood lust. A breath of madness seemed to have passed over this mob: from a wall children brandished indescribable trophies; women, dishevelled and emaciated, flung their arms about while uttering raucous cries, having apparently taken leave of their senses. I saw some of them weeping while they shrieked louder than others. Men were dancing about and jostling one another in a kind of savage fury. It was one of those extraordinary nervous outbursts, so frequent in the Middle Ages, which still occur amongst masses of human beings under the stress of some primeval emotion.

Suddenly a piece of artillery drawn by four horses drew up in front of the house. The confusion increased, if that was possible. Incongruously uniformed men on the horses were shouting out oaths. I saw a woman leap on one of the horses. She waved her hat, shouting 'Down with the traitors !' a cry which the mob took up *ad infinitum*.

For me the situation was becoming more and more dangerous. This crazed mob was looking at me suspiciously while uttering the cry of 'Down with the traitors !' Several fists were raised.

There was nothing more I could do in this place. I had not

been able to prevent the crime. It only remained for me to assure myself of the fate of the prisoners whom I had just seen taken away, and to prevent another mischance happening to the prisoners at the Mairie, against whom the hostility was very great.

I therefore did not go into the house, having a profound conviction that I should not come out of it alive. Thus I did not see the corpses, as someone alleges, in his statement that I watched the National Guardsmen executing a sort of *danse macabre* round the bodies.

I determined to proceed to the Château-Rouge to assure myself of the fate of the officers whom I had seen led away a little while before and on whose account I was not perfectly satisfied.

M. Sabourdy, to whom I communicated this idea, started to follow the road which the prisoners had taken. I stopped him and without giving any explanation told him that we must go down again by the Butte.

I have shown how hostile was the attitude of the National Guardsmen towards me while I was climbing the Butte. I had neglected to answer their threats because I still hoped to reach the Rue des Rosiers in time. Now I decided that if it was necessary to have an explanation with them it would be better to do so there on the spot and gain the credit for seeking this explanation, rather than expose myself at the Mairie to the risk of some unfriendly demonstration which might well result in the massacre of the prisoners.

I therefore turned and left the Butte with M. Sabourdy.[26]

The hostile feelings which the National Guard entertained towards me immediately became evident. I soon became the object of very pointed threats. They accused me of having plotted the removal of the guns; they expressed their joy at

[26] I believe that we left Mayer in the Rue des Rosiers. Ask Sabourdy. — *Note by Clemenceau.*

the murder which had just taken place; called out to me that there were others who had earned the same fate, and repeated what had already been said: that if I was not pleased about it they would do the same thing to me. They accused me of having wished to return the guns, which I was unable to deny. I only extricated myself from this dangerous situation by composure and coolness. Several men threatened me with their weapons. I retraced my steps and went directly up to them, asking them to explain their grievances against me. I told them several times they had just disgraced the Republic and that the murder on which they were congratulating themselves so heartily would inevitably bring the most disastrous consequences upon them as well as the country. My vigorous attitude caused them to retreat.

Nevertheless, it was with extreme difficulty and by parleying with them at every step that I reached the lower level of the Butte, where one of the guns was placed.

At this spot there was a group who manifested particularly strong hostility towards me. Very luckily M. Sabourdy was recognized by one of them and as he served as guarantor of my conduct it ended, not without difficulty, in their allowing us to pass.

The rest of the descent was accomplished with comparative ease, although through the midst of a crowd of National Guardsmen whose state of mind was unfriendly towards me. If a single man had uttered to my face certain definite accusations which were in the mind of all, thousands of voices would have been raised against me, and it is my profound conviction, as well as M. Sabourdy's, that I should have suffered the fate of the Generals.

The first word that M. Sabourdy said to me as we arrived at the foot of the Butte was, 'Without your sangfroid you would have been lost!'

THE narrative continues. Clemenceau proceeds to the Vigilance Committee in the Rue de la Chaussée-Clignancourt and asks what has become of the officers whom he met in the Rue des Rosiers. The answer is given that they are at the Château-Rouge and that the necessary steps will be taken to have them released in the evening. Satisfied on this point Clemenceau regains the Mairie; this day of blood and madness ends without further incident. It must have left a deep impression on his life.

# XXVI

## CILICIA — ATTEMPTS TO SABOTAGE THE PEACE TREATY — CLEMENCEAU TURNS PLAYWRIGHT

*17th May* 1928

CLEMENCEAU: Well, you know, I have looked at these two letter-books: and the more I think about it, the more it annoys me to have to give them to Poincaré. For thirty-six very good reasons, and especially because it might look as if I was wanting to resume friendly relations. Between Poincaré and me everything is finished.

MYSELF: But on the other hand you can't leave them lying about. There are no papers in the national archives whose publication would entail more serious consequences than these.

CLEMENCEAU: How about burning them then?

MYSELF: Oh, what a pity! [*To Piétri*] You haven't read them, have you? As one turns over these pages the entire war passes before one's eyes: the Allies. . . All the difficulties it was necessary to overcome. . . Cambon, Barrère worn out and receiving two or three telegrams on the same day: 'Go and see Lloyd George . . . Balfour . . . Orlando . . . Sonnino . . . insist! Show them that . . . Ask them if . . .'

CLEMENCEAU: There is one fellow in there. . . I wonder what became of him. I mean Orlando. He wasn't a bad sort. I think that he lived near us somewhere in the Midi. A chap who was a great deal more cunning was Sonnino. A Jew. . .

MYSELF: And a baron.

CLEMENCEAU: Jews are quite often barons.

PIÉTRI: You oughtn't to burn them. You haven't the right. I have an idea. . .

CLEMENCEAU: Ah ! Let's hear your idea.

[*Piétri sets it forth.* `Like our *Piétri's ideas it is full of good sense and reason. Clemenceau takes his side immediately.*]

CLEMENCEAU: Good ! It's decided. I should like now to speak to you of another of my crimes. . .

MYSELF: Still another ?

CLEMENCEAU: Yes — Mosul. I have been severely attacked because of Mosul and the oil fields. Well, yes, I gave up Mosul; but what they forget is that I used it as a bait in order to get Cilicia, which several of our good Allies very much wanted us not to have. Cilicia was, it might again become, a very pleasant country. Today its soil is uncultivated: nothing is grown in it: wherever the Arabs and the Turks have passed, they've brought the desert with them. . . But it must not be forgotten that when Cicero governed it, it was a country quite fantastically wealthy. What prevented us from restoring it to its ancient glory ? Unfortunately, in order to allow M. Deschanel to mount the throne of France, I retired from office, and the rest of the negotiations were conducted any old how. . . We gave up everything.[1] It had nothing to do with me.

Wait a minute ! I have a map of that country. Just look ! [*He shows me a little map of Asia Minor in which the countries under French mandate are coloured violet and those under British mandate pink.*] Here is Palestine, with Jerusalem. Naplouse, and on the coast Jaffa and Acre. All that belongs to the English. There is Syria, with Damascus, Aleppo and, as ports, Beirut, Tripoli, Latakia. That is ours.

---

[1] The treaty of Angora, 20th October 1921. Under this agreement the northern frontier of the French Zone was put back to the south of the Bagdad railway.

Then here on one side is Mosul with its oil fields, and on the other Cilicia, Adana. Here is Alexandretta and the Bagdad railway. Alexandretta is an excellent port to which to bring the oil from Mosul to the coast. We foresaw the construction of a pipe line for the purpose. The English were set on the idea of having this pipe line end at Jaffa, but it would have cost them something like a million and a half sterling to bring it into Palestine. All this proves that Cilicia and Alexandretta were not such a bad thing. I therefore said to the English, 'Which would you rather have, Mosul or Cilicia ?' They answered, 'Mosul.' I said, 'All right. I'll give it to you and I shall take Cilicia.' Can I be held responsible if, later on, the Turks chased us out of Cilicia and if M. Franklin-Bouillon, who was complaining that the Treaty of Versailles had not given us sufficient advantages, was called on to settle that matter? We have it, haven't we?

MYSELF: Certainly.

CLEMENCEAU: As for the Peace Treaty, never lose sight of the fact that there were two things to consider: what I got out of it, and what my successors got out of it. When I left office, Alsace and Lorraine had been given back to us; French troops occupied the left bank of the Rhine and the bridgeheads; Poland and Bohemia had been put on their feet; Roumania and Serbia enlarged; we had reconquered Morocco, put our hand on the Cameroons and so forth. After which came M. Millerand and others — and the Treaty fell to bits. All there was still to do, all the work to be partitioned out over the months and years to come, was given up. I had not been out of office a fortnight before they announced that they were not going to extradite William II and all those people who burned, pillaged, and so forth. Germany should have been made to disarm. . . At Spa and elsewhere she was granted delay after delay; we removed all our commissions of control — and now the Boche army is built up again, Boche factories are once more turning out cannon, machine guns — and everybody thinks that's perfectly all right.

Even better than that. The Treaty required Germany to deliver us coal free. . . At Spa we undertook to pay Germany two billions for coal, and it was paid — in the consulship of M. Millerand. The Treaty required Germany to pay twenty billion gold marks before some date or other in 1921. . . When the time for payment came, the Boche owed us twelve billion. . . So we said to them, 'Well, here is what you are going to do about those twelve billion: you are going to give us one of them right away, and as for the other eleven we'll just lump them in with the rest of your debt and give you seventy years to pay them.' And so forth, and so forth. Ten, twenty, thirty imbecilities of that kind! The Treaty has been practically torn to pieces. Wherever the Treaty says a hundred billions M. Millerand and his successors have said, 'No, no, it is much too much ! Give us fifty billions, thirty billions, and we'll let you off the rest.' Everything that I extracted from the Boches they give back to them. Everything that could be said against the Treaty to weaken it or even to wreck it was said. Millerand, as President of the Council, asserted before the Chamber, 'It is bigger with promises than realities.' Briand also declared, 'It is like Roland's mare: she had no life left in her.' What next ? What next ?

The moral of this story — that I was very wrong to be eighty years old in 1920. If I had been twenty years younger they would have thought twice before going on in that way. [*He is silent. His head is turned towards the garden and he is considering that battle which evaded him. Then*] Have you looked over my papers on the Commune ?

MYSELF: I've begun.

CLEMENCEAU: A funny business that also. When I think

of my life. . . I have always been surrounded by a lot of people who would very much have liked to see me dead and who wished for my destruction with a kind of mystic delirium.

MYSELF: Amongst your papers I found a play in which you express some less melancholy ideas. It is called *The Departure for Cythera*.[2] It is a manuscript which comes from Compère's Typing Bureau. I'll let you have it.

CLEMENCEAU: Pouh! It is just a joke. I also have this play: *The Pretence of Happiness*,[3] and another one, *The Strongest*, which I adapted from my novel. I had had several conversations about *The Strongest* with Porel[4] in order to get him to put it on. But Porel asked me to shorten the third act. I tried, but I couldn't do it. I found that everything I had put in it was necessary. Then I gave it up. That's all I've done in the way of playwriting.

MYSELF [*taking some papers out of the portfolio*]: Yesterday I was rereading this old letter of M. Viollette's. It bears the date of your first ministry, 1908, and concerns the dissolution of the C.G.T. [*Confédération Générale du Travail*].

---

[2] *Le départ pour Cythère*, a comedy in one act.

Cast : Mme. la Marquise d'Erlon, 30.
M. le Comte de Sombreuse, 40.
Mme. de Boisvert, 50.
Mlle. Dorothée de Boisvert, 22.
Mlle. Isabelle de Courvoisier, 60.
M. le Docteur Ferrand, 70.
Mme. Lelong, a companion, 60.
Rousseau, an old gardener.

The scene is laid at the Château d'Erlo about 1910.
It is a sentimental bit of work which takes place in high society and abstractions. The theme is whether marriage does or does not kill love. 'What !' says the Marquise d'Erlon, 'shall these hypocritical conventions arrogate to themselves the right to rule our every act, our every word, to the uttermost limit of hypocrisy, whilst that wondrous bloom, that veiled messenger of the supreme emotion, comes to the portals of a new life, and even the most delicate soul retiring within itself will see itself hurled to the coarse gossips of the streets ?'
Personally I prefer the Salernes speech.

[3] *Le Voile du Bonheur* was staged at the 'Renaissance' by Andrée Mégard and Gémier. The music was supplied by Gabriel Fauré. The piece was withdrawn after a few performances.

[4] Director of one of the principal theatres of Paris.

CLEMENCEAU: Oh ! What did he write ? Was he scolding me ?

MYSELF: No; he writes: 'You have gained my vote !'

CLEMENCEAU: That's nice ! [*Indicating other documents which I have just spread out*] And what are those ?

MYSELF: It is the correspondence between Poincaré and yourself. What a tone you adopt towards him !

CLEMENCEAU: Yes, I suppose so. I had had a visit from a certain Maurice Bernard, who said to me: 'If you have Poincaré elected President of the Republic he will at once have you made President of the Council.' I got up and showed Bernard the door. And I wrote to Poincaré: 'After the steps that you have dared to take with regard to myself it gives me great satisfaction to tell you that I no longer have the pleasure of your acquaintance.'[5]

PIÉTRI: Gracious ! When was that ?

CLEMENCEAU: 1913.

PIÉTRI: Already !

[5] On the 8th December 1917 in the esplanade of Metz, when they were presenting Marshal Pétain with his baton, M. Poincaré and M. Clemenceau went up to each other and embraced. But these cordialities were not renewed.

# XXVII

## 'I Should Choose Him Again'

*18th May* 1928

I ARRIVE at the Rue Franklin. Piétri is already there.

CLEMENCEAU [*seeing me coming in*]: Well?

MYSELF: I notice in these pages which you've given me to arrange a number of documents concerning the attitude of the Allies with regard to Foch. These documents are not signed; I wonder therefore what to make of them. Is it true that the Allies had protested against the attitude of Foch, who never stopped criticizing the Treaty of Peace? And that it was at your insistence that he was able to remain at the head of armies?

CLEMENCEAU: It's very simple. Foch only did what suited him. I had asked him one day to forward a letter to the general commanding the Army of Occupation in Germany. He returned it to me, and I was obliged to send it directly. So what do you expect? The Allies used to say 'How can we get on with a man who doesn't even listen to you?'

[*Albert enters and announces Dr. Laubry.*]

In my bedroom. [*Albert goes out.*] Have you found amongst the papers I've entrusted to you a rather long memorandum I wrote on my relations with Foch and what I thought of him ?

MYSELF: Yes. I'm just reading it. I'll return it to you shortly.

CLEMENCEAU: No, keep it; it's for you. You may have need of it. Are the conversations which Foch had with my brother Albert at Cassel discussed in that memorandum ?

MYSELF: I believe so.

CLEMENCEAU: Then that's it.

MYSELF: I'd like to put a question to you. It's about the defeatist propaganda during your ministry.

CLEMENCEAU: Go ahead.

MYSELF: You attacked M. Malvy with the help of the document which I observe over there on your table, and which is a long report issued by the Secret Service, reviewing in detail all the incidents of unpatriotic and revolutionary propaganda in the factories and amongst the labour organizations. Thanks to these pages — which read in a most sinister way — I don't know if you still remember them? . . .

CLEMENCEAU: Yes; they're appalling.

MYSELF: . . . You turned out M. Malvy. You came into power. You cut short the career of Messrs. Malvy and Caillaux. . .

CLEMENCEAU: And of several others as well, Martet. In more explicit terms: Bolo, Lenoir, and the rest.[1]

MYSELF: Yes. But there still remain a substantial number of people who will probably continue to hold the opinions which you have accused M. Malvy of having allowed them to hold. We have this paper on the defeatist propaganda in M. Malvy's time. But are you sure that there is not another paper like it on the defeatist propaganda in M. Clemenceau's time ?

---

[1] Executed for treason.

14

CLEMENCEAU: Well, it would surprise me. For defeatist propaganda in my time could not have been very powerful. Those fellows make a great deal of noise when they're permitted to, but if you tell them 'That's enough!' they keep quiet.

The revolutionary of that model is generally a failure who hasn't been able to succeed in anything within the ordinary framework of Society by the normal and legal means which it has established, so he tells himself that by dragging Society into the mud, he will be able to profit from the resulting mess. He is quite a pretentious being, with a very high idea of himself, who, on beginning life, expected to reach the top immediately, at one stroke, thanks to his abilities, his eloquence, and various other things of that kind. He perceived presently that, as far as the top is concerned, he is not more than the tram conductor or the street-sweeper. He concludes from this that there is no justice, or, if there is, it doesn't favour him — like everything else. They're fools, but fools who haven't much more courage than the bourgeois — and, good God! that's little enough.

It's ideas that give a man courage, and your revolutionaries are as gifted with ideas as my boot. They have spite, bitterness — but that doesn't get one very far. I saw them during the war; I have talked with them and tried to find something in them! it was pathetic. I've never had the least trouble with any of those specimens. When M. Malvy said to the Senate, 'Don't meddle with those fellows! There will be a Revolution,' he was pulling our legs. I didn't even have to engage in a struggle with them. They melted away like pale shadows.

I've had far less trouble with the anarchists than with Poincaré and Foch. [*Silence. Suddenly, and half-solemnly*] Speaking of Foch — well, you see, Martet, how Foch conducted himself towards me, all the shabby little tricks he played on me, how warily I was forced to proceed with him — yet despite all that he was the man we needed. With Pétain, a loyal and trustworthy man who behaved himself in exemplary fashion, the war would have lasted another year.

Who else was there? Mangin? You could expect anything from Mangin. He was capable of the best and the worst. Fayolle? Maistre? Castelnau? Guillaumot? I see no one but Foch.

During the final German offensive I was afraid; I was doubtful of him. I used to make it a rule not to meddle in military operations, but in certain cases I say to hell with rules — the country before everything. I therefore went to see Pétain. I asked him, 'Well, what conclusion must we draw about Foch?' And Pétain answered, 'I've seen his plans — there's nothing to say.' So I let him go on. The Chamber demanded his head; I defended him. Moreover, I spent two years defending him against everybody. And it was all the more to my credit that at that time I had already perceived his opinion of me, had already realized that I didn't like him, that I didn't like people of his kind, in whose souls ability and courage live side by side with — less attractive traits. I defended him because at bottom it was not a question in that situation of him or of me, but of the country.

Foch, who knew how far he could depend on himself, had this to his credit, that he leaned on Weygand. And he had fire! He had the fire of all the devils in hell. I admired him very deeply at Doullens. He went back and forth at the Front, saying, 'You scold and dabble, but you don't fight! I shall fight before Amiens, in Amiens, behind Amiens.' That's the way to talk! Whilst another of our great commanders — we were walking in the courtyard, this great commander and I — pointed out Haig, who was also going back and forth, and said, 'That man will have to capitulate in open country in a fortnight, and we'll be lucky if we don't have to do the same !' [2]

I repeat: if it had to be done again, even knowing what I had to expect from Foch I should choose him again. I don't regret anything.

[2] It is quite clear in the original text that Clemenceau's contemptuous contrast has only to do with the 'other of our great commanders' and in no way with the late Lord Haig.— *Translator's note.*

# XXVIII

## FOCH'S THANKS

ON THE 26th March 1918, at Doullens, the English and French Governments came to an agreement to entrust General Foch with the task of 'Co-ordinating the activities of the English and French Armies on the Western Front.'[1]

The battle before Amiens was ended. The front recovered a certain measure of quiet, occasionally broken by violent cannonading. There were several weeks of waiting, then suddenly the thrust at Château-Thierry.

During the night of May 26–27 the Germans launched a very violent bombardment along the entire sector between the Forest of Pinon and Rheims. On the morning of the 27th the attack was begun. 'The Franco-British troops,' said the communiqué given out at 2 o'clock, 'are resisting the German onslaught with their customary bravery; the battle is still raging.'

There's nothing to fear. Foch is on the job.

The communiqué issued at 11 o'clock that night observes,

[1] Many pieces of fiction have been written about the Doullens Conference. It has been said that Clemenceau was forced by the Allies to accede to the institution of the single command; this is based on a slight misconception, perhaps, of our Allies' mentalities. As a matter of fact Clemenceau had been preparing for this measure since he took office.

It has been said that Clemenceau would have preferred Foch's supreme authority to be limited to the operations before Amiens — this because Clemenceau wished to placate English susceptibilities.

It has been said that Clemenceau would have liked the command of the Allied armies himself. Clemenceau's comment on this was, 'I'd even had a uniform made—and the most gorgeous cap!'

'The struggle continued all day with extreme violence along the front of more than 40 kilometres, from the Vauxaillon region to the outskirts of Brimont. . . Several detachments of the enemy have reached the valley of the Aisne, in the vicinity of Pont-Arcy . . .' followed later by these words: 'The Franco-British troops are falling back in good order. . .'

Take up your maps once more — those maps with which you used to mark the breach in the English front two months earlier and which you perused so often with your eyes starting from their sockets. Observe the front before the attack: Noyons-Rheims; between these points Pinon. Cutting this southeast-northwest line from east to west is the course of the Aisne, and ten kilometres farther south the Marne. On the Marne and 35 kilometres from Meaux is Château-Thierry.

Château-Thierry is 80 kilometres from Paris. Notice the road which the Boches are going to take.

28th May, 2 o'clock communiqué: 'The Germans have crossed the Aisne between Vailly and Berry-au-Bac. The Franco-British troops, in the face of an enemy greatly superior in numbers, continued to withdraw in good order.'

The communiqué of 11 o'clock that night: 'The battle is developing with undiminished violence along the line of the Vesle, which the Germans succeeded in crossing this morning. . .'

29th May, 2 o'clock: 'The German thrust has grown in intensity . . . our troops are slowly retreating to the south and northeast of the heights above Saint-Thierry. They are holding between the Vesle and the Aisne canal.'

11 P.M: 'Soissons has been evacuated . . . we have given ground to the north of Fère-en-Tardenois.'

30th May: 'The Germans have gained possession of Fère-en-Tardenois and Vézilly. . .'

31st May: 'German detachments have reached the north bank of the Marne. . .'

MARSHAL FOCH

In five days they have crossed the Aisne and the Vesle, gained eighty-five kilometres — now they've got a foothold on the Marne. And the thought occurs: 'But Foch ! Where is Foch ? What's he doing ? What good is the elaborate paraphernalia of the unified command ?'

On the 1st June the enemy pushes his advance-guard to the outskirts of Château-Thierry. To the northwest of Château-Thierry he seizes Neuilly-Saint-Front. This attack has taken the form of a symbol — it is the sword which every day is thrust deeper into France's flesh, in the direction of the heart, Paris. And the 11 P.M. communiqué of the same June 1st says, 'The enemy forces are still numerically superior. . .'

In Paris there is tremendous commotion. The railway stations are overflowing with people who feel a sudden interest in the sunny slopes of the Mediterranean. The Chamber is dejected, panicky. Again, as two months earlier, I see hastening to the Ministry those men and women who 'want to know,' who feel 'that something is being concealed from them,' who 'heard the sound of gunfire' the previous night.

'What about it now? Foch has been taken by surprise, you see.'

'No — not really — you must give him time. . .'

'Time ? But look at the map. They're within twenty leagues of Paris.'

On the 4th there is a session of the Chamber. What will be the subject of interpellation ? Foch. Popular assemblies always clamour for heads. It's so simple ! Foch was a splendid idea which turned out to be deceptive. They expected victory from him: the Boches are at Château-Thierry. There is nothing in this battle — supported by us from beginning to end — to prove that Foch is a genius. He has hurled men in to fill the gaps as well as he could — but that's been done these four years.

One deputy shouted, 'Give us the sign for which we are

waiting.' Then Clemenceau ascended the rostrum. 'Nothing has developed since the brief but conclusive inquiry which I conducted to justify any steps being taken against anyone whatever. If it is necessary, in order to obtain the approval of certain people prone to hasty judgments, to abandon the leaders who have deserved well of their country, that's an act of cowardice of which I am incapable; don't expect me to commit it — our splendid soldiers have splendid leaders, great leaders, leaders worthy of them in every respect.'

The interruptions cease.

Clemenceau goes on: 'I repeat, I shall repeat as often as necessary because it's my duty to do so, that these fine soldiers have fine leaders — those two great soldiers called Foch and Pétain. General Foch enjoys the unanimous confidence of the Allies. . .' And the picture, the striking human picture which gives so great persuasive strength to his speech: 'Are we, because of a mistake which may or may not have occurred, going to require explanations from a man whose head I've seen fall exhausted with fatigue on a table piled high with maps? That I cannot permit. Expel me from the rostrum if that's what you're asking.'

Loud applause breaks out. Foch is saved.

Four months later an occasion presented itself to Foch for thanking Clemenceau. On the 5th of October Mr. Lloyd George sent him his 'sincere congratulations' on his birthday.

Marshal Foch replied: '*I am deeply touched, etc. I have not forgotten that it is to your firmness that I owe the position which I occupy today.*'

# XXIX

## Claude Monet

25 May 1928

YESTERDAY Piétri telephoned me: 'Cogné[1] is in Paris. We are going to see his bust with the President.'

I arrive at the Rue Franklin and find Clemenceau with Piétri.

CLEMENCEAU: So it seems that we are going to visit a sculptor called Cogné.

MYSELF: Good. Let's go.

CLEMENCEAU: I've something to tell you, Martet. I wanted to give you some of Poincaré's letters which it may interest you to examine later, but I can't get at them straight away; they're in the country.

MYSELF: Far from here?

CLEMENCEAU: Quite far.

MYSELF: Have you confidence in the person who's taking care of them?

CLEMENCEAU: Great.

MYSELF: Then it doesn't matter. They're as well there as elsewhere. I shall see them later. All I ask — just in case of

---

[1] Cogné is the sculptor of celebrities. From the Pope to M. Pierre Laval — taking in Messrs. Caillaux, Barthon and others on the way — he bustified the lot of them (*les a tous bustifiés*).
I met him through Bernier and had already been to his studio in the Rue de Villersexel to see the bust which he had made of Clemenceau *without even having seen the original*.

something unforeseen occurring — is that you tell this person not to refuse to hand these letters to me.

CLEMENCEAU: Granted. [*Indicating Piétri*] Furthermore, here is a man who can act as your witness.

MYSELF: Good.

CLEMENCEAU: So that's fixed up. [*Seeing me take some papers from my portfolio*] What's that?

MYSELF: Papers which it's better I shouldn't keep at my house and which I'm returning to you.

CLEMENCEAU: Put them there. I also have some papers to hand over to you — we've been exchanging papers in this way for some time — it gives us a somewhat idiotic appearance. [*He hands me a pile of papers.*] Look these over.

MYSELF [*reading*]: A typed memorandum on your encounters with Foch. I notice that a word is corrected in ink, and I think I recognize Mordacq's writing in this correction.

CLEMENCEAU: Good. Go on.

MYSELF: Some documents about General Leblois.

CLEMENCEAU: Oh, yes. He was a good fellow. What does he want?

MYSELF: He sends you a confidential memorandum concerning the request which he made for the reasons which led to the decision relieving him of the command of the Second Colonial Division, which he had held since the beginning of the war.

CLEMENCEAU: Well, what did he want me to do about it?

MYSELF: On the 11th January General Langle de Cary had sent him the cross of the Legion of Honour; on the 22nd Joffre relieved him of his command. He doesn't understand what it's all about.

CLEMENCEAU: Well, neither do I. Nor do I care. Meantime I'd like a word with you about another matter. Piétri has told me of the opinion you expressed about the book I'm writing. . .

MYSELF: Which book?

CLEMENCEAU: I'm only writing one. I've only one right hand.

MYSELF: The volume on Monet! I've no opinion about it; I haven't read it.

CLEMENCEAU: Quite so. Nevertheless, it appears that you think a book by me on Monet rather a slight affair, and that after having written *Au Soir de la Pensée* I oughtn't to talk about painting.

MYSELF: I find it a little off the mark. I shouldn't like people to think that your silence is merely a screen for trivial occupations.

CLEMENCEAU: Well, that's just the reason, you see — I'm writing this book precisely because it's different from *Au Soir de la Pensée*. If I wrote in the same vein, I should repeat myself. What do you want me to talk about? My little job on the Debts is finished: I've nothing more to do but revise it and strike out certain passages. The frame is too large, it would make a book — which I don't want. I shall publish it, however, after the elections. With Monet I'm doing something else — something which follows naturally, nevertheless, on *Au Soir de la Pensée*. I'm taking up a question of which I've never yet spoken but of which I ought to speak — the world's emotional impulse as expressed in religion or art. Well, I shall take art. I'm setting aside a page to link it up with what went before.

Amongst all the men I've known Monet is perhaps the one who most gave me an insight into all sorts of things. This describes him, doesn't it? He stands before a light, he takes that light, breaks it into its component parts, puts it together again. From the point of view of science there is nothing more interesting. Once I said to him, 'Monet, the rest of us fools, seeing a field or a sky, think "This is a field and that's a sky"; but for you that's not so. Those words "field," "sky"

have no meaning for you. And that must be a kind of in-
fatuation, an obsession with you, for wherever your glance
happens to fall you must wonder not "What is that ?" nor
even "What colour is that ?" but "Of what are those spots
composed ?" I should think your wits would be turned by
that sort of thing.' He answered, 'You can't have any idea to
what extent what you've just been saying is true. One day I
was at the deathbed of a woman I had dearly loved, whom
I still love dearly. I looked at her temples and said to myself,
"There is a kind of violet there — what is there in it of blue ?
of red ? of yellow ?" '

So you see how Monet lived. I shall tell a few other stories
to illustrate how proud and courageous he was. This one, for
instance: at the time Monet was selling his canvases for twenty-
five francs. One day, at Vétheuil, he had painted the sunrise
with the sun beginning to illuminate the mist. He took it to
a picture-dealer, who looked at the canvas and said, 'What
I buy, you understand, is painting. I don't know how you
made up your reckoning for that; it's only canvas; there are
a great many portions of it which aren't even covered. Put
some paint on it, and I'll buy it for fifty francs without haggling.' Monet said nothing — there was nothing to say. Five
or six years passed. One morning the picture-dealer came to
see Monet and noticed the Vétheuil canvas on an easel; he said
to Monet, 'That's very nice, that job over there. I'll give you
six hundred francs for it.'

'But don't you remember ?' said Monet. 'You refused it
once because there wasn't enough colour in it. Well, today
you'll have to get it through your head that if you offered me
fifty thousand, I'd rather destroy it than give it to you.'

He was a fellow with a knack, never satisfied with his work,
yet appreciating its worth — he found the means to reconcile
both those characteristics. I've known him in bad times as

well as good.  I owe it to him to write this book, don't you think ?

MYSELF:  Well, certainly, sir, but . . .

CLEMENCEAU:  Begin with the principle that there are always 'buts' in everything.  The entire question is knowing whether there are more 'buts' in favour of doing a thing than there are against it.  Do you want to be agreeable ?  Tell me that there are at least as many buts for writing *Monet* as against . . . poor Monet !'

MYSELF:  He must have passed the last days of his life in despair. . .

[*I mean his genius grew exasperated: the more he became master of his art the more he reached for distant and inaccessible goals.  Clemenceau believes that I mean the cataract which Monet developed.*]

CLEMENCEAU:  Not at all.  Despite his cataract (he was in a terrific funk of physical pain; he had undergone a small preliminary operation, but the extensive interruption which the second one would have entailed — I did all I could to make him have it — he was afraid of it) — despite his cataract he could see well enough to paint and even to improve his canvases.  Do you remember his water-lily studies ?  I had prevailed upon him to give them to the State.  He had said to me, 'Yes, I'll give them.'  But later he added, 'I'll give them, of course, but I don't want them removed now.  They can be taken away after my death.'  I wasn't at all reassured; I was afraid that he might mess them up.  I had seen at his house canvases of clouds which he had obviously spoiled, overloaded.  And I said to him, 'I don't feel very easy. . .'  But he didn't answer.  Later I went to Giverney.  He led me into his studio and showed me the canvases.  'How do they strike you ?'  A hundred times better — all illuminated, etherealized.

One of his things which I think exceptionally fine is his por-

trait of himself which I gave to the Louvre. Do you know it?
It's his masterpiece. You know, it was his habit to establish
himself on the bank of his little stream, to remain seated there
for hours, looking at the water and the reflections of the clouds
in it, the flowers — he used to return to his studio after that
and cover one of his large canvases in an hour. Well, that
portrait, it's he on the day he decided to begin on his great
water-lily frieze. His eyes are half-shut, he is looking at his
canvases, at all that will happen both of joy and sorrow. It
was a custom of his to destroy his pictures, to tear them to
ribbons by stamping on them or slashing them with a knife.
I was able to save that one. It was a bit of luck.

What I want to tell is the story of that conflict — a conflict
which ended both in victory and defeat, a victory because he
left behind a vast body of work, including many splendid
things, a defeat because in that domain there is no such thing
as success. And, between us, I shan't mind giving a lesson to
the art critics, whose number is ludicrous. Further, if I don't
take this subject, what subject shall I take? Politics?

MYSELF: You are quite right. Although, to tell the truth,
it's not subjects that are lacking. Have you read about the
triumph — as the newspapers call it — of the left in Germany,
and, at the same time, the explosion of the yellow-gas magazine in Hamburg?

CLEMENCEAU: Yes; that means that henceforward we can
sleep in peace. It appears that the League of Nations is going
to take up this 'incident.' So everything will be all right.
There is nothing to wait for now but the sanctions. Martet,
what a strange country ours is! To come back to Monet,
when my book is finished I'll show it to you, and you will tell
me what you think of it. I shall follow your advice. Let's
go to Cogné's.

[*We go out and get into the car.*]

# XXX

## Clemenceau at His Sculptor's

[*In the Citroen, a little coupé whose interior is lined with pearl grey. Brabant is at the wheel and handles the little darling a bit violently.*]

MYSELF: What a lovely new car you have! Is it your old Citroen done up?

CLEMENCEAU: I'll tell you what happened. I went to see Citroen. I gave him my old car and said, 'I need a new one.' He answered 'Good, but a man who has done what you have for the country isn't in the same category as an ordinary customer; I can't let you pay a penny.' I looked at him. I wondered if he was pulling my leg. For some years I've not been accustomed to hearing that sort of thing. I returned, 'All right. That seems a pretty good proposition to me. I accept your gift. But here's ten thousand francs which you will be so kind as to distribute amongst your workmen from me.'

PIÉTRI: You're forgetting that you handed over your old car. Moreover, Citroen wouldn't sell it again. . .

CLEMENCEAU: No. He's keeping it as a souvenir. He's a Jew, but a good Jew. There are some good Jews.

MYSELF: They didn't all crucify Jesus Christ.

CLEMENCEAU: Oh, everybody more or less crucified Jesus Christ. They still crucify Him every day. . .

MYSELF [*examining the accessories*]: And I see that there's a pretty little contraption for necessary articles like a powder-box, lip-stick. . .

CLEMENCEAU: Yes, indeed; I even said to Citroen, 'It's a pity that you can't throw into the bargain a little girl who might find these things useful.'

PIÉTRI: That bargain reminds me a little of the one you once made at Djipur. . .

CLEMENCEAU: Oh, yes. One day in a little village called Djipur, in the East Indies, I noticed at a dealer's a little statuette which represented a God and Goddess in the act of making love, saving your presence. I said to the dealer, 'I like your statuette. How much is it ?' He answered, 'Because it's you, seventy-five rupees.' I said, 'Because it's I, I offer you forty-five for it.' He raised his hands to heaven. 'Forty-five rupees ! You're making fun of me. What if anyone happened to hear of it ? People would say . . .' and so forth. I said, 'Forty-five rupees.' Then he made a fine gesture of indignation. 'Impossible. I'd rather give it to you.' 'Agreed !' I reached out my hand, took the statuette, stuffed it into my pocket, and said, 'You are extraordinarily kind, and I thank you. But it is quite evident that this gift can only come from a friend to a friend.' 'Yes, of course.' 'Consequently, you won't take it amiss if I in turn make you a gift.' 'Naturally not.' 'Well, here are forty-five rupees to use in good works.' He took the forty-five rupees and we parted enchanted with each other.

[*We arrive in the sad, grey little street called the Rue de Villersexel. Cogné's studio is number 9. We cross the court-yard. Cogné's assistant opens the door for us. Cogné comes forward, bows, 'Mr. President.' He is a small man, quite round and correct in every detail, rosette (of the Legion of Honour), eyeglasses, etc.*]

COGNÉ: I am greatly honoured by this visit, Mr. President.

CLEMENCEAU: Let's have a look at my bust.

[*We go into the studio, which is full of busts. Here are Caillaux, Laval, Barthou, as well as Maurice Rostand and the Pope. The bust of Clemenceau is set up in the centre of the studio, on a high pedestal. Clemenceau goes straight to it, looks at it, studies it with knitted brows, walks round it, shakes his head — all without a word. Cogné waits. Piétri and I also wait. This lasts a long time, perhaps a minute — and I am beginning to wish I were elsewhere.*]

CLEMENCEAU [*finally*]: Yes. [*Another silence; more headshakings.*] Yes. [*Same business.*] Yes. [*Same business again — and again.*] There's something there.

COGNÉ: Oh, Mr. President, now that I see you, I realize that it's imperfect. What a pity that I hadn't seen you before !'

CLEMENCEAU: Yes.

COGNÉ: Your eyes, for instance. I see that they are less deep set, more on a level with your face. But I did that from photographs; the shadows misled me.

CLEMENCEAU: And there's also the distance between the cheek-bones — do you see ? — it's not exactly like that — there's something of the Kalmouck in me. . .

COGNÉ: There is something of the Kalmouck beyond a doubt, Mr. President. . .

CLEMENCEAU: And there too — the jaw is more. . .

COGNÉ: And the ears — are a little less. . .

CLEMENCEAU: Exactly. The ears are much less.

COGNÉ: Oh, Mr. President, I see you now ! That's it. *Now* I see you. If I dared, Mr. President, I should ask you please to . . .

CLEMENCEAU: What ?

COGNÉ: I shouldn't abuse the privilege.

CLEMENCEAU: Go on.

COGNÉ: If you would allow me to take a few photographs ?

CLEMENCEAU: All right. Take away.

[*He sits down on a chair. In five seconds Cogné has arranged a lamp so that it pours its light on Clemenceau's face and is flourishing a photographic bulb, ready to press it, when Clemenceau, who had kept his hat on, decides to take it off.*]

COGNÉ: Oh, thank you, Mr. President! I didn't dare ask you. . .

[*And click! Click! And click once more. Clemenceau is taken full-face, right profile, left profile. Cogné comes, goes, presses, clicks. When the ceremony is ended:*]

COGNÉ: There you are, Mr. President. I've finished.

CLEMENCEAU: Is that all there is to it? I haven't suffered too much.

COGNÉ: And if I might dare ask one thing more, Mr. President — it will be the last — I'll leave you in peace after that. I should like to ask, Mr. President, if you'd allow me to take some measurements. . .

CLEMENCEAU: Take away. . .

[*Cogné provides himself with an enormous pair of compasses and measures the famous 'spread' between the cheekbones, the 'spread' between the ears, the height of the nose, etc.*]

CLEMENCEAU [*indicating the space between nose and chin*]: And this.

COGNÉ: You're quite right. We mustn't forget that!

[*He takes this final measurement, then bows and opens his arms wide to indicate it's all over.*]

CLEMENCEAU: Splendid.

COGNÉ: With these, Mr. President, I shall make a bust for you which shall have absolute truth—a perfect likeness. I think that I've caught hold of you now, Mr. President.

CLEMENCEAU: I don't doubt it.

COGNÉ: Do you know Laval, Mr. President?

CLEMENCEAU: Laval?

CLEMENCEAU INSPECTING THE STATUE
ERECTED TO HIM AT SAINTE-HERMINE

Cogné: Yes, the deputy . . . the Senator . . . the one who was a cabinet minister . . . here's his bust.

Clemenceau [*looking at the bust*]: Yes, of course. It certainly is Laval. [*Pointing at the bust of the Pope*] And who's that ?

Cogné: It's the Holy Father, Mr. President.

Clemenceau: The present one?

Cogné: The present one — and M. Barthou, Mr. President [*indicating the bust of Barthou: beard, eye-glass, smile*]. Do you recognize him ?

Clemenceau: I do. [*He returns the bust's smile.*] Barthou ! [*He points at a clay model of a Marshal of France on horseback holding the Marshal's baton impressively across his thigh.*] Why don't you make me look like that ?

[*And we leave. Cogné telephones me during the afternoon.*]

Cogné: What impression did the President form ?

Myself: He was charmed, quite enchanted. But he's a man you must get to know — he's not very demonstrative. However, with the photographs you took this morning. . .

Cogné: I've nothing but bad luck; my camera wasn't working.

# XXXI

## Across the Ages and the Arts

ALBERT shows me into the study. I wait for some time, perhaps ten minutes, amusing myself as best I can. I scan the books on the shelves — works on sociology, geography, philosophy.

There are photographs on the table, of pictures by Monet — *Vétheuil,* the *Women with the Parasol,* etc. Finally Clemenceau enters.

CLEMENCEAU: Ah, Monsieur Martet. Forgive me for having kept you waiting. I was engaged in making up my accounts with my valet. Do you realize something terrible is happening — the price of everything is double ?

MYSELF: I know. I know what I'm paying in rent.

CLEMENCEAU: But listen ! What's one to do ? There's no longer any way to . . .

MYSELF: I think the best thing is to get one's share of it.

CLEMENCEAU: That's all very well. Nevertheless, we must pay. And pay and pay. There are limits. Isn't anything being done to meet the situation ? I thought that commissions had been appointed to fight the high cost of living. Aren't you and everybody else tired of being throttled ?

MYSELF: But what would you suggest doing about it ?

CLEMENCEAU: Take a dozen individuals and hang them.

MYSELF: Yes, if that would lower the price of cauliflower. . .

CLEMENCEAU: Not a doubt of it. In twenty-four hours. But instead of doing that, people — I know what they do; they see that the cost of living is double, so they double their incomes. By stealing. They turn into thieves.

MYSELF: I haven't even that resource. . .

CLEMENCEAU: Then you're beyond forgiveness. In my time nothing more was necessary than to go out into the streets. [*He sits down.*] Sit down, Martet. [*I sit down and look at him. He looks at me.*] I'm bored.

MYSELF: Oh ! Why ?

CLEMENCEAU: I'm coughing. For two days I've been coughing like a horse. I'm tired. I've had enough of it. All this going back and forth — I've seen them doing it for eighty years. It isn't right. Poincaré — is there anything that looks more like Poincaré than Poincaré ? [*He yawns. After an interval*] By the way, you must give me back the memorandum I wrote on my relations with Foch. I must look it over. I wrote it quickly, and there are probably some things to change.

MYSELF: I'll bring it back to you. I haven't read it yet. I'm sorting out your papers on the Commune.

CLEMENCEAU: Are you finding anything in them ?

MYSELF: Some very interesting things.

CLEMENCEAU: What madness ! It is one of the maddest madnesses in all history. No one even knew what the Commune was about. Those people killed, burned, got themselves killed, at times magnificently, but they never knew why ! Did you go away for Whitsun ?

MYSELF: Yes, I went as far as the mouth of the Loire. I discovered a country called la Brière, which is heavenly. Marshes extending as far as you can see, with frogs.

CLEMENCEAU: Don't know it.   I went to Giverney the other day.

MYSELF: Are you working on your book on Monet?

CLEMENCEAU: I'm doing odd bits. You know, about Monet — I think that I can say quite a good deal about him. For forty years I had him at the other end of a wire. Monet took life as a struggle. I remember seeing him one day in his poppy field, with four canvases set up in front of him. He was going from one to the other, according to the position of the sun. Well, that's it, isn't it ? What's fine in Monet is that seriousness, that intensity. There are two self-portraits of Monet — the one I gave to the Louvre and the one that was at Giverney. In the latter he shows his quality — a look that pierces you; there's something cruel, savage about it. He is looking at his ricks. That was Monet; he threw himself into everything like a man possessed.

I don't like everything Monet did. Some of his things are mediocre — his *Cathedrals of Rouen*. They're anything you like but stone.[1]

MYSELF: He didn't want to reconstruct them architectur- ally. He only tried to reproduce the play of light and shade.

CLEMENCEAU: Nevertheless, they're bad. His impressions of Venice are bad. The light is depressing. I've seen Venice and I know what she is. I know that sun and that water — his are silly. But you still have his hayfields — which are prodi- gious. And his water-lilies. One should remove one's hat before those water-lilies.

MYSELF: Don't you find it odd that he was limited in that way and never tried to pierce through to the soul ?

CLEMENCEAU: To the what ?

MYSELF: The soul. He never attempted to portray human expressions. . .

[1] There was a time, however, when Clemenceau loved Monet's Cathedrals. 'I see rising,' he says somewhere, 'the monolith in its powerful unity, in its supreme authority — a flower in stone, vibrant, inundated with light. . .'

CLEMENCEAU: Don't take the soul too seriously, Martet. Do you really believe that men have souls? Do you believe that there is more of a soul in Gustave Hervé[2] than in a blade of grass? No, Martet, he didn't seek that — although in his two portraits, on that day, or rather on those two days, he did penetrate to the soul. But as you say, he was limited. Do you hold it against him? Not I. It is one of the forms of courage and power. Your first duty is to know yourself, and to limit your field of operations. He selected light — it wasn't a bad choice.

MYSELF: What did you go to Giverney for on Sunday?

CLEMENCEAU: I wanted to see the studies he made when he was living on the banks of the stream. They are very odd. They've nothing to do with any of the rest. He only wanted his effect. They're rough, wild, often melancholy. I was given two or three hundred letters, all those written to Monet by Mirbeau, Renoir, and myself. I'm engaged in looking through them now. Mirbeau was — yes, he was a man all the same. There was, naturally, a good deal of pose about him. He was a gentleman who adopted an air and stuck to it through thick and thin. One feels that he would have referred in the same terms to a bowl of strawberries and cream or the murder of an entire family. But after all his inspiration can only be praised. Do you like Mirbeau?

MYSELF: Yes, I consider him one of our greatest writers.

CLEMENCEAU: I'm of the same opinion. An odd fellow, rather tiresome, but with a splendid pen. His 628-E8 is a marvellous stunt. And his breeding, his courage, his generosity! Renoir's letters are also interesting. I don't like Renoir; Monet used to reproach me for it.

MYSELF: Renoir and Monet have many points of contact.

CLEMENCEAU: Not in their work.

---

[2] A journalist who, after having spoken of 'erecting the flag on a dung-hill,' became a passionate patriot.

MYSELF: No, but in spirit.

CLEMENCEAU: You know, I can't forgive him for having made woman a sort of monster. It's enough to disgust you with love forever after.

MYSELF: Are you in favour of love, sir ?

CLEMENCEAU: Aren't you ? Or do you prefer spontaneous generation? Have you seen the buttocks he gives those poor wretches ? It oughtn't to be allowed. Where did he ever see buttocks like that ? I've travelled quite a bit, but I've never run into them. But I realize — if it gives you any pleasure — that he was somebody. He sought.

MYSELF: And your letters to Monet ?

CLEMENCEAU: I don't know what they contain. Friendship and scolding, probably. That's what my life's been made up of. I can't like anyone without scolding him. I've always had great respect for Monet. In the first place we lived on two different planes — we never collided, never fought. There was never any jealousy or rivalry between us. In the second place he painted exactly as I should like to have done had I been a painter — stubborn, obstinate painting.[3] It's stupid to say that genius is merely long drawn out patience. Because in the first place patience itself doesn't mean anything — it requires more than patience to get what you want — you must go straight for it. And secondly, there is one kind of genius, perhaps the best and most precious, into which not a grain of patience enters. But there is another kind which is due to effort, a fierce application, and to that, for my part, I pay respect.

MYSELF: What is going to happen to the Giverney canvases ?

[3] Clemenceau once wrote in reference to the quays of the Seine: 'The panting crane, with the grating sound of iron, describes a large circle in the air. The great hampers dip suddenly and pour out the ochre-coloured sand or tawny slag in a sparkling golden shower. Huge slabs of Burgundy stone rear themselves into white walls, wooden planks are piled up in a homely sort of building construction, and the rose or amber of the pale bricks brighten the river with a caress of colours. . .' That's a Monet !

CLEMENCEAU: He left everything to his son Michel.

MYSELF: And his daughter-in-law, his son Jean's wife ?

CLEMENCEAU: Well, he left her without a penny.

MYSELF: Impossible.

CLEMENCEAU: Yes, it's true. I've told you before, Monet was afraid. He was afraid of physical pain, afraid of death. The operation I wanted him to have would have allowed him to use his sight to the end. He funked it. His courage left him at the thought of death — he didn't want to think about it. So he died without doing anything for his daughter-in-law.

MYSELF: Extraordinary. And she was so exceedingly good to him.

CLEMENCEAU: She was admirable, in every way. She took care of him, pampered him. She watched over him as if he had been her child. She helped him prepare his canvases; she took care of his investments.

MYSELF: I know.

CLEMENCEAU: Well, there you are ! He leaves everything to Michel's discretion, which means that I shall have the business on my hands. I said to Michel, 'What are you going to do for her ? Obviously you must repair your father's oversight.' Michel replied, 'Well, yes, I'm going to fix all that up.' I said, 'It isn't a question of fixing it up in the more or less distant future; you must do it right away !' I know that he'll do it. He's not a bad sort and his needs aren't great. He's having a little house built for himself on the banks of the Eure. He's living there. On behalf of the Louvre I said to him, 'You ought to set aside the *Two Women with the Parasol* for the Louvre.' He has done so. I also said to him, 'You ought to give a canvas to the architect who fitted up the Orangery — he didn't overcharge for it.' He did that too. He really does what he ought. Unfortunately there he is, in his car, running about the country — he'll break his neck one of these days and the little sister-in-law will be left without a penny. So there you are. That's how I'm diverting myself for the moment. A man's life is interesting primarily when he has failed — I well know. For it's a sign that he tried to surpass himself. Monet succeeded in his. He found fame, money. Nevertheless, I shall enjoy seeing him again in these letters, reconstructing him, finding an idea where he probably had only an instinct. I shall take the letters away with me to the Vendée. I shan't be bored with them. I prefer that past to your present. Have you read about the Colmar trial ?' [4]

MYSELF: Yes.

CLEMENCEAU: What do you think about it ?

MYSELF: It's very sad.

CLEMENCEAU: That Berthou [5] carried in triumph by the priests ! There's proof for you of the disorientation of everything ! And Fachot [6] insulted by a band of hoodlums who threw stones at him. And that lawyer from Quimper who declared, 'France must not be judged by the abominable verdict which has just been rendered.' What do you expect to do after that ? I have received a letter from a former deputy from that region who says, 'When you were young I followed and supported you. During the war I disagreed with you. In memory of your youth and the ideas which you formerly upheld, what do you intend to do by way of protest against the degrading spectacle at Colmar ?' That shows you where we are.

MYSELF: What's the solution ?

CLEMENCEAU: For myself I see only one — to die. I no longer care to hear those things discussed. France frightens me. People laugh, amuse themselves, understand nothing, or if they do understand, they don't care a hang. The future

---

[4] The autonomist's trial. The verdict was returned on the 24th May.

[5] Communist deputy, lawyer for the autonomists.

[6] The Public Prosecutor. Some time later he was shot by a fanatic and wounded.

no longer counts. Where shall we find ourselves one of these days, when we wake up ? As for myself, I shall be amongst the dead. I don't ask anything more.

MYSELF: When do you leave for the Vendée ?

CLEMENCEAU: At the beginning of July. If my book on Monet is good, I shall publish it; if it's bad, I'll toss it into the fire. Have you seen those photographs over there ? I don't know where they come from; they're interesting, although they're in black and white. You feel the seeking after colour — the pencil trying to drag it out. . . There's a struggle going on there. He has the secret of the convexity of the earth — have you noticed ? You feel that it goes on beyond the line of the horizon. The sky loses itself, it doesn't stop.

I'm going to an exhibition of Bourdelle's in the Rue La Boétie. Do you know Bourdelle ?

MYSELF: I know his work.

CLEMENCEAU: What do you think of it ?

MYSELF: Good Lord !

CLEMENCEAU: That's exactly my opinion. He does Greek sculpture according to the German. He does Gothic, Peruvian, Mycenian. Only there's one thing that bores me about him — he never does anything Bourdellian.

MYSELF: Perhaps because there has been a Peru, a Mycenæ. . .

CLEMENCEAU: And there's never been a Bourdelle ? It's quite possible.

In any case he has queer flights of fancy. Do you know what he nearly did for my *Démosthène* ? The publisher had ordered some bas-reliefs, from which engravings were to be made. Whereupon my Bourdelle had the idea of doing my portrait in the guise of Demosthenes, dressed in a toga, passing the dead in review in the Champs-Elysées. Do you get the picture ?

MYSELF: It's a pretty idea, as they say.

CLEMENCEAU: Can you see me in the Champs-Elysées, holding a review of Poincaré, Jules Ferry, Franklin-Bouillon, François Albert ? I said to the publisher, 'Oh, no, I won't have that.' Bourdelle executed another most extraordinary thing. It represents Xerxes on horseback, turning his mount round and saying, 'Don't let's go any further. The ground is dangerous.' The trouble is (I'll show you the thing presently) that Xerxes is on his horse and his feet are dragging along the ground. Personally I have never seen that happen. When I was young I now and then had occasion to ride a horse, and I always took care to select one tall enough so that my feet wouldn't drag in the mud.

MYSELF: Did Xerxes travel on horseback, then ? I always imagined him carried in a litter.

CLEMENCEAU: No, he must have been on horseback. Don't you remember how in Herodotus they decided to take for their King, the one whose horse neighed the first ? It's an idea like another — as good as a plebiscite, at any rate. And it was Darius's mare who emitted the first neigh. Bourdelle is a fantasist. He models his clay in such a way that it gives, at first sight, the impression of power, and at bottom . . . you feel what he'd like to do, what he's seeking, trying to do and can't do. But now and then he pulls it off. He performs a stroke of genius, with an air of swank — and it's serious craftsmanship. However, since I couldn't have Phidias they tossed me Bourdelle.

MYSELF: There aren't many French sculptors.

CLEMENCEAU: In return there aren't any foreign sculptors at all. Foreigners can carve cherry-stones or mountains, but as sculpture it simply doesn't exist. They do much better to leave the poor stone in peace or make roads of it. Amongst us, at one time or another, there have been sculptors who knew how to turn out an occasional good piece. There was Houdon

—there's going to be a Houdon exhibition. I shall go to see that. There was Rude. . .

MYSELF: And Carpeaux.

CLEMENCEAU: He's a little too Second Empire. His grace is languid, a bit stupid. He gave lightness to stone, but it's a question whether stone was made to be light. I don't like Rodin.

MYSELF: Nevertheless. . .

CLEMENCEAU: Well, yes, I grant that you must say 'nevertheless' — perhaps it's because I knew the man. He was stupid, vain, and cared too much about money. That's quite a bit against him, isn't it? When I returned from South America with the order for a bust I went to see Rodin, who said to me, 'They must be made to pay as dearly as possible.' It was his first thought.

MYSELF: There is the *St. John the Baptist* — and the *Man Walking*, tense, nervous. . .

CLEMENCEAU: Yes, yes — there is also the *Balzac*.

MYSELF: Well, don't you like the *Balzac*, sir? It's an admirable effort. It has probably nothing to do with the real *Balzac*. . .

CLEMENCEAU: Probably — and it's ridiculous.

MYSELF: But those two great eye-sockets — the carriage of the body — there's something rather magnificent in it.

CLEMENCEAU: Yes, yes. . .

MYSELF: When you compare the *Balzac* of Rodin with the *Balzac* of the Boulevard Haussman. . .

CLEMENCEAU: The man sitting in his dressing-gown? What a dreadful thing it is!

MYSELF: Have you seen Cogné again?

CLEMENCEAU: Cogné? Oh, yes — he came to see me the other day and photographed me again. He had forgotten to light his apparatus.

[*Enter Michel Clemenceau — tall, thin, dressed in grey, his temples delicately silvered and his bearing young. He bears an extraordinary resemblance to his father — a gentler, smiling version.*]

MICHEL CLEMENCEAU: How do you do, father?

CLEMENCEAU: Oh, there you are!

MICHEL CLEMENCEAU: I've just come from Holland. I went to convey your good wishes to the Burgomaster Six.

CLEMENCEAU: He's not very remarkable, is he?

MICHEL CLEMENCEAU: Remarkable! And the Draper's Guild! That's beyond words, too. And this. [*He indicates a yellowing photograph on the mantel-piece: five middle-class women in small white head-dresses, their lips pinched and their eyes dull or fierce. They are the Committee of an almshouse, captured, appraised, and fixed on canvas by Rembrandt. What faces!*]

CLEMENCEAU: What frightful faces! Philanthropy in all its horror!

MICHEL CLEMENCEAU: I like the *Night Watch* even less. There's an effect of light and shade. . .

CLEMENCEAU: Yes. It's easier. But the man putting on his gloves! He did that in two hours.

MICHEL CLEMENCEAU: On my way back to Paris I went to see my grand-daughter.

MYSELF: Your grand-daughter? Are you really a grand-father?

MICHEL CLEMENCEAU: Yes, George has a daughter.

CLEMENCEAU: She's a funny little thing. [*He gets up.*] Come along and see Xerxes.

[*We pass into the bedroom. He takes Bourdelle's bas-relief from a drawer and shows it to us. It is a Xerxes with huge arms and legs gesticulating violently. Bourdelle was embarrassed by the necessity of getting horse and man into so small a frame. He seems to have folded them up like lobsters being packed for shipment in the bottom of a basket. In addition Xerxes has the air of pointing out the way to his horse by saying to him, 'Come along. This way.'*]

CLEMENCEAU: What do you think of it ?

MYSELF: ? ? ?

CLEMENCEAU: Hold on — in return look this over for me. [*He shows me the catalogue of Bourdelle's exhibition. On the cover is a photograph of Bourdelle — spectacles behind which thoughts are soaring; hair through which the breath of inspiration is blowing.*] He missed his Xerxes, perhaps, but he succeeded with his Bourdelle, eh, what ? [*I notice the cast of the Samos stele fastened on the wall.*] You're looking at that ? You can look at it all your life without getting tired of it. When you are in Athens don't forget to stop in front of it: stop a bit also before the woman who's tying up her sandal. There's a movement of her shoulders. . . Ah, Martet, the man who did that ! [*Showing me out.*] So I ought to write *Monet* ? He's a man I loved. . .

## XXXII

### TWO FRIENDS

MONET returned his friendship. The old painter's last years were made wretched by his eyes — that sight which was becoming feebler each day, confusing the outlines of things and distorting their values. . . His *Water-Lilies* — those vast mad frescoes painted with great strokes of his fiery brush in passion and anguish, which he gave to the State and wanted to keep, gave again, took away again — his pictures were not finished — the Orangery was not ready — and all those phobias, those delusions of the sick old man, all those obsessions and childish rages, all those things he confided to Clemenceau in these burning letters, written in pencil in a trembling hand which painfully sought to be legible, letters in which one can guess the weakness and the suffering and which yet burn with virile and brotherly affection.

Here are a few unpublished extracts:

*11th September* 1916

'I get on quite well despite some moments of complete discouragement, and then I regain confidence just because I fear that I shall not be able to see my way out of this enormous labour. . .'[1]

[1] The *Water-Lilies*. The fresco was divided into fifteen canvases.

*12th November* 1918

'Dearest friend, I am on the point of finishing two paintings to which I want to affix the date of the victory, and I should like to ask you to act as intermediary in offering them to the State.[2] It is a small thing but it is the only way I have of taking part in the victory. I request that these two panels be hung in the Museum of Decorative Arts[3] and I should be happy if they were chosen by you.

I admire you, and greet you with all my heart.'

*10th November* 1919

'As I telegraphed you yesterday, I have given mature thought to what you said to me yesterday,[4] which proves the friendship which you have for me. But what can you expect? I am very much afraid that an operation will be fatal to me, that once the malady of the one eye is overcome it will be the turn of the other. Then I prefer to enjoy my bad sight, even to give up painting if necessary, but at least to see to some extent what I love, the sky, the water, and the trees, not to speak of the friends who surround me. And since I remember that a talented artist whom I know has just been operated upon, I am prudently going to find out the condition she is in after her operation, and then I shall be able to make up my mind and turn to you again. I hope that you understand my reasons. . .'

*3rd April* 1921

'I am going to Paris to see about my eyes and to make up my mind.'

*29th June* 1921

'I am continuing to work with keenness but the highly changeable weather is playing me dirty tricks.'

[2] In the end Monet offered the State all his canvases.
[3] The *Water-Lilies* were not placed in this museum. A special position was found for them in the Orangery in the Tuileries.
[4] Clemenceau was advising him to be operated on for cataract.

16

*6th September* 1921

'I have done a great deal of work and am still working.'

*25th November* 1921

'Everything is all ready except arrangements with the architect about the plans.[5]   I have invited him to come on Sunday to give me some necessary details without which nothing can proceed.'

*8th December* 1921

'As for the Orangery I am afraid the architect is finding himself in difficulties and that he is only thinking of keeping expenses down; nevertheless, I think that he should be asked frankly if the gift which I am making does or does not deserve that everything necessary be done in order that my decorations shall be exhibited as I want them to be.'

He was sick.   When he was better.

*13th December* 1921

'I am quite well.   I was able to leave my room yesterday and today I have started work again.   So life is lovely.'

*8th January* 1922

'What am I doing in this world ?   Well, I paint and then I wait for the appearance of the *Echo National*,[6] especially if you are writing in it.'

Clemenceau is in the United States.   Claude Monet writes to me:

*22nd February* 1922

'Since you were kind enough to promise me news of M. Clemenceau I should like to ask you what you know about him, about his health particularly, and to let him know how

---

[5] The plans of the Orangery.
[6] André Tardieu's paper.   M. Clemenceau never wrote for it.

often I think of him and how happy I should be to hear from him personally and learn if he is satisfied with what he sees. He has so accustomed me to his visits that I miss him exceedingly — tell him that, please, and tell him what pleasure it would give me to have a line from him.'

The Orangery was not advancing. Monet wrote to Paul Léon.[7] No answer.

*6th March* 1922

'I am pledged therefore and he is not, and to judge by the way things are going I am very much afraid we shall not get anywhere. The Beaux-Arts is overflowing, without a penny and only looking about to gain time.'

*4th May* 1922

'I am passing through some rather unhappy days. My sight, alas, is going completely, and if you knew what that means to me ! It would do me good to see you. . .'

*16th May* 1922

'Two words to let you know that the wistaria [8] is just coming out, that it will be beautiful in a few days, and that a visit from you is required.'

*22nd May* 1922

'I had hoped to see you yesterday. You did not come, which I greatly regret because the wistaria has never been so beautiful and in this heat it cannot last very long. Everything is splendid at the moment and this light is dazzling.'

The bad time has come:

*18th July* 1922

'Despite all my will and my keenness for work I have only had disappointments; nevertheless, I feel that I could have done good work.'

[7] Head of the Beaux-Arts.
[8] In the garden at Giverney.

*9th September* 1922

'Went to Paris yesterday for a consultation. Result: the sight of one eye completely gone, an operation necessary and even inevitable in the not distant future. While waiting, a course of treatment which might make the other eye better and allow me to paint. That done, I wanted to look over the work in the Orangery. Not one workman. Absolute silence. Only a little pile of rubbish at the door.'

*13th September* 1922

'You are decidedly a marvellous man and I grow prouder and prouder of your friendship. I am happy to be able to tell you that the drops which they are putting in my eye have had an extraordinary effect and that I can already see better than I have for a long time.'

Finally the decision was taken. The operation was to be performed.

*18th December* 1922

'I have only one wish: that it should take place as soon as possible, towards the 8th or 10th January, for I can scarcely see any longer.'

The operation is performed. Monet regains his sight. He sees the sky once more, the water, and the clouds — all that enchanted and tortured him. The Orangery is nearing completion — for everything comes to him who waits: an exquisite frame where Monet's genius can be displayed in the kind of peace which befits Eternity.

His work is finished: that is, if work can ever be said to be finished. . .

Then he dies.

# XXXIII

## On a Few Soldiers — Paris or Calais ? — Casablanca

*4th June* 1928

I WAIT a minute in the study. Clemenceau enters carrying a framed engraving by Daumier, *Don Quixote and Sancho.*

CLEMENCEAU: Monsieur Martet, I shall give myself the pleasure of depositing this in your hands so that you can present it as a gift from me to your seventh child.

MYSELF: Thank you. It will remain on deposit a long time.

CLEMENCEAU: Oh, why ?

MYSELF: I cannot do everything: have children and dream.

CLEMENCEAU: What if everybody said that !

MYSELF: It would settle everything.

CLEMENCEAU: That appalling dictum is not altogether devoid of sense. [*Showing me the engraving.*] Do you notice that if the horse takes another step he will have all his four hoofs off the ground ? And yet Don Quixote's air of assurance up there on top of him is magnificent. What a wealth of ideas ! It is even fuller of them than Cervantes. Daumier was a grand fellow. . . Naturally he wasn't appreciated until as late as possible. That's the rule. Well, have you brought me my paper on Foch ?

MYSELF: Yes, here it is.

CLEMENCEAU: I'll look it over.

MYSELF: I want to ask you a question: are you going to give it back to me ?

CLEMENCEAU: Yes, of course. It's yours. I don't want to keep anything.

MYSELF: Good. Because I find that this paper lacks a conclusion. It stops short. It seems to me that there should be something else. . . What ? I don't know.

CLEMENCEAU: It couldn't do anything but stop short. I wrote it one fine day in the Vendée and, getting interested in something else, I put down my pen and didn't take it up again.

MYSELF: I find the tribute which you paid to Foch very touching.

CLEMENCEAU: Because of Doullens I can forgive him everything. There was always Doullens.

MYSELF: You grant some fine qualities to Weygand. . .

CLEMENCEAU: It's because Weygand is somebody. He is ugly, deformed, twisted, and doesn't give a damn for anything. He is a man who must have had a good many kicks on the behind when he was still in limbo. But he is intelligent and he has a sort of indescribable sombre fire. I was annoyed because he came and talked at the Allies' Council of War. I said to Foch, 'You haven't even the right to come here yourself. You are only here to answer when you are called into consultation. At least make him keep quiet.'

Weygand is a man — how shall I say ? — dangerous, able in a moment of crisis to go far, to throw himself into things headlong — and intelligently, a good deal more intelligently than Mangin, who would have plunged in headlong anyway.

Dangerous but valuable. And having one rare quality — the ability to do his work without talking and without having it talked about. He went to Poland. I don't know what he was up to there — but whatever there was to be done he did it. He put everything back in its right place. The question was settled. He came back, didn't swagger, didn't say anything. No one knows what he's doing or where he is. It's rather fine. It isn't that Foch was silly, but his genius was of a good, childish, simple kind. The other had in addition something subtle and deep about him. Up to his neck in priests, of course.

MYSELF: Free-thinking soldiers aren't very amusing.

CLEMENCEAU: No, that's true.

MYSELF: Sarrail. . .

CLEMENCEAU: Oh, don't speak to me about him! And Percin, poor Percin!

MYSELF: He was put up in my district at the last elections. He got one vote.

CLEMENCEAU: It wasn't mine.

MYSELF: Do you remember Breymann?[1]

CLEMENCEAU: Yes, he was quite nice.

MYSELF: He had an exaggerated sense of justice. Injustice made him quite ill.

CLEMENCEAU: They amuse me with their justice. If you're too strong for justice you don't go into the army. [Reflectively.] You don't go anywhere.

MYSELF: You were speaking about Mangin a little while ago. . .

CLEMENCEAU: Yes.

MYSELF: What sort of fellow was Mangin?

CLEMENCEAU: The dogged sort. He did what he had to do in the African campaign and there was nothing more for him to do. He turned up at the front again and reckoned that it was the same sort of thing. And from time to time it was the same thing: a matter of waiting, power, push. . . But at other times it was necessary to look further than

[1] Breymann was a Commandant when Clemenceau came into power. I had him attached to the Military Cabinet. A week later Mordacq had taken a dislike to him.

that. It was I who reinstated him. He had practically every-body against him.

MYSELF: Will you allow me to ask you one question? But I am afraid of bothering you. . .

CLEMENCEAU: Go ahead! The more you ask me the happier I shall be.

MYSELF: Do you remember a quarrel which took place between you and M. Poincaré in March 1918, an exchange of letters or telephone calls — I don't remember exactly — on the question of whether or not Paris should be evacuated before the German advance?

CLEMENCEAU: Yes, I remember very well. I had tried to find men to work on the defences round Paris. I had ransacked the bottom of every drawer — when I found men for the purpose they took them away from me and put them somewhere else. In consequence Paris was an exposed city. So I had decided to leave Paris if the Boches came and to continue the war in the provinces. Poincaré wanted to stay — what would that have led to? To having himself captured. The English had asked me, 'Which do you want to defend, Paris or Calais?' I answered, 'Calais!' For, once at Calais, the Boches would have held the Channel and everything would have been over. Poincaré never understood that.

Moreover, I was never able to come to an understanding with Poincaré. Perhaps three weeks or a month before the Armistice Mangin [2] wrote to me, 'My troops are advancing. We have obtained results. But the men are tired.' Tom, Dick, or Harry would have said — for example Pétain, who paid a bit too much attention to the pros and cons — that it didn't matter. But in Mangin's fist the word 'tired' signified something. I said, 'Stop!' I communicated this to Poincaré, who raised his hands to Heaven exclaiming, 'What? Stop?

[2] Clemenceau was mistaken. It was Gouraud.

CLEMENCEAU AS HE LOOKED ON HIS VISITS TO THE FRONT

But you'll hamstring our soldiers.' Just that! Then I got extremely annoyed.[3]

As for the matter about which you were speaking, the question of whether we should abandon Paris, I don't believe there is a trace of a record left of my discussion with Poincaré. . . [*Reflectively.*] Although . . . he must have written me one or two letters about it. . .[4]

MYSELF: There is also that old story — but I am afraid I shall annoy you by jumping about this way. I was putting my records in order. . .

CLEMENCEAU: Go ahead!

MYSELF: There are some facts which I have been trying to fix and for which. . .

CLEMENCEAU: Go on then. This old story?

MYSELF: It is the Casablanca affair. It has often been said that Prince Radolin, the German Ambassador in Paris, had come and said to you, 'I am compelled to ask for my passports,' and you answered, 'What time does your train go?'[5]

CLEMENCEAU: Yes — it's a little too simple the way you tell it. The truth is that we just missed going to war that time. I hadn't slept for two nights. I no longer remember what we had done — I believe we had been pressing the Germans and that Germany was asking impossible conditions. I didn't feel like granting them. But if in the end it had

---

[3] This annoyance, which was serious, was on October 8, 1918.

[4] M. Poincaré wrote many more than two letters.

[5] 'When the German ambassador threatened to demand his passports, which was equivalent to a rupture, Clemenceau was not frightened. He simply took out his watch and advised his German Excellency to hurry up because "the Paris-Berlin express leaves very shortly." ' — Régis Michaud in his biographical notice of Clemenceau in the *Pages Françaises*.

A more detailed version: 'The German ambassador came to see the President of the Council, "If complete satisfaction is not given to my Government," said he, "I shall be constrained, on the orders of His Majesty the Emperor, to ask for my passports." M. Clemenceau suddenly stood up, took out his watch, looked at it and answered impassively, "Your excellency, the train for Cologne leaves at nine o'clock. It is now seven. If you do not want to miss it you will have to hurry." Never was a man more dumbfounded than the German Ambassador, who went out after stammering a few polite words.'—Abbé Wetterlé.

been necessary. . . I questioned poor Picquart, who was Minister for War: 'Can we risk it ?' A thing which I should certainly not do today, for Picquart was quite the last man to whom one could put such a question. Picquart said, 'Give me two days to answer. At the end of two days he came back and said, 'We can.' So I refused what the Germans were asking. In order not to seem to be doing it in any unfriendly spirit, I on my side proposed a quite reasonable solution, which was to take the question before the Hague Tribunal. And, the Boche having by luck accepted, the question was submitted to the Hague Tribunal, which returned a judgment practically consistent with sound reason. At least I think so — and it no longer mattered in the very least.

MYSELF: But Radolin ?

CLEMENCEAU: Oh yes, Radolin ! I got on very well with Radolin and we used to chat freely. He was a Pole who had married a Frenchwoman, a Talleyrand-Périgord. Why did Berlin send us that fellow ? Probably to put us off the scent. He said to me one day, 'We beat you in 1870 — it wasn't very difficult. We shall probably beat you a second time; perhaps we shall beat you a third time, and then we may find as a result of having beaten you so many times we shall have accumulated an enormous pile of money.' Don't you find that amusing from the lips of the German Ambassador ? Hence it is possible that Radolin came and said to me half-jokingly, 'Oh, come along now; you aren't going to force me to ask for my passports,' to which I may have replied, smiling and bowing, 'Well, if that is your decision I can only regret it and ask you what time your train leaves, so that I can come and see you off at the station. . .' or something like that. It might have taken place that way. But baldly, as you tell it, it's not in my style.

MYSELF: There is also this telegram which you drafted with

your own good pen and which was so abrupt that Pichon,[6] afraid, distracted, would have refused to send it.

CLEMENCEAU: Poor Pichon! It wouldn't have been the first time that events disturbed him a bit. What is true is that I did send an uncoded telegram so that the Boches should know about it. I said: I have come to the end of my concessions.' That's all. What else do you want to know?

MYSELF: Nothing more today.

CLEMENCEAU: I believe that with *Monet* I have enough pleasure and enough work for a little while. I went back to Giverney the other day. I saw that garden again. I remember all that. . .

MYSELF: When did Monet come to live at Giverney?

CLEMENCEAU: It must have been 1883.

MYSELF: Did the highroad and the railway go across his garden then?

CLEMENCEAU: More accurately, his garden went to the highroad and he had not yet acquired the ground where the stream and the little bridge are. He bought it when he wanted to study the water, and when he wanted to paint the *Water-Lilies* he had his big studio built. Before that he had his workroom on the first floor of the summer-house. I remember I was in that workroom one day chatting with him. He showed me some water-lilies, not very interesting and quite sober, but which I found very pretty. I said to him, 'Monet, you ought to hunt out a very rich Jew who would order your water-lilies as a decoration for his dining-room.' I believe that the *Water-Lilies* in the Orangery emanated from that idea. I went to the Orangery the other day and looked at them. . . I must go back there once more. I shall then have absorbed what I require of them. They are truly sublime.

MYSELF: They are the interpenetration of everything.

[6] A member of Clemenceau's first Cabinet.

CLEMENCEAU [*pointing his forefinger at me*]: That's it! It's a lesson about the universe which is worth all the books in the world. Poor Monet! He suffered, you know. . . One must suffer. One must not be satisfied. Renaudel is satisfied. It's very bad. Monet threw himself on his canvases, kicked them to bits savagely. He destroyed two very fine portraits of himself in that way. The portrait which he gave me he brought out to me to my car — I had gone to see him and was leaving. . . 'Take this away — I might destroy it!' With a painter who slashes his canvases, who weeps, who explodes with rage in front of his painting, there is hope.

[*Albert announces Maurice Winter.*]

CLEMENCEAU: Show him in.

[*Enter Maurice Winter. He is gentle and timid.*]

MAURICE WINTER: How do you do, Mr. President? How are you?

CLEMENCEAU: I feel like a toy blacksmith who cannot wield his hammer unless you pull the string. Martet is giving himself the devil of a lot of trouble so that I shall survive beyond my lifetime.

MAURICE WINTER: As a dying man you have just written a book of twelve hundred pages; that's a fairly good proof of vitality.

CLEMENCEAU: What's become of your chief?[7] They say that he would like to return to Indo-China.[9] That's a strange idea. I should like to write a life of Sarraut. What do you think? [*Turning to me.*] There are two things that I have against Plutarch: (1) that he didn't write the life of Aristotle,

---

[7] Son of an excellent man who had been Clemenceau's secretary for many years. Maurice Winter is an Inspector-General at the Ministry of the Interior. Clemenceau had entrusted him with the position of Director of National Safety during his ministry.

[8] M. Sarraut, Minister of the Interior.

[9] M. Sarraut was formerly Governor of Indo-China.

and (2) that he didn't write a life of Phidias. Why didn't he write them, Martet ?

MYSELF: Probably because it was beyond him.

CLEMENCEAU: He owed it to us. Phidias . . . Phidias. . . What an extraordinary thing. There was something which came from God knows where — nothing can explain it, neither the Orient nor Egypt. . . something which realized itself and was ended. That was Beauty's one day. Plutarch owed us the story of it.

It is true, as you slyly hint, that Plutarch wasn't very discerning. All he could do was the lives of soldiers. You can always manage the life of a soldier. Winter, I have fixed up a job for myself.

MAURICE WINTER: Bravo. You won't have taken a very long rest !

CLEMENCEAU: One shouldn't rest too much: that's what you die of. I am writing a book on Monet. It's a rather beautiful thing, the life of a man who only knew joy in suffering. Why does Sarraut want to go back to Indo-China ?

MAURICE WINTER: Doubtless for the pleasure of being a king.

CLEMENCEAU: In the heat they must be having out there ! What a kingship ! I had experience one day of the heat in Ceylon. I was sitting in the shade of a tree, the river in front of me and the other side of it the jungle, a twisted mass of tropical creepers. I knew that if I took three steps away from that shade towards the river I should fall dead. [*To me.*] You will find it hot in Athens.

MAURICE WINTER: You are going to Athens ?

MYSELF: At the very height of August.

CLEMENCEAU: He's crazy. That is the only way you can explain him. You must see Delphi. There is a lady of my acquaintance who came back from Greece — she hadn't even been to Delphi! What a fool! At Delphi, with that land-scape and those mountains — the things that happened there couldn't help happening. Thus it was written. Then Delos! You must see Delos! In Athens I was stopping at an hotel in the Place de la Constitution. During the night I heard under my windows a noise like babbling streams — it was the Greeks walking backwards and forwards talking politics.

## XXXIV

## The Stabilization of the Franc — The First Journey to America — At Maxas

*7th June* 1928

I go into the bedroom. Piétri is talking with Clemenceau about an inscription in *Au Soir de la Pensée* to a Mr. MacPherson. Clemenceau scrawls the inscription.

CLEMENCEAU: Martet, what do you think of the Mestorino affair ?[1]

MYSELF: I think that President Mangin-Bocquet[2] was so unmercifully pushed about by the public which wanted to enter the court. . .

CLEMENCEAU: I saw that and my heart rejoiced at it. For your Mangin-Bocquet did a thing which ought not to be done: he brought his wife along with him. A judge who does that is condemned out of his own mouth.

MYSELF: Moreover they say that Madame Mangin-Bocquet's pearl necklace was stolen and that her son had a thousand francs pinched from his pocket.[3]

CLEMENCEAU: Oh, so the whole family was there, was it ? I was ignorant of that tasty morsel. Well, Martet, for once God acted like a man of spirit. . .

[1] The story of the jeweller who assassinated one of his customers to rob him. The murderer was brought before the Seine Assizes.
[2] President of the Assizes.
[3] This was on June 6th. 'A crying scandal !' said the newspapers.

And those fellows [4] who saw Truphème killed, who saw him lying there on the ground, heard him crying for mercy and said nothing, who didn't even move! Aren't they going to lock them up? What's happening, Martet? What are our people coming to?

MYSELF: The crowd at the Assizes were no less extraordinary. At various times they burst out laughing. Bull-fighting, gladiatorial combats have been suppressed. . .

CLEMENCEAU: But they've left the Assizes. There's not so much blood in evidence. [*Turning to Piétri.*] Well, are they stabilizing or are they not stabilizing?

PIÉTRI: I believe that they are going to stabilize.

CLEMENCEAU: That seems to me completely insane. But since it's so, since the franc is at four sous and since absolutely nothing has been done to keep it from falling to four sous, well, they ought to keep quiet about it! Why the devil do they feel the need of crying, 'Do you realize, we are going bankrupt for the other four-fifths!'?

PIÉTRI: It seems that the Bank of France can no longer stand the racket.

CLEMENCEAU: Perhaps it wasn't necessary to let it go as far as that! I repeat: what did they do for the franc? Nothing. M. Poincaré balances his budget—and afterwards? What is the budget anyway? Nothing. The State's budget is not France's budget. It's necessary to balance the budget first, cost what it may, but after that it's necessary to do everything that has not been done, everything that hasn't even been attempted. But those fellows don't care about anything but sparring for time! And how did they balance the budget? By crushing us with taxes on the one hand—I don't know if you suspect it but, the more taxes there are, the more the country is impoverished—and secondly by bringing about in-

4 Mestorino's employees.

flation. M. Herriot was responsible for inflation and loud cries went up — but I don't believe that M. Poincaré abstained altogether from the practice !

PIÉTRI: Yes. But M. Herriot didn't have the authority for it.

CLEMENCEAU: That's the only difference ! M. Poincaré had a nice little law passed. What was done to restore equilibrium and stability in this maze and chaos ? In selling, buying, production, export, import ? How does it happen that livestock is diminishing and that the price of chops goes up every day ? I urge you to believe that if I'd been head of the Government things wouldn't have dragged out like that ! I would have chucked a certain number of individuals into prison — not the little fellows, not the beggars, but the big ones, those important gentlemen who live in pompous houses. I'd have restored order. Last year it was recognized that there was a surplus in the Exchequer of I don't know how many millions — a hundred or two hundred. What did they do with those millions to lower the cost of living ? They tossed them to the bureaucrats ! Thereby they increased the buying power of thousands and thousands of people. They thereby encouraged the merchants to abuse this increase of buying power. They thereby raised the cost of living. It is clear that the whole thing is idiotic.

PIÉTRI: Recently, in a restaurant opposite the Renault [5] factory, where the workmen have their mid-day meal, chops were priced at two francs. One fine day the proprietor put them up to 2.25 without notice. The workmen complained. The proprietor said, 'You've just had your wages raised !' 'No, we haven't,' answered the workmen. 'It's not till next week that the rise takes effect.' 'Oh, I see,' said the proprietor. 'I beg your pardon !' This time he only charged them two

[5] The motor car manufacturer.

francs for the chops, but the following week calmly put them up to 2.25. And the extraordinary thing about it is that this time the workmen didn't say a word but paid their 2.25.

CLEMENCEAU: The French people are getting it in the neck. And those economies ? What economies have they effected ? They should be able to swallow any measure. They wiped out the sub-prefects, that's all ! But, mark you, they wiped out their work but not their pay. The office was eliminated but not the office-holder. So when you say to me, 'There is nothing else to be done but stabilize,' I answer you, 'Of course. When you are chucked in the water with your hands tied behind your back and a fifty-pound weight tied to your feet, you can't do anything else but go to the bottom !'

MYSELF: How's your book on Monet ?

CLEMENCEAU: Well, the *Water-Lilies* make me unhappy.

MYSELF: Oh, so it's your turn. They made Monet unhappy enough.

CLEMENCEAU: I went to the Orangery yesterday. There wasn't a soul there. During the day forty-six men and women came, of whom forty-four were lovers looking for a solitary spot. You see how the crowd rushes to admire him. Well, looking at the *Water-Lilies* I realized that everything I had said should be torn up. I take it all back.

MYSELF: The other day I went to the Pavillon de Marsan to see the exhibition of ancient American art.

CLEMENCEAU: Oh, the pre-Columbians, all those things. . .

MYSELF: For five francs I was allowed to contemplate several dozen old pots and stones on which they tried to cut things.

CLEMENCEAU: Quite ! There is no ancient American art ! Now they are throwing themselves upon a mass of absurd objects, and beautiful women are swooning in front of a kind of peep-show manufactured by negroes. . . [*Taking a magazine from his table.*] Here, look at that. Our ancestors of five thousand years ago. . . [*He shows me the magazine. There is an illustrated article on some ruins discovered in the Indies. Fragments of sculpture: a man's head, a lion's head.*] Personally I prefer Praxiteles. . .

MYSELF: Speaking of ruins, have you seen the tombs which they have discovered near the site of Ur ?

CLEMENCEAU: No, but I must tell you that I have no confidence in Ur.

MYSELF: In those tombs they found, round the dead king, his wives, his soldiers, his coachmen, his horse . . . all butchered.

CLEMENCEAU: That's very nice. It's from those people that we're descended. Doesn't it annoy you to be a man ?

MYSELF: What would you like to be ? A praying mantis ? She eats her lover. That's no better.

CLEMENCEAU: But I believe that man is the only animal who kills·without reason or for reasons which are more or less metaphysical. He's a kind of buffoon ! When you leave this world you ought to breathe a sigh.

MYSELF: That's called yielding up the spirit.

CLEMENCEAU: There is a very pretty allegorical picture to be drawn from that: 'Lord, here is my spirit. It embarrasses me and in the long run it even disgusts me a little.' There is neither sense nor cleanliness except in complete extinction.

MYSELF: Do you know that I have decided to go and celebrate the Capture of the Bastille with you in the Vendée. . .

CLEMENCEAU: Good idea ! We'll light the lanterns.

MYSELF: There is one thing that puzzles me: I should like to know whether, if the Bastille were to be retaken, you would have it back. . .

[*No answer.*]

CLEMENCEAU: I'll show you my flowers, Martet. I have some flowers which grow in the sand and obtain their nourishment from Heaven knows where. It's a mystery. We'll look at the ocean and exchange, as one might say, philosophical thoughts.

MYSELF: You won't have Mandel?

CLEMENCEAU: Are you afraid of Mandel?

MYSELF: I am a little afraid of eloquence. . .

CLEMENCEAU: Mandel comes without being invited. In return for which I forget to keep him for lunch. But don't speak badly of that prodigy. Mandel has no ideas but he would uphold them to the death.

MYSELF: I have a question to put to you, sir. I shan't pretend to you — I am trying to put myself in order and it isn't easy.

CLEMENCEAU: You are like Pelloquet, then?

MYSELF: Pelloquet?

CLEMENCEAU: Don't you know Pelloquet? Pelloquet was a kind of art critic. One day he was going to lecture and so stammered out some vague remarks on art, painting, and so forth. Suddenly he gathered up his notes, put them under his arm and left the platform, saying, 'I beg your pardon but there is no more order in my ideas than in my notes!' He charged five francs for the lecture. It's the same Pelloquet who was once beaten in a duel — do you know why? Because of the bouquet in Manet's *Olympia*. He declared that what caused the beauty and greatness of the picture wasn't the woman but the flowers. Gallant Pelloquet! There he was, wounded in the palm of his left hand — they said to him, 'But, my poor friend, you've caught your opponent's sword with your hand!' He answered, 'No, but I had that hand behind my back like this. I was merely trying to steal away unnoticed. . .' What was your question?

MYSELF: I should like to know why you went to America in 1865?

CLEMENCEAU: Oh, that's a large question. Because I had just qualified as a doctor. I felt that democracy was going to come into its own here. I said to my father, 'I should like to go and see how it works over there.' He said, 'Go ahead.' I went, I saw. . .

MYSELF: And ?

CLEMENCEAU: And nothing. Democracy is democracy. It isn't a devasting success. But in the first place it's the inevitable result of human experience. In the second place, democracy, aristocracy, plutocracy . . . what are all those 'ocracies worth ? There is only one good 'ocracy and that is theocracy. Provided there is a God.

MYSELF: You were speaking to me one day about the relations between the whites and the blacks in the United States.

CLEMENCEAU: Dickens described his trip over there in a book. He reproduced the advertisements to be found in the American newspapers: 'Lost, a negro recognizable by a missing eye and a broken jaw. Please return him to. . .' And another one: 'Lost, a negress answering to the name of Eliza and recognizable by the fact that her ears have been cut off.' That was the state of slavery in the United States[6] seventy years ago.

MYSELF: Nevertheless, Dickens had a great success in America with his lectures.

CLEMENCEAU: He didn't speak to them about that. I was present at his lectures. He confined himself to reading passages from his books: the death of Dora and the house of little David with its crows' nests . . . do you remember ? And the Micawbers. . . What a man that Dickens was !

MYSELF: And when did you come back from America ? In '69, I think ?

CLEMENCEAU: In '69.

MYSELF: What did you do ?

[6] 'Think of the abominations of Christian slavery in the United States. . .' — Preface to the *Mélée Sociale*. 'Read in the American newspapers before 1860 the descriptive notices of fugitive slaves. There are only marks of branding irons, shattered jaws, eyes gouged out, limbs mutilated or cut off. Is this the work of Christian and civilized white men ?' — Quotation from the *Mélée Sociale*.

CLEMENCEAU: I returned to my father's house and there I did what he did himself. I practised medicine and rode horseback over the countryside.[7]

MYSELF: And then you came to Paris?

CLEMENCEAU: The war broke out so I came to Paris. Since I didn't know where to find lodgings I stopped with one of my friends, Lafont, who lived in Montmartre. The 4th September came. There wasn't anyone in Montmartre capable of taking an interest in things. . . The Government appointed me mayor. Some time afterwards there were the elections. Two or three friends and I drew up a poster. The people announced that it was in conformity with their tastes. They elected us. That was the beginning of my troubles.[8]

PIÉTRI: Hadn't you been in prison before your departure for America?

CLEMENCEAU: Yes, in '61 or '62.

MYSELF: What had you done?

[7] I had the good fortune to find the book in which this young doctor of under thirty kept a record of his consultations.

It is a book of 142 pages bound in green. On the cover Clemenceau had stuck a little pen and ink drawing showing two skeletons holding a kind of shield. One of the skeletons holds a candlestick with a candle, and the other is armed with a scythe.

The patients' names are entered alphabetically. For instance:

| Baumard | Nov. 20 1869 | 2 | visits | | 2.50 |
|---|---|---|---|---|---|
| | | 1 | " | | 3.00 |
| Barbot (La rochette) | " " " | 1 | " | at 5 francs | 33.00 |
| | | 1 | " | at 0 | |
| Marie Biré | " " " | 6 | " | at 4 francs | 24.00 |
| Bonnet (Libaud) | Nov. 21 1869 | 1 | " | | 2.50 |
| " " | Nov. 22 1869 | 1 | consultation and | | |
| | | | operation | | 5.00 |

etc.

A consultation and operation for five francs: charges were very reasonable.

Sometimes Clemenceau indicates the complaint. 'Prunet: umbilical hernia. . .' And there is this account: a patient owes him 275 francs for a long course of visits. We read: 'Bill totalled up to 275 francs, 50 of which were paid in August 1870. Balance due: 225 francs. On October 16th, 225 francs paid, less one franc I lose for leaving it out, and half a franc which she asked me to knock off. Credit: 223.50.'

From 1869 to October 1871 Clemenceau earned 1900.50 francs.

[8] Clemenceau was appointed mayor of the XVIIIth Arrondissement of Paris on September 5, 1870: he was elected on November 9th. On February 12, 1871, he was elected Deputy for the Seine in the National Assembly. On March 26th he resigned.

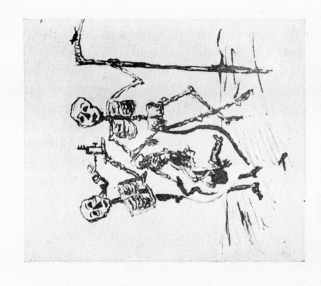

FANTASTIC SKETCH BY CLEMENCEAU
MADE WHILE HE WAS PRACTISING
MEDICINE AND DISCOVERED IN HIS
APPOINTMENT BOOK

TITLE-PAGE OF CLEMENCEAU'S
MEDICAL THESIS PUBLISHED IN 1865

CLEMENCEAU: *Opposed the policy of the Empire.*[9] I stayed
at Mazas two months. That reminds me of an incident in a
comedy by somebody or other. There was a son-in-law who
thus reproaches his father-in-law: 'You were six months in
prison at Mazas !' The other answered, 'Oh, that prison's
been pulled down !'

MYSELF: Now I want to bring you back to the war. . .

CLEMENCEAU: Which war ?

MYSELF: The war of 1914.

CLEMENCEAU: Oh, I've had so much of it.

MYSELF: You are accused of not having tried to isolate
Germany. . .

CLEMENCEAU: How useful that is ! In what way would
you want me to isolate Germany ? Don't you see what's happening today ? I must repeat to you that I alone was representing Continental interests: against me were England and
America.

MYSELF: It is quite certain that with all those dynasties
expelled from their thrones Germany is more united than
ever. . .

CLEMENCEAU: And afterwards ? I know only too well !
How could it have been otherwise ? The Dorten affair indi-
cates so well what could have been hoped for in that direction.
In a city occupied by a French garrison, under the very eyes

[9] Clemenceau had organized a demonstration which was to take place in the
Place de la Bastille on the 24th February 1862. It was to celebrate the inaugu-
ration of the Republican Era.

On the 11th April, records M. Camille Ducray, Clemenceau was seated in the
dock of the Sixth Correctional Chamber, with Me. Hubard as his defender, and
the court was about to pronounce its judgment:

'It is established by the charge and the arguments that on the 23rd February
Clemenceau committed the offence of direct provocation to an armed gathering,
with no harmful effects;

'That he did in fact write and distribute, affix and cause to be affixed, a certain
number of posters in which he summoned various persons to an assembly in a
place previously determined, with the intention of convoking a mob capable of
disturbing the public peace;

'Therefore Clemenceau is sentenced to prison for one month and to pay half
the costs.'

At that time preventive detention was not confused with punishment.

of our soldiers and their officers, the Germans seized the Rhine-landers who wanted to secede, to inaugurate and maintain friendly diplomatic relations with France — in fine, the great idea of Mangin and Poincaré — and cut their throats. A frightful business! Isolate Germany! Like those people who wanted to make a crime out of my being satisfied with the frontiers of 1870. They would have liked those of Charlemagne. . . I tried to get Landau. One day I said to Balfour, 'Before Waterloo we had Landau: it's a bit of French soil. I don't ask it of you but if you would offer it I should be pleased.' Balfour put his hand on my shoulder and said, 'My poor friend.' Mind you, two days before the ratification of the Treaty, they nearly upset everything. It was then that Wilson said to me, 'You are not going to send me back to face my own country without something having been done!' I answered, 'I should be heartbroken, but I can't do anything more than escort you to your boat.' That's how I got the Sarre. . . And what has been done with the Sarre? Ask Poincaré and Briand what they have done with the Sarre! Ask them what they are busy doing with Alsace! [*I get up.*] Do you know what happened to Piétri one day in Java? He said, 'Listen! I think that I have hit the wife of the Prefect of Police in the eye!' I sought further information. . . What did I discover? It was only the wife of the Sub-Prefect of Police.

PiÉTRI: Since Martet is engaged in taking notes for History. . .

CLEMENCEAU: Yes, so he is. Martet is here, he is listening. . .

PiÉTRI: Tell him in detail what happened at Bandong.

CLEMENCEAU: And when Piétri left, the unfortunate woman was heard singing on the river bank:

*Nicolas! Nicolas!*
*Don't desert me!*

There are dramas in Piétri's life. Au 'voir ! Come again. Come often. Put your questions. Push me into a corner. I'll answer. [*While showing us out.*] There have also been people who have accused me — I have been accused of everything — of saying to Czarnin, 'You're a liar !' Briand referred to this in his characteristic voice, 'You shouldn't have done that. I don't speak that way.' That blessed Briand ! Admit all the same that this planet is an extraordinarily queer object.

## XXXV

### There Are Some Bad Consciences About !

It was on the 28th March 1918 that the German offensive against the Anglo-French front was shattered.

The first French communiqué announced the loss of Mont-didier, the second (issued at 11:00 P.M.) said:

'The enemy, continuing his thrust in the Montdidier region with powerful forces, has attempted during the day to enlarge his gains to the west and the south of this town.

'But with magnificent dash our troops counter-attacked and at the point of the bayonet drove the enemy out of the villages of Courtemanche, Mesnil, Saint-Georges and Assainvilliers, which we have regained and are holding firmly.

'The gain thus achieved along a front of ten kilometres exceeds two kilometres in depth.'

It was the first serious counter-attack by our troops. The reserves had arrived.

On the 29th 'our forces, continuing their success, seized Monchel after a violent struggle.' The communiqué stresses 'the indomitable resistance of our troops.' We are 'victoriously' keeping the enemy in check. On that day Pershing came to see Foch, 'All that we have is yours. Use it as you like.' One felt the formidable weight of this new sword falling into the balance.

And then, on the 30th, the battle was resumed 'on a front of forty kilometres from Moreuil to Lassigny ——' (The two o'clock communiqué.) The front is extending. 'The struggle is raging along a front of sixty kilometres ——' (The eleven o'clock communiqué.) The German onslaught is checked everywhere. A tremendous Boche effort. A tremendous and heavy repulse.

On the 31st there was confirmation of the repulse. 'Moreuil, taken by the enemy, regained, lost again, has been retaken at the point of the bayonet by Franco-British troops mingling in the same ranks.' On the 1st April the battle was continued; all the enemy's assaults were repulsed. Clemenceau left Paris in the morning, accompanied by M. René Renoult. He returned on the 2nd: the danger was over. M. René Renoult declared that he was 'highly enthusiastic.'

It was over — for the moment. . .

THEN, steel having failed, other tactics were employed. The Czernin affair.

On the 2nd April Count Czernin, 'Minister of the Royal and Imperial Court and of Foreign Affairs of Austria-Hungary,' received a delegation from the municipality of Vienna. Naturally he made a speech and said, 'M. Clemenceau made inquiries, a little time before the beginning of the offensive on the western front, as to whether I was ready to enter into negotiations and on what terms.'

On the 3rd April the speech was reported in Paris. Clemenceau had left for the front that morning. They telephoned to him. The Government statement appeared on the 4th in the newspapers, 'On reading the despatch . . . M. Clemenceau simply made this comment, "Count Czernin lied." '

On the 6th the newspapers published a fresh statement, 'M. Clemenceau on coming into office had found conversations going on in Switzerland, on the initiative of Austria, between

Count Revertera, a personal friend of the Emperor, and Commandant Armand, of the Second Division of the General Staff, appointed for this purpose by the then Minister for War. He did not think that these conversations should be broken off. But he gave this instruction, "Listen and say nothing." '

It was now up to the Hapsburgs to speak. The newspapers published a long statement from the Austrian Government on the 9th. 'The conversations took place on the 22nd and 23rd August 1917. They were resumed in January 1918 at the behest of M. Clemenceau. . .'

Clemenceau answered, 'A diluted lie still remains a lie.'

On the 12th the French newspapers published a letter from the Emperor of Austria to Prince Sixte de Bourbon, his brother-in-law, which had been presented to the President of the Republic on the 31st March 1917. It read: 'I beg of you to convey secretly and in confidence to M. Poincaré that I shall use all the means in my power to satisfy the just claims of the French with regard to Alsace-Lorraine. . . We must work to prepare the ground of understanding for a basis on which official *pourparlers* may be entered into.'

In the newspapers of the 14th the Austrian Government declared, 'The letter is a forgery,' which drew from Clemenceau the celebrated reply, 'There are some bad consciences about.' 'The original document was transmitted in the presence of M. Jules Cambon, General Secretary to the Ministry for Foreign Affairs, delegated for the purpose by the Minister, to the President of the Republic, who with the authority of the Prince conveyed a copy of it to the President of the Council.'

Clemenceau's reply went even further than these 'bad consciences.' We read, 'Finding no way to save his face, the Emperor Charles stammers like a man who has been caught out. . .'

Before this new style: 'Count Czernin lied . . . there are bad consciences about . . . stammers like a man who has been caught out'; before these publications of ultra-confidential documents and this kind of raking fire which traversed Europe from right to left—bang ! bang !—there was a great tumult in the camp of traditional diplomacy. I remember M. Jules Cambron. . . . This very courteous and correct man was completely aghast. He raised his hands to Heaven. He looked at me for four or five seconds and I thought that he was going to open his heart to me. . . He contented himself with tapping me softly on the shoulder, shaking his head and going out. . . He expected even worse things. They had never before experienced these roarings of the tiger—what was going to happen ?

This:

The Emperor Charles telegraphed to William II on the 16th April: 'I have no intention of continuing the discussion with France any longer. . .' On the same 16th April the newspapers announced, 'It is learnt from Vienna that the Minister of the Royal and Imperial Court and for Foreign Affairs, Count Czernin, has offered his resignation to the Emperor who has accepted it.'

It was the last ministry which Clemenceau was to bowl over. Something had given way on the other side.

And on the 17th, at dawn, in the ditches of Vincennes, a man was shot: Bolo.

There was no connexion of course between Bolo and the conversations in Switzerland. But there was, willy-nilly, in that roll of musketry a kind of savage full stop to those troubled days when the word *peace* had been circulated.

# XXXVI

## TRAVELS

*12th June* 1928

CLEMENCEAU: I've been dreaming about Psichari. . .[1] What's become of him?

MYSELF: Isn't he dead?

CLEMENCEAU: I don't know . . . people come, they go. . . There's a man who adored me. He must have come to a bad end.[2]

---

[1] The author.

[2] During the war Psichari had sworn an overflowing and flaming passion for Clemenceau. He spent his time composing sonnets to his glory and sending me these sonnets at the rate of five or six a week:

25th December 1919

> Here it is piping hot,
> But I must bind you to silence.
> Not a word,
> The second is in the press, the most beautiful of all.
> Yours,
>
> JEAN PSICHARI

Then follows a sonnet entitled *Silence* which begins with these words:

> Yes, you have borne the brunt; not to speak, but
> To act!

The next day:

26th December 1919

> Dear Sir,
> Here it is, the loveliest sonnet.
> Well, no, it seems to me less successful than the others.
> Yours,
>
> JEAN PSICHARI.

Followed by:

> O Georges, who amongst us understands your sombre spirit?

concluding with these lines:

> You know how to hide, under a virile lightness,
> Under an iron glove the velvet hand!

MYSELF: Are you working?

CLEMENCEAU: Yes. I am not satisfied. I am doing a job which isn't coming out; to crown my good luck I fell the other day in the garden. . .

MYSELF: Really!

CLEMENCEAU: I had great trouble in getting up again. I was covered with mud; for two days I suffered from a kind of shivering. Where are the days when I vaulted the streams of the Marais [3] with a pole? I tried to make Geffroy [4] do it. . . He couldn't find anything better to do than break his arm.

MYSELF: Didn't you hurt yourself when you fell?

CLEMENCEAU: No, I don't think so. Then I wondered if I didn't have too much sugar in my blood. I had an analysis made — I haven't. But it is quite certain that I eat things which don't do me any good.

MYSELF: Why?

CLEMENCEAU: Why? Because one gets tired of everything, even of taking care of oneself. And you? What's become of you?

MYSELF: Great news! I've decided not to go to the Orient.

CLEMENCEAU: Really! Why?

MYSELF: In order to work.

CLEMENCEAU: At what?

MYSELF: Something I am doing at the moment.

CLEMENCEAU: Something serious?

MYSELF: Yes.

CLEMENCEAU: Good. Moreover you know that the best journeys are those which you never make. The best thing about a journey is the railway timetable.

MYSELF: I announced the fact to my wife. . .

CLEMENCEAU: And she clawed your eyes out?

MYSELF: No. She said, 'All right, let's stay.'

[3] In the Vendée.
[4] Gustave Geffroy, the author, who was an old friend of Clemenceau's.

CLEMENCEAU: Well, you can boast that you have a wife of a kind they don't make nowadays. Where'll you go then?

MYSELF: To a place called Theron, near Pornic.[5] The country is terrible, so much so that I shan't be tempted to stroll about.

CLEMENCEAU: I think you're right. We shall be neighbours. You will be able to come and see me. How far is it from me?

MYSELF: Less than a hundred kilometres, and if the roads are good I should do it in two hours.

CLEMENCEAU: If I can't put you up at my house I have another next door, where you will be better off in any case than on a bench. Will you bring your wife?

MYSELF: If you will allow me to.

CLEMENCEAU: I felt that the tour of the Mediterranean which you were contemplating was not the thing for you. You know: Syria, Palestine, Jerusalem, they're all a kind of lice heap. When I was at Alexandria I wondered if I ought to go there. I had read things about them that deprived me of any desire to go nearer. Where else were you going?

MYSELF: We were going to make a little tour in Egypt. We were planning to go as far as Constantinople, coming back by way of Athens.

CLEMENCEAU: Well, you will do that later: you will do it as it ought to be done. Egypt should have a whole journey to herself. Or else it's a farce. You must see Khartoum. Once when I was at Khartoum someone said to me, pointing out a woman who was passing, carrying something or other on her back, 'That's a slave.'

'Oh, how can you tell?'

'By a mark which she has. . .'

You should see the White Nile and the Blue Nile join without mingling . . . two streams which flow on side by side.

[5] On the Atlantic.

It's at Khartoum that the English under Kitchener gave that drubbing to the Mahdists. At Wadi-Halfa I saw the Mahdi's second in command in prison . . . what was he called ? . . . Osman Digma . . .[6] a fine fellow with eyes like coals and a great beard. His prison was the kind of place which you can leave just as you like if you have the slightest desire to. Osman Digma didn't dream of going away. Which is obvious proof that it is only in prisons that you can have quiet. . .

MYSELF: And freedom.

CLEMENCEAU: Not a doubt of it ! And freedom, if you take 'freedom' in its noblest sense. He stopped there, seated on a bit of straw, leaning against the wall, and spent his days repeating his prayers. I don't know what he ate — bits of wood. But he was very happy. When I came in he got up — I tell the story in *Au Soir de la Pensée*. He said to me: 'Oh, M. Clemenceau !'

They asked him: 'But do you know M. Clemenceau ?'

'Certainly, and I was expecting him. . .'

They tell a good story about Osman Digma. Kitchener went to see him one day. He came in and said, 'Don't you recognize me ?'

'No.'

'I'm Kitchener.'

'Kitchener ?'

He had never heard Kitchener's name. And Kitchener, who had come there to astound him, to crush him under the weight of his laurels . . . came out heartbroken. It eluded his soldier's brain.

Well, one day when the Governor was hunting over that way, his bearer said to him, 'I beg your pardon, Mr. Governor, but do you intend to release Osman Digma ?'

'Well,' said the other, 'we are keeping him a bit unjustly,

but he doesn't make a row; he never makes any complaint. I think that we shall keep him like that till the end.'

The man answered, 'You do well to, because I warn you — he tore my father's eyes out and my mother's, violated my sister. . . He wouldn't be out of prison an hour before I should have cut his throat. And I'm not the only one to entertain those sentiments towards him.'

Osman Digma, outside these little whims, was a very nice fellow.

And Egypt is a lovely country.

At Khartoum the Governor lives in a building whose windows were completely without glass. This turned out to be rather embarrassing. One day when we were eating there, some birds who had built their nests behind a picture came out in the middle of the meal and cleared all the food off the tables.

Do you like trees?

MYSELF: I find them a very pleasant addition to the landscape. . .

CLEMENCEAU: Well, in Egypt there are trees — yes, I suppose you might call them trees — palms, which look like plumage, and baobabs, which are like thick towers, and enormous, with branches high up where a kind of nut grows. They are very ugly. The peasants hollow out the trunks and fill them with cement. That makes a cistern where the rainwater lies stagnant. They drink this water: it's filthy.

One day we were at the foot of one of these trees and tried to knock down some nuts; there was nothing we could use, neither stones nor sticks. We threw camel droppings. We looked a bit silly, I fancy. An old woman came along, old, ugly, and said to us: 'You know, in my time, I was very attractive and pretty — I was the Mahdi's slave!' Just as she might have said, 'I was the queen of the world.' And she added, 'When men took their pleasure with me, well, you can believe me, they didn't regret it !' As if she might have said, 'I took all the prizes in my class !'

Travel, Martet. You'll see how strange the world is. One day I was hunting something or other — the marabout or the tufted crane . . . the marabout is a sympathetic animal. I could quite willingly join up with a marabout. You might with accuracy call him a peasant who loses himself in his work. I was there with my gun, looking at the animal — I didn't even think of firing — when suddenly they all flew away and I saw a man with gold spectacles appear. I said to him, 'What are you doing here ?'

He answered, 'I am a Dutch missionary.'

'Oh, and are you succeeding in your efforts ?'

He answered, 'They are a little obstinate.'

I asked him, 'Are you sure that they don't say the same about you ?'

MYSELF: As if Egypt hadn't already enough gods. . .

CLEMENCEAU: One day we were following the course of the Nile. There was a man who wore two pairs of braces to support one-third of a trouser, and who stopped me and asked me who I was. I said to him, 'And you ?'

'I am the American bishop of this station.'

Then I told him who I was. He took me home with him. He lived in a house built of a kind of metallic canvas as protection against the mosquitos, with a disagreeable kind of wife, who in herself must have been worse than several million mosquitos and three or four swarms of locusts. He must have married her as the consequence of a deadly sin, to mortify himself.

I wanted to know how the natives went about making a fire with two sticks. The bishop's wife wouldn't allow it. 'Not here ! Do it outside !'

I said, 'No madam, it must be done here.'

'You will burn my carpet.'

'We will extinguish it for you. Go ahead, light it !

As you see, an impossible woman. Then I saw how they made a fire. A man took a stick of hard wood, and one of soft; in the stick of soft wood he made a hole with the point of his knife; he sharpened the stick of hard wood, twisted it round with his hand . . . there was some smoke . . . he breathed on it and that caused a flame.

MYSELF: But don't they also make a fire by rubbing two flints against each other ?

CLEMENCEAU: No; one thing that you don't know — your ignorance is incredible. . . What did they teach you at school ?

MYSELF: At the 'Varsity there was a man who examined me on comets. I hadn't any trouble in telling him what their tails were made of.

CLEMENCEAU: It's appalling ! So you simply don't understand anything about anything ?

MYSELF: Not very much. . . But is there anything very much that one can understand ?

CLEMENCEAU: You can put questions to yourself. Then put this one about flint. Two flints knocked against each other don't give out sparks.

MYSELF: Oh, why not ?

CLEMENCEAU: Because you must have iron.

MYSELF: Why ?

CLEMENCEAU: Because that's the way it happens to be. When I was young, at a place called Mouilleron-en-Parads,[7] I rubbed two stones together like that; they gave out a phosphorescent gleam which had a rather queer odour. I tried to find out where this odour came from. . .

MYSELF: What did Science have to say about it ?

CLEMENCEAU: She didn't know anything about it. In all these proceedings there wasn't the least suggestion of a flame.

[7] The village in the Vendée where Clemenceau was born.

Because what makes the flame is the particles of iron which separate and ignite on contact with the air.

My bishop and six women servants who spent all their time with jugs on their heads going to get water from the Nile, to fill a kind of cistern. He seemed to find everything quite satisfactory. It must have reminded him of the Samaritan. He had taylorized the Samaritan. He took me to his church, a kind of hut with two or three benches, one of which had three legs, and a pulpit which was made of an old broken soap box — and that was the lot. I asked him, 'Have you many of the faithful ?'

'Well,' he answered, 'I have six, my six servants, but when I fire them they go back to their own religion. Otherwise it might breed bad feeling and no one would speak to them any longer.'

MYSELF: It sounds successful.

CLEMENCEAU: It isn't bad. He gets five thousand dollars for it. I think it's five thousand or six or something like that. Add the heat, the terrible noise of the sun making everything dry up, boil, crackle; add the Nile — then you have Egypt. . . And you see people living on the banks of the Nile making a species of boat out of a wood, as hard as stone, from which they have removed the pith. They hunt the hippopotamus in them.

MYSELF: Are there hippopotamuses ?

CLEMENCEAU: There are. The hunters have a bow and arrow and a rope. They fire at the beast; when the hippopotamus has had enough, they pull the rope; you see an enormous, slightly comic mass appear which they eat.

MYSELF: And the desert ?

CLEMENCEAU: It's strange. I've crossed it. Carcasses of camels, varieties of white partridges. . . There are plenty of things to die of. Once I was sleeping in a train; it was like sleeping in an oven. There was one of us who had an ingenious idea. In order to get to sleep he lay down outside on the ground. Then some people came along. He received a heavy shower of blows with cudgels. . . He didn't do it again.

I went to Berber. It's there they take the india-rubber from Port Sudan on the backs of camels. It's a very impressive business. Under a tent you have women who roll the balls of gum between their fingers and throw them in the air to rid them of dust. As the tent is traversed by the rays of the sun, the result is millions of stars dancing silently. Go and see it.

MYSELF: But you've been everywhere. . .

CLEMENCEAU: I have been to all the places where they said it would perhaps be better not to go. They are very nice, very kind people, but you feel that for a yes or no they might cut your throat; they don't attach the least importance to this gesture.

MYSELF: What is the most beautiful thing you saw ?

CLEMENCEAU: Oh, the second cataract. A volcano of black stones. Did I ever tell you this ? Our boat, a little steamer, got out of order, nearly foundered. An Arab came to tell us that it was going down. It was certainly the last place for a shipwreck. For there wasn't anything there. . . I heard them tapping on iron. They patched it up again as best they could, thanks to which the boat was able to wait till it reached port before going to the bottom.

MYSELF: And Karnak ?

CLEMENCEAU: Well, at Karnak you see columns formed of clustered papyri from which emerges a tuft of foliage which is the capital. There are columns which are veritable monuments. When you compare them with the little Greek columns of the Parthenon or of the Asclepieion, there is something ridiculous about it. You shouldn't limit yourself to Egypt, Martet. You ought to see India.

MYSELF: I know. One should see everything.

CLEMENCEAU: India is something quite insane. You know that it's not very long since the English forbade the funeral pyres on which they used to burn widows. But there still remains the marriage of ten-year-old children with men of sixty. On the following day they are in such a condition that they go into hospital. There is an American woman who saw that and who exposes its horrors.

MYSELF: What do you think of the Indian dancing girls?

CLEMENCEAU: Well, once I came to the outskirts of a town (I don't know what its name was) on the banks of some sacred stream or other, and half a dozen very beautiful women came up and surrounded me. I made signs to them. I thought that they were like all other women. The Englishman who was there with me said:

'In Heaven's name, I beg of you not to speak to them.'

'Oh? Why not?'

'If you speak to them it will cause a terrible scandal. When you address those women you are disgraced. It would be in all of the papers the next day.'

Brr! I'm terribly afraid of the *Little Benaresian* and of the *Haidarabad Beacon!* So I had them dance. They executed a few indifferent steps which reminded me, in a less exotic way, of the Universal Exhibition of 1878 and I continued on my way.

MYSELF: You must have met some missionaries out there also.

CLEMENCEAU: Yes indeed. At — oh somewhere — in the jungle were two missionaries who had seen me at the front. They wanted to meet me again. I asked them:

'Well, what are you doing here?'

They said:

'The natives are bored, so we tell them stories and play with their children.'

'Do you also talk to them about religion?'

'Oh, yes, at the right time.'

There's another most ludicrous thing, the caste system. There was a Rajah who wouldn't dine with me because it would have contaminated him. Since I didn't specially want to dine with him, I was quite satisfied just to sit at his table. I presided at the dinner and after the food he came over. We sat down together on a divan and began to tell each other stories. There is your caste system.

MYSELF: And the women ?

CLEMENCEAU: They're not up to much. They only know how to laugh and produce children. They spend their lives being pregnant. When you say to them, 'Still another ?' they laugh. It's appalling.

MYSELF: Are they happy, those people ?

CLEMENCEAU: When they're made to work, no. You force civilization on them, make roads, and bridges for them: they don't understand and they die. But I remember one day we were travelling along a road by car. There were crocodiles crossing the road in order to get from one pool to another. . . I noticed roads which broke off completely and became buried in the jungle. They reminded me strikingly of the little sunken roads of the Vendée. I said to the man who was guiding me: 'Let's go that way for a little while.' We plunged in. But we weren't able to go very far. At the end of twenty minutes I had to stop — the road had become a kind of chaos of stones and trees. Then the folk who live in the jungle came up to us and began to talk to us about all sorts of things. They appeared to be delighted with life.

MYSELF: But the famines.

CLEMENCEAU: There are famines. . . Then they die off like flies. It's one of their established routines. . . There are some countries where you die of arterio-sclerosis or alcoholism. Out there you die of hunger. During my entire journey I saw

only one old man. You ought to see what they eat — a kind
of black preserve which tastes like rotten fish. And the dogs !
Species of skeletons running about — not one ounce of flesh
on them, and eyes distracted with hunger. There isn't anything, not even refuse. They eat whatever they find, even
stones.

Because of the widows reduced to a state of slavery, and
the little girls violated under pretext of marriage, India sends
a kind of shiver over you. The English point at all that and
say, 'You see. It's been a good job, nevertheless, bringing civilization to those people.' But all they would have to do would
be to forbid those horrors and they would disappear. There
might be some difficulties, but you'd only have to fire on them
once or twice — everybody would be on the side of the
shooters.[8]

MYSELF: My next voyage will not be to India.

CLEMENCEAU: Oh. Where will it be ?

MYSELF: To Greece.

CLEMENCEAU: You're right. You should always begin with
Greece. You should also end with her.

MYSELF: In spite of the Greeks. It's rather sickening to find
Pangalos installed there after Pericles.

CLEMENCEAU: It is certainly very trying. They've inherited
nothing from their ancestors except their garrulity. What
talkers they are ! You'll see them, while they eat curious
objects which they call artichokes and which are merely thistles
— they dip them in salt — talking, talking inexhaustibly. See
Olympus. Do you know that Pausanias was still able to see

[8] Clemenceau left Paris on the 21st September 1920. He embarked at Mar-
seilles on the *Cordillère*. He telegraphed from Port-Said on the 27th, 'Good cross-
ing. Health fine. Everything all right.' From Colombo on the 2nd October,
'Excellent health. Weather splendid. Excursions Sunday and Monday.' From
Singapore on the 17th, 'Arrived safely. Health excellent. Leaving Friday for
Batavia.' Then he was in India. He stayed there three months. On the 13th
February 1921 he telegraphed from Mysore, 'Everything fine. We left Colombo
23rd. Barring the unexpected shall be at Marseilles 13th March.'

wooden columns at Olympus in the second century? I went to a place where they said it was impossible to go, and as a matter of fact, it wasn't very easy—to Phigalia.

MYSELF: Where is it?

CLEMENCEAU: In the north of the Peloponnesus. It's a place which was full of temples. You still see them on the ground. You can take a stroll amongst the architraves. It's an impressive sight. Also see Agrigentum, Syracuse. . .

MYSELF: Pæstum!

CLEMENCEAU: Naturally you'll see Pæstum!

[*Albert announces 'M. Jaeger.'*]

CLEMENCEAU: Yes. In my study. He's the son-in-law of Dr. Bucher.[9]

MYSELF [*getting up*]: I'll disappear. Presently I should like to ask you why you were born at Mouilleron-en-Pareds.

CLEMENCEAU: Why I was. . .

MYSELF: Yes.

CLEMENCEAU: Ah, you're on that subject now, are you? It's very simple: because my mother, who came from the petite bourgeoisie — her brother's father was a solicitor at Saint-Jean d'Angély — the Clemenceaus were of the bourgeoisie before the Revolution, a fact of which they were as proud as peacocks — my mother didn't want to have her confinements at L'Aubraie, where she would have had to stay with her father-in-law, who was an old imbecile and didn't like her. She went to Mouilleron with her parents.

MYSELF: The Clemenceaus came from L'Aubraie?

CLEMENCEAU: No, the Clemenceaus were from Mouchamps. Don't you know Colombier? It's the little family château. One day I'll take you to see the house where I was born, at Mouilleron, and the bit of earth where I shall be buried, at Colombier. Those two points will mark the span of my sad rainbow. . .

---

[9] Editor of the *Alsace Française*.

CLEMENCEAU AT SIXTEEN

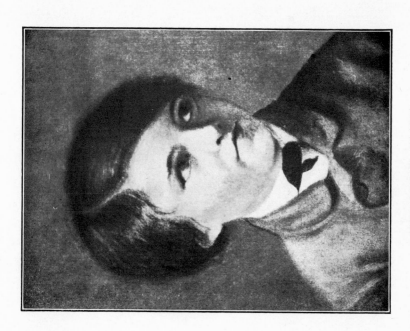

CLEMENCEAU AT TEN

*From a pastel by his father*

My father was a doctor, my grandfather was a doctor. He went to inspect the cows in a white tie and a high hat. When he met me in the courtyard of the château, he used to say to me, 'Where are you going, little fellow ?' I would answer, 'I'm going to the kitchen.' He would reply, 'Your place isn't in the kitchen, it's in the drawing-room. In the drawing-room there was, by way of amusement, my aunt who used to read Mme. de Sévigné. It was very dull. When I was able to ride and take a gallop in the fields, life was attractive. Until then it was deadly. I can understand why my mother preferred to undergo her confinements elsewhere.

MYSELF: How did L'Aubraie [10] happen to come into your family ?

CLEMENCEAU: My great-grandfather acquired it through his wife. His wife's family was very proud of it and always for the same reason: they had had it before the Revolution. It wasn't national property.

MYSELF: And what did your great-grandfather do ?

CLEMENCEAU: He was also a doctor. He had been one of the Five Hundred. After this he was appointed sub-prefect of a sub-prefecture which no longer exists: Montaigu. He took advantage of the appointment to make speeches and issue proclamations on the glory of Napoleon, to his heart's content.

[*I noticed on his table a pamphlet*: Clemenceau's geistliches Vermaechtnis.]

MYSELF: Aha !

CLEMENCEAU: Yes, it's by a Boche. He's probably abusing me violently. *Vermaechtnis?* What does it mean ? *Impotence ?*

MYSELF: No. *Legacy.*

---

[10] In *The Strongest* there is a description of a château which point for point resembles L'Aubraie — it's the manor house of Henri de Puymaufray. 'Situated in the rectangle made by the muddy waters of its mote, the wan château raised towards the skies its expressionless three-story façade with its latticed, funereally black windows. The drawbridge, whose shaking supports have for two centuries been sunk into the stone, is affixed to the arch, surmounted by battlements, which gives access to the fortress.'

CLEMENCEAU: Oh, really ? Are you sure ? That surprises me. . . *Ver* . . . *Ver* . . . [*He goes into the hall and looks for a book on the shelves.*] I had a German dictionary, but everything disappears round here. Somebody must eat them. . . Ah, here it is. [*He begins to turn the pages.*] *Ver* . . . *ver* . . . *vermaechtnis* . . . *legacy.* . . That's funny !

MYSELF: *Clemenceau's Spiritual Legacy.* At least he doesn't abuse you in the title.

CLEMENCEAU: These Boches, all the same ! Extraordinary people. There's an inscription by the author which takes ten lines. Is he pulling my leg, I wonder ? No, he's simply a fellow without malice. Their great quality lies here; they don't become enfeebled. They'll fall on us at exactly the right moment. [*He gets up.*] I'll go and see the little Jaeger.

I OFTEN observed that Clemenceau was not very familiar with his family's history. Fortunately there is an abundance of information elsewhere.[1] In going through the legal and parochial records of various villages of the Vendée — Mouchamps, Mareuil-sur-le-Lay, Saint-Michel en l'Herm, etc., it appears that there was formerly a certain Jehan Clemenceau, the protégé of Mgr. de Sacierges, bishop of Luçon.

Jehan Clemenceau had been apprenticed to the Marnef brothers, who were printers in Portiers. He had learned his trade and returned to his native village, Mareuil-sur-le-Lay, where Mgr. de Sacierges had his palace. He had opened a printing-works and a stationer-bookseller's shop and married Isabella Voyneau, Lady la Touche, of Dissais, near Mareuil, on 12th January 1498. The business had prospered and Jehan Clemenceau had become a person of importance. By letters patent of King Louis XII, given at Blois the 5th February 1508, he had been exempted from all public duties.

Jehan Clemenceau had two sons. The younger, Jacques become, in 1547, vicar-general to Mgr. d'Hilliers, who had succeeded Mgr. de Sacierges; later he was 'Master of the Music to the Cathedral Chapter' — an office of high dignity.

[1] See especially a remarkable study by Henry Cassira — *J'ai Vu*, 15th December 1918. M. Cassira mentions the researches made by M. Louis Brochet, an archivist.

The elder, François, lord of la Couffardière, was Seneschal of Luçon and of Moustiers-sur-le-Lay. In this capacity he held, on the 23rd January 1570, an inquiry into the depredations committed by the protestants on the houses of the bishops and canons of Luçon and Moustiers.

François Clemenceau married Jehanne Orceau, daughter of the Revenue Officer of the manor of Moustiers-sur-le-Lay. He had one son, from whom sprang the two branches of the Clemenceaus, those of La Serrie and those of Colombier.

The generations passed on. The Clemenceaus formed a Clemenceau line. In 1623, Squire Clemenceau, a doctor at Nantes and a man proficient in his art, was ennobled by letters Patent of King Louis XIII, who gave him arms 'divided, in the one half gules with a key argent, in the second a seal of gules on argent.'

On the 8th March 1709, Pierre-Benjamin Clemenceau was born: he studied for the bar and became a Parliamentary advocate. He married as his second wife, in 1748, Charlotte-Anne Bouquet, daughter of Paul, lord of the manor of Chadelière, and of Anne-Louise Chapeau.

A son was born the 29th May 1749 and called Pierre-Paul Clemenceau. He practised medicine for several years and later was elected, on the 2nd September 1791, a member of the departmental administration of Fontenay-le-Comte. In 1792 he was mayor of the commune of Mouchamps.

The insurrection broke out in the Vendée. Pierre-Paul Clemenceau was appointed a medical officer in the Armies of the West. At the beginning of the year VIII he was head of the municipal administration of the Canton of Mouchamps. In Floréal [Revolutionary month 20th April — 19th May] he was appointed sub-prefect of Montaigu. He was a conscientious and zealous official. I have several of his reports to the Prefect of the Vendée — they are marvels of bureaucratic style. He served the Emperor faithfully. His superiors were delighted with him. He received letters of warm commendation[2] and finally, coming to Paris, was received at the Tuileries:

'Sir,

The Court Chamberlain, in obedience to the command of his Majesty the Emperor and King, has the honour to inform you that there will be a levée at court on Monday, 24th March 1806, at 9 o'clock in the evening. R.S.V.P.'

He was invited to the wedding ceremony of His Royal Highness the Prince of Baden to Her Imperial Highness the Princess Stéphanie Napoleon. Cardinal Caprara asked him for the honour of his company at dinner, 'on next Monday, the 5th of May, at five o'clock sharp, at the Hotel Biron in the rue de Varennes. There will be no ladies present.'

And this little card, which was sent to him by the Grand Master of Ceremonies:

'The Grand Master of Ceremonies, in obedience to the command of his Majesty the Emperor and King, has the honour to announce that the marriage of His Majesty with the Archduchess Royal Marie-Louise will take place in the grand ballroom of the Louvre.

'You are invited to be presented in the first drawing-room in the Museum Gallery, next the Chapel.'

['This ticket is for personal use only, to be presented on entering. Entrance will be by the two side stair-cases of the Clock Pavilion from the side of the river-bank or of the Carrousel. The doors will open at seven o'clock and shut at midnight. Ladies will wear Court dress and gentlemen evening dress or uniforms.']

In 1776 Pierre-Paul Clemenceau had married Charlotte Mail-

---

[2] These letters, printed in the original, are omitted here because of their length. — Translator's note.

lot, daughter of Charles, Squire of l'Aubraie, in the parish of Mouchamps. He died in 1825.

His eldest son, Paul Jules Benjamin, born the 22nd of June 1777, was a doctor, like his father. In 1801 he married Marie-Thérèse Gabrielle Joubert, by whom he had one son, Paul-Benjamin, in 1810.[3]

Paul-Benjamin, a doctor like his father and grandfather, married, in 1839, Sophie Emma Eucharis Gautreau, of Mouilleron-en-Pareds, by whom he had three daughters, Emma, Adrienne, and Sophie, and three sons, Georges, Paul, and Albert.

The register of Georges Clemenceau's birth reads:

'In the year one thousand, eight hundred and forty-one, on the thirtieth of September, at five o'clock in the evening, there appeared before us, the Mayor and Public Officer of the State for the Commune of Mouilleron-en-Pareds, Canton of la Chateigneraye, Department of the Vendée, M. Paul Clemenceau, physician domiciled at Nantes, who presented for registration a child of the male sex, born on the twenty-eighth of this month at half-past nine in the evening, at the home of Monsieur François Gautreau, landed proprietor resident in the borough, and his wife Madame Sophie Eucharis Emma Gautreau: he declared his intention of giving to the said child the Christian names of Georges Benjamin; the said declaration and presentation took place in the presence of Messrs. Pierre Auger, baker, aged fifty-two and Jacques Lazare Chabinier, carpenter, aged thirty-two, both domiciled in the borough of Mouilleron and friends of the child's father; and both appearing signed this instrument after reading.'

[3] Born at l'Aubraie 28th April 1810. Died at l'Aubraie 23 July 1897.

# XXXVIII

## COLONIAL POLICY — FERRY, GAMBETTA, THIERS, JAURÈS

*19th June* 1928

MYSELF: You were speaking to me the other day about your 'crimes' — I should like to ask you about another 'crime' with which you have often been charged—your struggles with Jules Ferry. You accused Ferry of two things — with not organizing the Republic with sufficient speed and system. . .

CLEMENCEAU: Yes.

MYSELF: Secondly, you criticized his foreign policy and his colonial policy. As far as his domestic policy goes, they might answer you that, if Ferry did not want to hasten democracy's triumph after the fall of the Empire, it was because he was inclined to distrust democracy, its possible results and the difficulties into which it might lead the country — and seeing what has happened, perhaps he wasn't altogether wrong. In regard to his colonial policy, it can't be denied that the colonies supported us in our struggle, shared our sense of national honour, and gave us men.

CLEMENCEAU [*who has been listening impatiently*]: Is that all ? Martet, I'll answer you. I must tell you in the first place that I'm not a simple ideologist who made a cult of the Revolution. At l'Aubraie there were portraits of Robespierre, of

273

Saint-Just and other such marvels in all corners of the house.
My father used to tell me that they were gods and that there
were none beside them.  My father brought me up a Republican.  I fought under the Empire for the Republic.  The 4th
of September came. . .

One day I found myself face to face with Ferry.  I understood that Ferry was incapable of bringing the Republic to
realization.  You tell me 'If he didn't organize democracy
sooner and more quickly, it's because he distrusted democracy.'
That's a mistake, Martet.  It's only because he couldn't do any
better.  He wasn't a dishonest man.  But in the matter of
intelligence he was sub-normal, unable to do anything, even
to put two words together.  These fellows usually have at least
the gift of gab—they may not have anything but hot air to
express, but they express it.  When you went to see him he
looked at you with vacant eyes, made banal little jokes, and
that was all.  And if they made him President of the Council,
it was precisely because he was of no use for anything.

Well, in those days my great scheme was, as you know, free
and compulsory secular instruction.  With Barodet and a few
others I went to see Ferry.  I told him all that.  He said,
'Free instruction.  It's impossible.  We haven't the means.
What I'm trying to do now is to increase the subsidies.  Compulsory?  What are you asking!  The people would never
permit it.'

And that's how things are going on today and will continue
to go on so long as they continue to make laws without the
will to enforce them.  The Republic turns out quantities of
laws — she forgets to station a policeman beside them.  Every
now and then she even makes laws which say that such and
such a thing is forbidden by virtue of such article in such law,
that this article has not been enforced but that beginning today
all that will be changed — and you soon see that it's merely
tantamount to the law proclaiming its own bankruptcy.

'As for secular instruction,' said Ferry, 'it's not to be thought of; there would be a revolution.'

Whereupon, after having assured us that the three things were impossible, he did them; he spoke one way and acted another.

As for his foreign policy, he succeeded in his pretty little *tour de force* of throwing Italy into the arms of Germany by putting his hands on Tunis. I blamed him for that in no uncertain terms. I even — a memoir, Martet ! — remember making a little speech on this subject one day, a little speech for which I had prepared carefully. Some time later the Berlin correspondent of the *Times,* whom I knew, went to see Bismarck. The latter asked him, 'Who is this Clemenceau ?'

'Well,' said the other, 'he's a young man, a doctor who's this and that. . .'

'Oh,' said Bismarck, 'he said a thing or two the other day — he's a lad to keep your eye on.'

As for colonial policy, I blamed Ferry for throwing away our men and money on remote expeditions when we needed them a good deal more urgently at home.

MYSELF: If you had it to do over again, would you still oppose that colonial policy ?

CLEMENCEAU: In the same way, Martet, and with the same energy, if we still had the German menace always before us, a declining birth rate, an army and navy barely sufficient to defend the metropolis, and if, finally, France persisted in wanting colonies without colonists. The French don't want to leave Paris, Bordeaux, Marseilles. The French don't want to have children. What's all this fuss about colonies then ?

Furthermore, I blamed Ferry for making these colonial expeditions — I also blame him for the way in which he made them. You can't have any idea of the stupidity, the incompetence which ruled these undertakings. One day Ferry said to me from the rostrum, 'A battle has taken place near a town which isn't marked on the map.'

I replied, 'Excuse me, but the town is marked on the very maps which you distributed to us. And that town is. . .' He hadn't even looked at the map ![1]

The people and the millions they gambled with, without knowing where or against whom — and all the corrupt dealing that went on behind it. A colonial policy is a good thing, Martet, when it uncovers a few genuine truths for export to the poor devils, black or yellow, who otherwise wouldn't care a hang most of the time. But when it merely serves to enrich a few people, to found companies, to exploit capital resources, to make these same yellow and black folk sweat gold, then, with your permission, it doesn't arouse much enthusiasm in my breast. There is a great drawback attached to colonies, namely that in general they are very far away and almost anything can go on there without anyone ever going out to have a look, and when investigators are sent out they come back two or three years later when the matter is no longer of interest — and usually they return delighted, for some mysterious reason, with the result of their investigations.

Myself: But the help which the colonies sent us during the war.

Clemenceau: Yes, there is that. That brings to mind this story which I heard in India. There was a man who rose early every morning and went out into the country with his gun. Every time he heard a nightingale sing he killed it. One day his wife said to him, 'See here, you're killing all these poor little beasts; it's horrible. It's a kind of killing that serves no purpose whatever.

[1] Speech of the 27th November 1884 on affairs in Tonkin:

The President of the Council, 'The action took place near a town whose name is not on the map.'

M. Clemenceau, 'I regret exceedingly, Mr. President, to call your attention to the fact that the name of this town is certainly on the map which you distributed to us — it's the town of Hung-Quan. You haven't looked at the map — that's your excuse.'

'You shouldn't say that,' answered the man. 'If I didn't go out to kill those little beasts I should remain in bed, and I find it does me good to take a little walk in the morning.'

Even the stupidest actions have their good side — the colonies gave us Mangin. He was a dangerous man, and if he had lived he would have done things which it would have been better not to do. But he knew how to fight, and in that underbrush and in those marshes of his he caught the flavour, the meaning of combat. He made war like a soldier and not, as did a pack of others, like an office-holder.

And there were not only the whites who went and saturated themselves and took shape in Africa or Asia. There were the blacks, the Senegalese, whom I used to see going by in lorries, serene and smiling, and who fought like wildcats.

One day at the front I saw a detachment of these fellows from a distance, with a man on horseback circling about them. I asked who they were, and was told that no one knew. So I went up to them in the car. They were blacks who were just coming out of the trenches, where they had been forgotten for eighteen days. You can imagine what they were like — lumps of mud. They were returning with their rifles broken, their clothing in rags — magnificent. When they saw me they began to play the *Marseillaise,* with anything whatever, tapping on stones and bits of wood — it was the answer to my attacks on Ferry. I spoke to them. I don't know if they understood. I told them that they were engaged in liberating themselves by coming to fight by our side, that through blood we should become brothers — sons of the same civilization, the same philosophy. Words — small enough in truth in comparison with them, their courage and nobility.

They were splendid. The Boches complained because we sent blacks against them. But there is no Boche, no doctor of the University of Berlin or of Munich, who is as handsome or magnificent as any one of these Senegalese. What have they anyway, the Boches ? Their science ? They're gifted in semantics ? in psychology ? What does that amount to ?

Yes, I know all that. Nevertheless, the fact remains that when Ferry pushed us toward Tonkin — 'because we found it did us good to take a little exercise in the morning' — he diverted us from the one thing it was imperative that we should heed and fear — Germany; whilst I knew well that it was not at Tonkin that our destiny would be decided, but right here, where it actually was decided.

MYSELF: There's one thing I don't understand very well, sir, and that's this: it is said that Bismarck did everything in his power to encourage our colonial schemes in order, as you say, to divert our attention. I wonder, therefore, why we didn't in our turn apply the same policy to Germany and why we took her colonies away ?

CLEMENCEAU: Because in the first place, I had that grudge on account of the snippet of the Congo which Caillaux had turned over to them. It was a dishonourable business. It would have been better to give them the whole Congo. So we took that, the English took something else, all that they could take; finally everything was taken from them. And I don't regret it. When a people have done what the Boches did in Belgium and France, it is hardly for them to say, 'We want to civilize Africa.' They'd do better to civilize themselves first.

MYSELF: And Gambetta ? What did you think of him ?

CLEMENCEAU: Gambetta was a man of another stamp, another spirit, than Ferry. He was a foreigner, who relied greatly on the sonorousness of his voice, from which, however, he obtained striking effects. Not many ideas. He had conducted the war — both well and badly, but more badly than well — but he certainly did conduct it, and as well as he could. And he had profoundly generous impulses — his philosophy was beautiful and noble. I liked Gambetta, and respected him. He didn't know very well where he was going, but he went with ardour.[2]

MYSELF: And Thiers?

CLEMENCEAU: Thiers? That's very easy: the Versaillais, returning to Paris,[3] killed 20,000 men, women, and children. One day I went with my sister to Mouilleron-en-Pareds. We met a man who had just left the military service. My sister said to him jokingly, 'Ah, Untel! You must have played some scurvy tricks while you were in the Army of Versailles.'

He answered with the air of a good fellow, 'Well, miss, scurvy tricks are all accordin'. All I can tell you is that with my last shot I fired into the stomach of a woman who was near the end of her carrying period.'

Thiers was the savage, limited type of bourgeois who steeps himself in blood without flinching.

MYSELF: A little while ago I put this question to you about the war you waged against Ferry—it's quite certain that if you had known then what you know today, if you had been acquainted with democracy as you are. . .

CLEMENCEAU: Yes—well?

MYSELF: Would you all the same . . . ?

---

[2] I found amongst Clemenceau's papers this letter, addressed to M. Georges Clemenceau, Mayor of the XVIII Arrondissement, Paris.

Bordeaux, 3 February 1871

My dear Clemenceau:

Paris has fallen. But we must still think of France and the Republic, and look in the provinces for the co-operation on which we have a right to count.

There is a large city which demands at its head an ardent republican, a man of courage yet of broad and conciliatory spirit. Challemel-Lacour fulfils these qualifications in the highest degree; but his strength is exhausted, and it is necessary, in order not to jeopardize so valuable a life, to find a successor who shall be worthy of him and of Lyons.

It is you whom I have selected. You were held in Paris by the expressed wish of your fellow-citizens and by your duties; unfortunately the cessation of hostilities does not permit you to believe that you are as necessary as you were, and I need you for a more urgent post.

Come then, without raising objections, for it is still a question of serving the Republic. Come.

Fraternal greetings,
LÉON GAMBETTA.

[3] After the Commune.

CLEMENCEAU: What is there beside democracy — will you tell me that ? Democracy is men — it is man. If man is foolish and stupid, obviously it's very embarrassing. But I don't see any remedy for it. All systems have ended in the same way — in the mire. It is humiliating for a country to have had men like Louis XIV and Louis XV, who were streets below Fallières.[4] You shouldn't growl against the Republic and democracy just because you see them embodied in chimney-sweeps. Monarchy would probably be embodied in the same individuals, and if it were embodied in others, the latter would be no better than the former. The annoying and irremediable thing about it all is that, whether you have a Republic or a Monarchy, there will always be at the head of the state a Doumergue, a Deschanel or a Charles IX, that is, there will be men, nothing but men.

MYSELF: In ten years, between 1885 and 1895, there was such a change in the situation, such disillusion.

CLEMENCEAU: Yes. It ended with Jaurès. When the Republic was set in motion, everything cleaned up, the way prepared, then the Socialists turned up with Jaurès and plunged in — and that was the beginning of the end. Till then our struggles were kept within the borders of the country — they threw wide all the doors.

Jaurès had enormous talent. But there was something mischievous in the man. He had extraordinary gifts, which I myself had difficulty in resisting, but he was without greatness or dignity or generosity . . . or humanity. Yes, he was without humanity. Probably that's why he named his paper as he did.[5] Behind Jaurès' humanity and humanitarianism there was always something hostile and threatening. Behind his idyllic pictures you could see rising the smoke of civil war. He had none of the qualities which bestow the true love of

---

[4] Recent President of France.
[5] *Humanity* was founded by Jaurès.

humanity on a man — neither the smile, nor the tolerance nor self-doubt, nor skepticism — nothing. Humanity was, to Jaurès, numbers, the mob, brute strength. He fought for the side which was bound to win. I prefer Baudry d'Asson, who fought for hopeless causes and gathered painfully behind him three dozen rattle-pates.

I remember Jaurès during the Rochette [6] business. I got Lépine [7] to imprison Rochette without notifying Briand, who was Keeper of the Seals. Why? because I had no confidence in Briand, who had caused the release of one of his socialist friends the day before. I said to myself, 'If I speak to Briand about this, the beans are spilled.' Well, Jaurès got wind of it, and did everything in his power to embarrass me. I wouldn't tell him, 'It's because I distrust Briand.' He would have gone at once to his followers and told them about it.

Yes, a mischief-maker, and dangerous. If we had had him about during the war, we should have lost.

MYSELF: How do you think it's all going to end?

CLEMENCEAU: All what?

MYSELF: The experiment in democracy we're in process of making?

CLEMENCEAU: I don't know. Probably with a general who, having decision and system, will sweep it all away as he likes. Then you will see the Empire once more, the priests. . .

MYSELF: And it will all have to begin over again.

CLEMENCEAU: Yes. But I shall no longer be mixed up in it. Let them scramble out of it themselves. I've done enough fighting for liberty, and enough fighting against myself to make that same liberty secondary to the safety of the country. During the war I trampled on everything, had people shot — it would be true to say that shooting often brushed by me, and very closely.

6 The financier.
7 Prefect of Police.

One of my worst memories is the time I left Paris during the Commune. I said to myself 'They are going to shoot all the people under my jurisdiction. I can't however give it the sanction of my authority.' One of my friends, an American, gave me his papers and I left. I took the train and went as far as Saint-Denis, where the Versaillais troops were. A man stopped and questioned me. I answered in English, treating the man affably and joking. After a minute or two of this little game he had enough and let me go on my way. I wanted to go to l'Aubraie. I thought 'I shall be fairly quiet there.' In order to go to l'Aubraie I had to go first to Alençon and then to Nantes, where Father Waldeck-Rousseau, an old Catholic and a worthy man, gave me a fictitious passport. Provided with this passport I arrived in Luçon on the day of the fair. I found my father and it was all over.

MYSELF: Didn't the Government disturb you ?

CLEMENCEAU: No.[8] On one occasion I was asked for my passport, and I showed it. An excellent passport ! It all amused me very much. . .

[8] The Government did not seem at bottom to regard Clemenceau with any great fury. In this connexion Bernier sent me three documents which are not lacking in relish.

The first is an anonymous letter addressed to the Ministry of the Interior, where it was recorded on the 14th June 1871:

'A friend of order warns the Minister that comrade Clemenceau, an ex-mayor of Paris, sent to Bordeaux to incite that city to insurrection, is hiding in the Vendée with his father, a league from Sainte-Hermine. He does not go out by day; the authorities are unaware of his presence, but he is there and can be taken whenever you wish. The entire country will greet his arrest with pleasure, for everyone detests these Red scoundrels and especially leaders as dangerous as this Clemenceau. Sainte-Hermine is the country-seat of the canton, near Luçon arrondissement of Fontenay (Vendée). Let justice be done.'

The second is a telegram from the Ministry of the Interior to the Prefect of the Vendée; it is dated 16th June. 'An anonymous letter informs me, etc.'

The third is the Prefect's answer. 'La Roche-sur-Yon, 19th June 1871. The information in the anonymous letter is correct. This person, according to the sub-prefect of Fontenay, is actually with his family at Sainte-Hermine; the neighborhood is so little in sympathy with him that he dare not go out for fear of being hooted at. His political ideas are very radical, but I think opposed to the Commune and to the atrocities which it committed.'

With which M. Thiers' Government appeared to be satisfied.

THE documents which Clemenceau collected concerning the 18th March 1871 are innumerable; there are fewer on the weeks which preceded the drama; I find only these old yellow papers:

## THE REPUBLIC OF FRANCE

### MAIRIE OF PARIS

### *The Mayor of Paris*

### NOTICE

THE CITIZENS whose names follow herewith are appointed Mayors of the twenty arrondissements of Paris:

. . . . . .

### *18th Arrondissement*
### GEORGES CLEMENCEAU [1]

. . . . . .

Given at the Hotel de Ville at Paris this 5th day of September one thousand eight hundred and seventy.

ETIENNE ARAGO

[1] He was living with his friend Lafont, 19, rue Capron at the time.

OFFICE OF THE
COUNCILLOR OF STATE                    Paris, the... 186
SECRETARY-GENERAL


*Memorandum*

CITIZEN CLEMENCEAU, having been appointed mayor provisionally is required to proceed at once to the Mairie of the 18th arrondissement and take possession of it.[2]

> Paris, the 5th September 1870
> The Mayor of Paris
> ETIENNE ARAGO


> THE REPUBLIC OF FRANCE
> MAIRIE OF PARIS
> *Mayor of Paris*


NOTICE

THE CITIZENS herein-named are appointed assistants in the twenty arrondissements of Paris:

. . . . . .


18th *Arrondissement*  { LAFONT
                       { SIMONOT

given at the Hotel de Ville at Paris the 6th September 1870.

> ETIENNE ARAGO


[2] From this day the task began. It was a heavy one. Food had to be found for the civil population; children required milk and it had to be found. Shelter had to be found for the refugees. Coal and oil were urgently needed. The National Guard had to be armed and drilled. The ramparts had to be inspected. As if that weren't enough this youthful mayor of 29 undertook to secularize the schools.

[A poster]
## REPUBLIC OF FRANCE

LIBERTY — EQUALITY — FRATERNITY

*Mairie of the 18th Arrondissement*

CITIZENS:

SHALL France be swallowed up in the abyss and disappear, or shall she resume her former rank in the vanguard of the nations ?

That is the question which presents itself to us today, and which it is our duty to answer.

The enemy is at the gates of the city. The day is not distant, perhaps, when our breasts will be the country's last rampart.

Every one of us knows his duty.

We are the children of the Revolution. Let us find our inspiration in the example of our forefathers, and like them we shall conquer.

*Vive la France!   Vive la République!*

Paris, the 23rd September 1870

*The Mayor*

*Associates:*
J. A. LAFONT
A. SIMONOT

G. CLEMENCEAU


[Another poster.]
## REPUBLIC OF FRANCE

LIBERTY — EQUALITY — FRATERNITY

*Mairie of the 18th Arrondissement*

THE CITIZENS of the 18th Arrondissement protest with indignation against an armistice which the Government can only agree to by committing treason.

Paris, the 31st October 1870

*Associates:*          *The Mayor of the 18th Arrondissement*

J. A. LAFONT                    G. CLEMENCEAU

A. SIMONOT

The November elections took place:

*Republic of France*
*Mairie of Paris*

Paris, the 9th November 1870

To CITIZEN CLEMENCEAU, Mayor of the 18th Arrondissement

Citizen,

According to the abstract of the returns with which I have been provided, it appears that you have been elected Mayor of this arrondissement.

I ask you therefore to assume the direction of the Mairie immediately, and to request your associates, who have also just been elected, likewise to enter upon their duties.

*Fraternal greetings*
The Mayor of Paris
*Etienne Arago*

[A Poster]

## REPUBLIC OF FRANCE

LIBERTY — EQUALITY — FRATERNITY

*Mairie of the 18th Arrondissement*

CITIZENS:

Your suffrages, so freely given, impose serious duties upon us. We shall endeavour to fulfil them.

The hour of sacrifice is about to sound. By your self-denials for the republic, by nobly bearing with stubborn patience the long trials before you, you will ensure the safety of our country.

*Vive la France! Vive la République!*
Paris, the 10th November, 1870.

*Associates:*        *The Mayor*
J. A. LAFONT        G. CLEMENCEAU
S. DEREURE
(JACLARD, unable to sign)

ON THE 8th February 1871 he was elected a Deputy for Paris.[3] He proceeded to Bordeaux.[4]

The *Laissez-passer* which was delivered to him on the 5th carried the following details:

*Name:* CLEMENCEAU
*Christian names:* Georges Benjamin
*Occupation:* Doctor of Medicine
*Residence:* 19, rue Capron
*Age:* 29
*Purpose of voyage:* Delegate to the Convention (Gironde)
*Route followed:* Via Toulouse. (Hell Gate)

The seals of the Prefecture of Police and of the general staff of the army of Paris are affixed to the document.

On the back in Gothic characters:

FRENCH REPUBLIC

The person herein described has permission to pass through the German lines, etc.[5]

ON THE first of March, after one quiet trip to Paris on personal business, he was back in Bordeaux — which did not prevent him from having the following poster stuck on the walls of his arrondissement in Paris:

---

[3] By 96,000 votes. The armistice had been signed ten days.
[4] Leaving Lafont in charge of the Mairie.
[5] In German — *Translator's note.*

## REPUBLIC OF FRANCE

LIBERTY — EQUALITY — FRATERNITY

*Mairie of the 18th Arrondissement*

CITIZENS:

One last trial has been reserved for us, a fearful and humiliating trial — that of seeing the enemy enter Paris.

We have been handed over without conditions.

All resistance has been rendered hopeless. Any act of aggression would be fatal to us.

If any of you still believe it to be their duty to die and to bury their wives and children under the ruins of the city, let them think of the futile results of so hopeless a struggle, let them think above all of the Republic.

Only the Republic can revenge and repair our disasters.

The Republic cannot perish if all its citizens stand to arms to defend her when the time comes.

You showed your confidence in us on the day after our proclamation of the 31st of October. It was our duty, before the following day, when we went to present our credentials, to warn you against fatal disturbance.

Citizens, on your calmness depends the safety of France and the Republic.

*Vive la France !  Vive la République !*

Paris, the first of March 1871.

*Associates:*                                     *The Mayor*

J. A. LAFONT                                    G. CLEMENCEAU

S. DEREURE

JACLARD

Eighteen days after this appeal for composure the Commune broke out.

FIRST of March 1871, in the auditorium of the Louis Theatre at Bordeaux. Jules Grévy presides. Some figures are handed

# REPUBLIQUE FRANCAISE

LIBERTÉ, ÉGALITÉ, FRATERNITÉ

# MAIRIE DU 18ᵉ ARRONDISSEMENT

## *Citoyens,*

Aujourd'hui, à midi, la Mairie du 18ᵉ Arrondissement a été envahie par une troupe armée. Un officier de la Garde Nationale a osé sommer le Maire et ses Adjoints de remettre la Mairie aux mains d'un délégué du Comité central de la Garde Nationale.

Le Maire et ses Adjoints, revêtus des insignes municipaux, ont, en présence de tous les Employés de la Mairie, sommé le chef du poste d'expulser les envahisseurs. Celui-ci, après en avoir conféré avec son commandant, a répondu qu'il se refusait à obtempérer à cet ordre et qu'il était disposé à prêter main-forte aux violateurs de la Loi. Le chef des envahisseurs a alors mis en arrestation le Maire et deux de ses Adjoints, qui ont été conduits au poste entre deux haies de Gardes nationaux. Quelques minutes après, on venait déclarer au Maire et aux deux Adjoints élus du 18ᵉ arrondissement qu'ils étaient LIBRES de se retirer.

## CITOYENS,

Nous avons à cœur d'éviter un conflit dont les résultats désastreux nous épouvantent. Voilà pourquoi nous cédons à la force sans en appeler à la force. Mais nous protestons hautement contre l'attentat dont la Garde Nationale du 18ᵉ arrondissement s'est rendue coupable sur la personne de Magistrats républicains librement élus, et qui se rendent ici publiquement le témoignage qu'ils ont accompli leur devoir.

### VIVE LA FRANCE! VIVE LA RÉPUBLIQUE!

Paris, le 22 Mars 1371.

Le Maire du 18ᵉ Arrondissement,

## G. CLEMENCEAU.

Les Adjoints au Maire du 18ᵉ Arrondissement,

### J.-A. LAFOND, V. JACLARD.

PROCLAMATION ISSUED BY CLEMENCEAU AS MAYOR OF MONTMARTRE, 22 MARCH 1871

up to him. He announces the result of the vote on the peace preliminaries: 546 deputies have voted in favour of ending the war, 107 against. Amongst those opposed was Georges Clemenceau.

On the following day he signed the following letter, addressed by 37 deputies 'to the Representatives of the Departments of the Lower Rhine, the Upper Rhine, Moselle, Meurthe, and the Vosges':

*Dear Colleagues and Citizens:*

Yesterday we associated ourselves, by our cheers, with the declaration which one of your number [6] made from the rostrum on the subject of Alsace and Lorraine — we wish to assure you that the representatives of Republican France still share your sentiments and opinions. We feel ourselves as strongly bound to the heroic populace which you represent as they feel themselves bound to our common fatherland. Moreover we have declared and we do again declare that the National Assembly and the French people as a whole have no right to make a single one of your constituents a subject of Prussia. Like yourselves we maintain that any law or treaty, vote or plebiscite which shall cede any part whatever of Alsace or Lorraine is null and void in advance. Whatever happens the citizens of those two regions shall remain our compatriots and brothers, and the Republic promises never to surrender its claim on them.

We cordially accept the hand which you tender us.

*Fraternal Greetings.*

Nothing remained now but to wait forty-seven years. . .

[6] Keller.

# XL

## THE DREYFUS AFFAIR — CLEMENCEAU IN AMERICA

*26th June* 1928

MYSELF: Good morning. You're smiling.

CLEMENCEAU: I've always got a smile, Martet.

MYSELF: I've known you at times when you didn't have very much of one.

CLEMENCEAU: For instance ?

MYSELF: On the 16th July, when, having made your first speech against Malvy in the Secret Committee,[1] you had only five or six votes including your own. Are you working ?

CLEMENCEAU: Yes. I shall have finished before I leave.

MYSELF: How can you work in this frightful heat ?

CLEMENCEAU: I'm very comfortable here. I have my window open — when I'm tired I go and pick a rose in the garden. [*On the table there are four or five yellow roses, their thorns trimmed off and arranged in a little Japanese vase of bronze or earthenware.*] That one over there is of a most extraordinary colour — like a young girl to whom you've just made a slightly improper remark. Speaking of roses, I've just had a visit from Mandel. He sat down in that chair and poured out a most magnificent flow of words, which didn't convey any exact meaning to me. Mandel is of the line of the Prophets. He is quite content to remain in a haze. . .

[1] Of the Senate.

MYSELF: Did he vote for the four sou franc ?

CLEMENCEAU: No. He voted against it.[2] He has one virtue, has Mandel: he pushes straight on and doesn't mind in the least being alone. Perhaps it's because he only looks for ideas in himself instead of going begging them from other people. Will the Jews go to Paradise ? It would annoy them to be separated from Mandel. . .

MYSELF: God would never do that !

CLEMENCEAU: So there's my report, Martet. What's yours ?

MYSELF: Oh, I've fifteen things to tell you.

CLEMENCEAU: All right. Begin with the fifteenth.

MYSELF: Your memorandum on Foch ?

CLEMENCEAU: I'll get at it as soon as I'm near the end of *Monet*. Fourteenth ?

MYSELF: Didn't you tell me once that you had some letters from Matthew Dreyfus which would clear up certain points in the Dreyfus affair and that, if you found them, you would give them to me ?

CLEMENCEAU: I don't remember. I don't think that I kept Matthew Dreyfus' letters. If I did, I have no idea what I did with them. Documents and I, you know. . . Moreover, I don't know what these letters could clear up for you. Besides, Matthew Dreyfus is a very good chap — I'm sure that if you were perplexed and needed information, he wouldn't refuse it to you.

MYSELF: What were the relations between Alfred and Matthew ?

CLEMENCEAU: They're brothers.

MYSELF: I mean — how do they compare intellectually ?

CLEMENCEAU: When Dreyfus came back from Devil's Island, Matthew Dreyfus wrote me, 'I'm going to bring him to see you.' He was a curiosity — Fancy ! a traitor who hadn't

---

[2] The whole of the scheme of the Monetary Act was passed in the chamber by 450 votes to 18. Amongst the 18 was Mandel.

committed treason. Matthew Dreyfus turned up with his man. I looked him over and said to myself, 'Really, this can't be his brother — what kind of fellow can he be ?' He looked like a pencil-seller. That was Dreyfus.

MYSELF: What did he make of the Dreyfus affair ?

CLEMENCEAU: Nothing. He's the only one who didn't understand it. He was I don't know how many abysses beneath the Dreyfus affair. It's much better so, however. They can't accuse us of having allowed ourselves to be seduced by his personal magnetism. He didn't have three ha'pence worth of it. Poor Dreyfus. Everything that happened to him was, as you can well understand, completely, ludicrously, his own fault. You know, they made him write something — his hand trembled — they said to him, 'Aha ! Your hand's trembling, captain.'

He would stammer something or other. He should have answered, 'My hand's trembling ? Well, what of it ? What do you conclude from that ? That I've committed treason ? I warn you that your superior rank doesn't mean anything to me — if you attempt even to insinuate that sort of thing, I'll slap your face.'

That would have calmed them down a bit.

MYSELF: You began by believing in Dreyfus' guilt, didn't you ?

CLEMENCEAU: Naturally. You had to begin with that assumption.[3] What a period that was ! And yet in the end it did good, it caused a house-cleaning. We couldn't have gone to war with that canker in our midst. Of course, once the affair was over, everybody went his own way and things returned to where they were — but the useful work had been done.

During the war I met every sort, Dreyfusards and anti-Dreyfusards, and, amongst the latter, rabid anti-Dreyfusards who

---

[3] He had written in *Justice* 'Alfred Dreyfus is a traitor and I shall not insult any soldier by putting him in the same category as this scoundrel.'

saw red and threatened to have a stroke every time you opened
your mouth on the subject — lunatics for the most part — and
others — that's odd — who were men of sense with a head on
their shoulders, but who didn't like Jews. So they thought
that through hatred of the Jew and love of a kind of ex-
pressly manufactured, imaginary fatherland, they could flout
reason, justice, and humanity. That was going a bit too far.

MYSELF: Nevertheless it's difficult to doubt Esterhazy's
guilt. . .

CLEMENCEAU: He confessed everything. But you know an
incident like that becomes a matter of faith, of mere hyp-
notism — like Jesus walking on the waves. You may say to
such people, 'But it's impossible to walk on the waves !' They'll
answer you, 'Explain it as you like — I saw it.' To which
there is obviously no reply. From the moment that the discussion ceases to be whether or not Dreyfus is guilty but
whether or not Jews are birds of ill-omen, whether or not it
is desirable that a Jew be the guilty party, whether it is bad
for the country and the army that a court-martial may have
been in error, and so forth, arguments of that sort can just
drag on until the world comes to an end.[4]

MYSELF: You also told me that you would show me your
article on the Debts. . .

CLEMENCEAU: Yes that's easy. It's over there, in a
corner. . . I'll give it to you presently. Next, Martet.

MYSELF: Next, sir — it's rather complicated. I should like

---

[4] On the eve of the Armistice Clemenceau received the following letter:
*"Dear Mr. President,*
  I wanted to let the flood of congratulations which you received on your birth-
day go by before sending you my own on the occasion. I am not forgetful of
the past and I have a faithful memory. But what I want to express to you today
is the sentiment which we all hold on this march to victory, a sentiment which
has led our soldiers to bestow on you the very charming nickname of "Father
Victory."
  Please accept this expression of my loyal devotion.
                                                        ALFRED DREYFUS
Lt. Colonel Dreyfus
Commanding the artillery arsenal at Orléans'

to ask you how your mind was moulded. I own that it rather confuses me. I don't even perceive the influences which acted upon you.

CLEMENCEAU [*at first opened his eyes wide. After a few seconds his surprise disappeared and he began to disentangle and arrange his ideas.*] Well, I think that the only influence which had any effect on me was — yes, my father's.[5] Where did he imbibe his ideas ? Certainly not from his family, which was practically all unfriendly to him. I believe that he got them from Michelet, of whom he always spoke with the greatest respect. My father was at bottom a romantic who had carried the literary theories of Victor Hugo and those people over into politics and sociology.

In the ordinary course of the day I didn't see my father much — he didn't do a great deal, and like all people who don't do anything, was always very busy. But at table — my father wasn't a man who attached great importance to the pleasures of the table — he spoke largely of his reading, enunciated his philosophy in fits and starts and, little by little, I absorbed it. He used to talk about Danton. I must say that I wasn't for Danton.

MYSELF: Nor Robespierre either ?

CLEMENCEAU: No, by God. What a mongrel lot of fellows they were ! Mangy dogs ! My father's influence began to get hold of me when I entered the Academy at Nantes as a student in philosophy. I was a day-scholar. So, in the evenings, at dinner, my father. . .

MYSELF: Were your parents living at Nantes then ?

CLEMENCEAU: Yes.[6] My father was practising medicine in a vague way. Luckily he never had a single patient — he'd have killed them abruptly. He used to ask me at dinner,

---

[5] Geffroy has drawn a very vivid picture of Clemenceau's father: 'His hands clasped behind him under his grey coat, wearing his straw hat and his coarse, heavy shoes, his face shaved to the eyes which flashed behind gleaming spectacles, a half-smile playing about his carefully shaved lips . . .'

[6] 8, Rue de Calvaire.

'What did you learn today?' I would tell him. I would repeat the clerical theories which had been served up to me during the day, on the soul, on life, death, and so forth, and he would discuss them. I was caught between two fires. The next day in class I would turn to my philosophy instructor — I was very outspoken — and say to him, 'But there is a counter-argument, sir, to what you're saying. How can you reconcile this one and that other. . .'

MYSELF: It was your debut in interpellations. . .

CLEMENCEAU: Once, pointing my finger at my instructor, I said, 'But you're losing the thread of your argument.'

His answer was, 'Leave the room!'

At Nantes my father used to go to a reading-room — I saw the house again some time ago — it belonged to Père Plançon — I don't know if the reading-room still exists. It was a large room, a little larger than this one, where people came to read and gossip — odd folk, who had seen the Revolution and Napoleon. My father pointed one of them out to me and said, 'Do you see that man over there. He's an old friend of Marat.'

I wasn't very clear as to who Marat was or what he had done, but Marat was a colossal name which struck me because of its association with all that blood, that bathtub, Charlotte Corday. Therefore I had a great respect for this old fellow.

All these people were peaceable and tolerant bourgeois, but naturally there were some police-spies amongst them. My father used to walk back and forth in this room, holding forth on the Empire and the priests. He did it so often that in 1858 they arrested him. It was in relation to Orsini's attempt at assassination. There's no need to tell you that my father had been involved in Orsini's affairs about as much as you or I. I remember going with my mother to see him in prison, and bringing him his little valise, for he was going to be sent to Algeria; in front of the spies I went up to him and said, 'I'll avenge you !'

He answered, 'If you want to avenge me, work ! [7]

He went away. Whereupon they must have realized that he wasn't very dangerous. He had a little money and therefore wouldn't want to bring society down. . . He arrived at Marseilles and was about to embark when the order came to let him return. Then there was a terrific scene between my father and the prefect of police. My father, shouting at the top of his lungs, said to the prefect, 'You'll see, I've no need to bind my son to Hannibal's vow. You'll have enough trouble with this lad yet !' [8]

MYSELF: Did your father go back to Nantes?

CLEMENCEAU: Yes. He had to, not being allowed to leave it. Then, since his family had taken refuge at l'Aubraie, he left the windows and shutters open, in order to make it seem that there was someone in the flat — we lived on the ground floor and the whole place might have been burgled — he leaped on a horse and arrived at l'Aubraie, having evaded the police.

And it would all have gone off very nicely if my sister Emma — the only one of my sisters still alive — hadn't gone mad on learning of my father's arrest. She remained in that condition eighteen months — she had to be taught to read all over again.[9]

---

[7] Certain people have tried to fix this scene seven years earlier. Geffroy, particularly, writes, 'Arrested at the time of the Coup d'Etat of 1851 . . .' Georges Clemenceau would have been rather young. . .

[8] A little pamphlet mentioned by Mr. Henry Cassira, *The Suspects of 1858*, gives the names of M. Clemenceau's 'accomplices' — 'Several days after Orsini's attempt, the report spread to Nantes that orders had gone forth to arrest a number of respectable citizens who were known as republicans. Their names were: Clemenceau, doctor of medicine, Masselin, printer, Even, tiler, Pageot, tanner, Leseux, labourer.'

[9] *The Suspects of 1858:* 'Doctor Clemenceau had nothing of the conspirator about him; but, of a fine and subtle mind, he had more than once vented his sarcasms at the expense of certain persons who hated him because of his pointed and biting epigrams. He was about to be embarked for Africa when a grave occurrence, which had profoundly agitated public opinion at Nantes, compelled the authorities to give way. At the time of his removal, in fact, his daughter, a

I recall two scenes connected with my father, who was an extraordinary man, reserved yet ebullient — they may have been told me or I may have witnessed them. The first happened during the June uprisings, I should tell you that I had an uncle, Paul Clemenceau, my father's brother, an altogether charming man, a bit reactionary. . .

MYSELF: What did he do?

CLEMENCEAU: He hunted. He was never known to do anything else. He had a pack and a whipper-in with which he went hunting with the bloods of the countryside, self-invited — he was a bit of a gate-crasher — and we never overlooked a chance of rubbing it in. Well, when the Assembly felt itself threatened, it appealed for help to the provinces against the Parisians. All the Vendeans had armed and equipped themselves and one day, I remember, I went into the kitchen and saw my uncle's whipper-in melting up bullets. My uncle Paul was getting ready to go! My father was informed and came in as if blown by the wind. He said to my uncle, 'Paul, if you go to defend those swine, I'll go too — I'll go and join the Parisians.'

So in the end no one went. The two brothers were very fond of each other. My uncle Paul was a naturally pleasant and charming man. . .

MYSELF: What's become of him?

CLEMENCEAU: What becomes of all of us? He died, of scarlatina — which enabled my father to bring us up properly. For my father wasn't rich. With my uncle's money, since my father was a good manager and economical, he was able to make ends meet.

MYSELF: What was the other scene?

young woman of marked talent, had been suddenly struck down by catalepsy, in consequence of which she lost her speech. For several months she hovered between life and death. The entire city of Nantes participated in the sufferings of this unhappy family and such severe censure was expressed that the authorities had Dr. Clemenceau brought back without delay.'

CLEMENCEAU: It took place when my father was arrested in 1858; there was a friend of his, a good fellow, but not very clever, who turned up and said triumphantly, 'I've been able to get a letter of introduction for you from the Bishop of Nantes to the Bishop of Algiers.'

'Leave me alone, you idiot. It's you and those like you who are sending me there.'

And he tore up the letter.

MYSELF: How old were you when you left Mouilleron ?

CLEMENCEAU: I must have been two or two and a half.

MYSELF: Where did you go ?

CLEMENCEAU: We went to Nantes.

MYSELF: Didn't you go to l'Aubraie ?

CLEMENCEAU: Well, we went there now and then. My father adored horses. My brothers and I were brought up on horseback.

MYSELF: And your studies ? Before you went to college ?

CLEMENCEAU: It was my mother who first undertook them. I should add that she taught all my sisters. There wasn't one of them who went to boarding-school. My mother was an extraordinary woman. She learned Latin in order to be able to teach it to me. After that I went to a little private class. Then to the academy. I remember that I entered in the fifth form.

MYSELF: What sort of memories have you of it ?

CLEMENCEAU: Pleasant ones. I realize now that they didn't teach me anything they should have taught me. My instructor in the fifth standard was the father of Vallès, a violent man who always seemed on the point of swallowing everybody up, but there was no harm in him. I had an instructor in history and geography — what was his name ? Gregory ! He wrote some quite well-known books. Well, just think, he taught us geography without an atlas. He dictated his lessons: 'The Loire has tributaries on the right. . .' And history in the same way, 'Dagobert II ascended the throne in. . .' Is that how they always teach in the schools ?

MYSELF: I had an instructor of anatomy who dictated his courses in the same way: 'The back of the eye is covered with the filaments of a nerve (he pronounced it nervvv) which is called the o-pe-tic nervvv. . .'

CLEMENCEAU: It's dreadful. They made me translate Demosthenes at the rate of three lines a month. Just the thing to make me disgusted with him forever. When I wanted to get a translation of Demosthenes in French in order to try to understand something, I had to get my father's permission. There I remained until I took my bachelor's degree.[10]

MYSELF: Were you a good student ?

CLEMENCEAU: Not too good. I don't think that I took many prizes.[11] My father promised me ten francs if I passed the examinations for my degree. I did pass them. I'm still waiting for the money.

MYSELF: After taking your degree did you at once take up medicine ?

[10] On the 27th May 1922 Clemenceau was present at the unveiling of the Monument to the Dead of the Nantes Academy. He made a few short speeches. In one of them he said, 'I went through this old academy. At that time children weren't very sensible. They had impudent faces, sharp tongues, and a mischievous light in their eyes. They have become men — at what a cost. I don't know how you regard me exactly — perhaps like one of those old owls, beating his wings against the breeze, whom our country-folk nail to their barn doors for the crime, according to the story-teller, of being able to see by night. In Athens the owl was the bird of wisdom. . .'

[11] It was amusing to look up the prizes and honours won by Clemenceau as a student:

Fifth standard: Fourth honours (*accessit* — next to prizeman) in Latin composition.
Second honours in classic oratory and elocution.
Fourth standard: None.
Third standard: Second honours in English.
Second honours in elocution.
Second standard: Third honours in chemistry.
Third honours in oratory.

In rhetoric the highest standard but one, and in natural history the second prize. Honourable mentions in French oration and in English. In philosophy Clemenceau demonstrated his powers: he carried off the first prize for Latin translation and the first prize for his French essay.

CLEMENCEAU: Without delay. My father had been a doctor, so had my grandfather and great-grandfather. I took my examinations and entered the School of Medicine.

MYSELF: Are your memories of it pleasant?

CLEMENCEAU: Very. If you want to study medicine properly, there's no doubt you must do it in the provinces. There's no lack of 'cracks,' and the atmosphere is right. Bonds are forged between professors and students which do not exist in Paris. There was only one boring feature — the good Sisters. I would go into their garden and eat their apricots. Then I'd say to them, 'What difference does it make to you, since in any event they don't go to the patients?'

I was suspended a fortnight for my pains. I went back there a little while ago, and it was exactly the same. I wanted to see the operating-theatre and was told, 'It's very tiresome, but a Sister has the key and she's at Mass.'

MYSELF: At heart you have a delightful quality of youth. . .

CLEMENCEAU: Yes, I realize it. Add to the above a distant cousin of my grandfather's who nearly married him and who in the end married one of Charles X's bodyguard. While riding in the Champs-Elysées this bodyguardsman and his wife were run over and she, having broken something that ought not to be broken, couldn't have any children; they lived in a pretty château, Vachonnière near Mortagne. They had some fine property in Mortagne as well. It now belongs to a M. de Grandcourt. We'll go to see it. When I wanted to go off on a jaunt with a girl, I'd establish my alibi there. I would spend a fortnight at Nantes and a day at Vachonnière.

MYSELF: And then you did your thesis. . .

CLEMENCEAU: Yes. On the *Generation of Anatomic Elements.*

MYSELF: I haven't read it. I should like to.

CLEMENCEAU: Oh, it's of no interest. It's a compilation. But there are two or three passages which might amuse you.

*[He gets up and takes a book from the chest of drawers.]*
There you are. It's the second edition, the one with Robin's preface. It was published by a man called Germer-Baillère, who offered to republish my thesis in exchange for a translation of one of Stuart Mill's books. When I left for America I took the Stuart Mill volume with me, and translated it there. It was my apprenticeship to English.[12]

MYSELF: You left for America in 1865 and returned in 1869. What did you do out there?

CLEMENCEAU: Because of two or three ladies who were interested in me I established myself in New York, afterwards I gave lessons in a school for young ladies at Stamford, Connecticut. I went there on Mondays and came back on Tuesdays, sleeping there on Monday nights. What did I teach them? A little French — I also taught them riding. Now and then they'd tumble off into a ditch. It was there I got married.[13]

MYSELF: Have you kept up relations with your old schoolmates at Nantes?

CLEMENCEAU: Well, there were four of them who could excel in whatever subject they chose. One has become a tax-collector somewhere, another a customs clerk, the third a notary's clerk and the fourth — I forget what — even less than

---

[12] *Auguste Comte and Positivism, a translation by Dr. Georges Clemenceau.* Paris, Germer-Baillère, 1868. A new edition was published by Alcan, in 1893.

[13] 'The Mayor of the Commune of la Réorthe, canton of Sainte-Hermine (Vendée), certifies that he has published and posted on successive Sundays, the 9th and 16th of the present month, the proclamation of marriage between Monsieur Georges Benjamin Clemenceau, Doctor of Medicine, aged 27, born at Mouilleron-en-Pareds and resident at Réorthe, bachelor, the legitimate son, of full age, of Monsieur Benjamin Clemenceau and his wife Emma Gautreau, householders, resident at la Réorthe.

'And Miss Mary Plummer, householder, born and resident at Springfield, Massachusetts, United States of America, aged 19, spinster, minor and legitimate daughter of Mr. Plummer and his wife Mary Taylor resident at Springfield.

'We further certify that we have been notified of no opposition to this marriage.

Mairie de la Réorthe, 23rd May, 1869

*The Mayor*
A. GAULY.'

The marriage took place in New York on the 23rd of June.

the others . . . which proves that you mustn't attach too great importance to scholastic success.

MYSELF: Do you like to call up memories of your youth?

CLEMENCEAU: Ah, what a youth I had. I see all those people again — there were mediocrities amongst them — and superior people as well — very superior. My grandmother Joubert was a fine pattern of a woman. She was the one who was present at the capture of Montaigu by the Chouans.[14] The Chouans had for artillery one old cannon which came somehow or other from the château of Richelieu. I've told you also how, on seeing a Chouan who was armed only with a stick she said to him, 'But what are you going to fight with, my good man? Haven't you got a rifle?'

'Oh, no, Madame, there aren't enough for everybody.'

'What are you going to do, then?'

'Well, when the battle begins, I'll kneel in a corner and tell my beads.'

Not a bad idea, eh?

There's another I regret, my uncle Paul. Everybody loved him. One day my brother Paul had gone to l'Aubraie. My grandfather looked at him, like this, and said to him, 'You bear a name which is very dear to us.'

My grandfather was Mayor of Réorthe, which includes l'Aubraie. When my father was released in 1858 he went to my grandfather and said, 'You're going to resign as mayor at once, do you hear, or you'll never see me again in all your life.'

That was the tone he used to him. You can understand why my grandfather's favourite was Paul, who was always smiling and care-free.

MYSELF: Can't you give me your article on the Debts?

CLEMENCEAU: Oh, yes. [*He takes the manuscript from his wardrobe.*] There. I'll throw in the dust as well.

[14] Vendée rebels in the Revolution.

MYSELF: Will you allow me to come back this week ?

CLEMENCEAU: Do come. I haven't told you everything. I haven't given you my recollections of prison. When I've told you everything I'll take you to the Vendée and lead you to strange nooks and corners, where, one day in my life, there appeared to me such. . . The Copse is a mysterious thing. I'll show you that Wood of Madness, which is certainly an ancient sacred grove. It's there, dominating the entire country. No one lays a hand on it. The people say that it's a landmark for boats. It's not true. They leave it unmolested because from generation to generation the word has been handed down. . .

You will see — the Vendeans are agreeable folk. The Vendean women are small and well-knit; they don't seem to stir, they don't say anything, whatever the situation. There was — still another story, Martet — a girl whom we used to know. One day she appealed to my father. Something had gone wrong. It came out that she was about to have a child. My father said to her, 'But how did it happen ?'

'Well,' she said, 'a commercial traveller was going along the road on horseback.'

'I see. He began to tell you jokes, you answered — and the needle was threaded. . .'

'No. He got off his horse, tied it to a tree, and that's how it happened.'

'But didn't you say anything ?'

'No. What could I say ?'

# XLI

## THE DEBTS — CLEMENCEAU AND THE PRESIDENCY

*29th June* 1928

CLEMENCEAU: I've just discovered a book. Guess what it is.

MYSELF: ? ? ?

CLEMENCEAU: Mommsen's *History of Rome.*

MYSELF: Hadn't you ever read it ?

CLEMENCEAU: Yes, but I'm reading it again. What do you think — I've had the idea of writing a book on the decadence of Rome.

MYSELF: A good idea. It will be a pendant to *Démosthène.* You can never tell these people too much about decadence, how certain ways of looking at things are bound to lead to their destruction.

CLEMENCEAU: That's so, isn't it ? I think I'll be able to entertain you with it. . .

MYSELF: I've brought back your article on the Debts and your medical thesis. I won't compliment you on your work on the debt question — you're making fun of it. But it's all right. All the arguments are there. It's written with a loftiness and at the same time a brutality that should shake without wounding. Even the Americans can't fail to understand.

CLEMENCEAU: I think that Hoover will be elected. Smith has the fact of his being a Catholic against him.

MYSELF: Oughtn't it to be ?

CLEMENCEAU: No. That sort of thing's very bad. Observe that Catholicism over there is not a State institution, as here. It's a religion. What difference can it make to them if a man eats a wafer or a piece of bread ? But they are like that. I shall not publish my article until after the election. Even not then unless the question of the debts comes up. If the discussion is opened I shall say, 'Excuse me, but I too have a word to say.'

MYSELF: Next, your medical thesis. . .

CLEMENCEAU: Did it put you to sleep ?

MYSELF: Not at all. On the contrary I found it very interesting. Fifty years removed, it's yet the first seed of *Au Soir de la Pensée*.

CLEMENCEAU: Really ?

MYSELF: Yes indeed.

CLEMENCEAU [*reflectively*]: It's true — there's that in it.

MYSELF: There are the same ideas and the same manner. People who reproach you for your changeableness have only to read that thesis.

CLEMENCEAU: Oh, the people who reproach me for changeableness. They're the ones who consider constancy to be the act of thinking of nothing. A bit of crust in a corner doesn't change its opinions. They forget one thing — that the bit of crust has no opinions.

MYSELF: All your theories of matter which appeared in *Au Soir de la Pensée* are in your thesis. You haven't changed them in the least. . . I'm surprised at one thing — how did your examiners in 1865 have the courage to accept that thesis ?

CLEMENCEAU: Not only did they accept it, but they gave me a specially good diploma.[1]

---

[1]      THE FRENCH EMPIRE
       DIPLOMA OF DOCTOR OF MEDICINE
          *In the Name of the Emperor*
THE Minister and Secretary of State for the department of Public Instruction.
Having examined the certificate of proficiency for the rank of Doctor of Medicine

MYSELF: They were hardly the ideas of Napoleon III, however.

CLEMENCEAU: Not exactly. But don't deceive yourself, my poor friend — they hadn't read it.[2] It was a thing outside of their line and it didn't interest them. Instead of questioning me on my thesis, as they should have done, there was a member of the Board, Potain, who examined me — can you guess on what — scarlet fever ! That made Robin, who was in charge of the thesis and who understood its argument, burst into an exclamation. Have you read what he wrote in the preface to the second edition ?

MYSELF: Yes, I also read, in that second edition, your heated arguments on the origin of things and what you had to say, without evasion, of those people who claim that you can derive something out of nothing.

CLEMENCEAU: Really ? What did I say about that ?

MYSELF: It's an observation at the end of the book [*Reading*] 'Great caution should be exercised lest we attach the meaning "beginning" to the word "origin." As a matter of fact "beginning" is something of which we can form no conception having never seen and being unable to imagine the possibility of it. If matter could issue from "nothing," unquestionably it would begin. But what is "nothing" ? How can we represent it to ourselves ? What conception can we

granted, on 13th May 1865, by the Faculty of Medicine of the University of Paris, to Monsieur Georges Benjamin Clemenceau, born at Mouilleron-en-Pareds, department of the Vendée, on the 28th September 1841.

Having examined the approval given to this certificate by the Rector of the said University.

Now ratify the said certificate and

Give by these presents to the said Clemenceau the diploma of Doctor of Medicine, to enjoy it with all the rights and prerogatives therewith associated by laws, decrees, and regulations.

30th May 1865

[The signatures follow, including that of the recipient.]

[2] Raoul Ducray states that 'theses of the doctorate type were very much in vogue at that time. Ferdinand Taule, Clemenceau's comrade who contributed with him to *Travail* and who was acquainted with the same judges and the same prisons and was for a long time director of the Lariboisière Hospital, had also submitted one of these materialistic theses.'

CLEMENCEAU IN 1872

CLEMENCEAU DURING HIS
STUDENT DAYS IN 1862

form of it ? If I go directly to the meaning of this word, I find a negation and nothing else. Our minds can grasp matter and only matter. When we express the thought of "nothing," we merely picture a negation of matter. It is very simple to recognize that that is purely subjective and without reality. . .'

CLEMENCEAU: But of course !

MYSELF: '*Nothing* equals *not something.* Something is an objective conception. The absence of something is a subjective one. Being unable to understand *nothing,* we find ourselves unable to conceive of a beginning. And not only can we not conceive of it, but we can assert that there can't be any. . .'

CLEMENCEAU: Otherwise, reason has no meaning and there's no purpose in writing books. . .

MYSELF: '*Ex nihilo nihil.* Even if that nihil had any reality, any beginning would nevertheless remain an inexplicable thing. The coming-into-being of matter would imply, in fact, an origin outside itself, a force without a base to rest on, a quality without a possessor, a non-sense, in a word. . .'

CLEMENCEAU: All of *Au Soir de la Pensée* is there !

MYSELF: 'This idea of "beginning" is therefore completely devoid of meaning; it is counterfeit money which should be left to the Don Quixotes of Pure Reason to use as currency amongst themselves. What they, in fact, call the origin of things is the beginning of the world, a thing impossible to explain which they nevertheless do explain, a thing beyond understanding (I mean for a healthy brain) which they make it their profession to understand.'

CLEMENCEAU: It's very entertaining. I don't remember having said that. I can turn my pen in the inkwell three times and try to give thirty-six turns to my thoughts; I shall never be able to think in any other way. There will always be a great many people to tell you, 'On Monday God created light; on Tuesday He created the sun.' For according to the Bible that's how the good God worked. First He created light and then he created the source of that light. There are millions of people who read and repeat that. They believe in it unshakably. You know, there are two ways for man. There is the domain of the reason and the domain where reason has no place — where it is forbidden to reason to enter. That can go on a long time. Don't forget, presently ask me for my book. My first edition.[3] Now put your question.

MYSELF: Well, amongst your papers I came across the trail of a man with whom you were very close before leaving for America in 1865, a man called Jourdan.

CLEMENCEAU: Jourdan. Yes indeed.

MYSELF: Who died of cholera in 1866 and seems to have played an important part in your life. . .

CLEMENCEAU: Yes, that's right.

MYSELF: Who was this Jourdan ?

[3] The cover of the first edition reads:

DE LA GÉNÉRATION
DES
ELEMENTS ANATOMIQUES
PAR
le Dr. George [sic] CLEMENCEAU
Ex-interne des Hôpitaux de Nantes
Ex-interne provisoire des Hôpitaux de Paris

Paris
J.-B. BAILLIÈRE ET FILS
Libraires de l'Académie Impériale de Médecine
Rue Hautefeuille 19.
1865

Robin's preface is missing. Instead there is a 'declaration by the author.'
'The exact observation of phenomena is science's point of departure — to group and analyse them is its purpose. I bring forward no new discoveries; I merely assemble the facts.
'I alone am responsible for the opinions I express. I do not hold them because I have written this work; I have written this work because I hold them.

I hope that M. Robin will accept my thanks for his kindness in allowing me to make use of him, helping me with advice and providing me with whatever information I required.'
M. Robin's preface to the second editions begins with these words, 'M. Clemenceau's purpose has been to exhibit the whole group of facts, specific and general, the study of which has led him to the conclusions he expresses relative to the manner in which anatomical elements are generated. "Substitute" the manner in which anatomical elements are generated "by" the problem of the universe' and you have an excellent description of *Au Soir de la Pensée*.

CLEMENCEAU: I had known him while I was a medical student in Paris. I had met him at the café at the corner of the Boulevard St. Michel and the Boulevard St. Germain. Do you know it ? It was there that people like Andrieux, Lefont, and others used to meet. Jourdan was about twenty years older than I. He was descended from the Marshal Jourdan, the Fleurus man. He was a fellow with brains, strength, and fine spirited eloquence. He had had the rare good luck to be appointed Crown solicitor by Louis Philippe in that island called — is it Bourbon Island ? No — La Réunion. Bourbon Island became Maurice.

MYSELF: I think Maurice had been the Ile de France.

CLEMENCEAU: Then that's it. It's Bourbon that became la Réunion. You get lost in all those islands.

I remember — it's an amusing tale — meeting the Governor of Maurice Island at Ceylon, during a voyage to India. . . He spoke French as well as you or I, and when I showed my surprise, he said, 'But I'm compelled to. Everybody speaks French out there, the newspapers are published in French, the plays are performed in French. Sometime ago some people came to me and said, "We'd like to belong to France again." I replied, "I don't see anything against it, but don't forget that England bought you last year for twenty millions in sugar." So they went away. Next day they returned and said, "Well, there's no hurry about it." So that's how it remained.'

Where was I ?

MYSELF: Jourdan. . .

CLEMENCEAU: Oh, yes. He had married a wife who had been married before and brought Jourdan a small fortune. Jourdan, who wasn't rich and had great delicacy in these matters, although a former Crown Solicitor, showed the greatest respect for his wife, always called her 'Madame,' and in order to be sure to derive no advantage from this money lived completely apart. I don't even know if he shared his wife's bed — he was probably afraid of wearing out the sheets. It was quite a strange household. Jourdan introduced me to his wife, and I became a friend of hers; after Jourdan died she made me her residuary legatee. She left me a Poussin — I kept it with me, or near me, for many years. Then I grew tired of it — it's easy to grow tired of Poussin. So I sold it. It's now in America. As regards Jourdan I had a great friendship for him combined with a deep respect. When I left for the United States in 1865 we agreed to keep up contact and write each other. The other day I found some letters addressed to Jourdan from me. I burnt them.

MYSELF: You were wrong.

CLEMENCEAU: Oh, burning's a good thing. And Jourdan used to write me — When he died I really felt as if I had lost the last support to which I could cling — I was alone. It was a deep sorrow. [*He muses.*] Jourdan — I'm glad you spoke to me of Jourdan. I've got a photograph of him, I believe. If I find it I'll give it to you.

MYSELF: I notice amongst your papers that your father took you to London to see Stuart Mill before you left for America.

CLEMENCEAU: Yes.

MYSELF: What did he talk to you about ?

CLEMENCEAU: Oh, various angles of positivism. I was going to translate a book by him on the subject. We had a talk about it. [*He gets up, leaves the room, and returns with a shockingly dirty book.*] Here's my thesis. It's the copy which I took to America with me. Hold on — there are some leaves which I gathered out there in it. [*He offers it to me. A silence.*] Poor Jourdan. I see him again, in that café. . .

MYSELF: Democracy was a lovely thing in those days. . .

CLEMENCEAU: Yes, like all things which are yet to be born.

MYSELF: I also found amongst your papers some documents relating to the 16th May. There was a sort of committee of delegates from the left, amongst whom were Gambetta,

Charles Floquet, and others, who used to meet at Léon Renault's — you were the secretary. Who was Léon Renault?

CLEMENCEAU: Well, he became Prefect of Police, poor devil, and I think he's still living in some corner or other. Can you imagine Gambetta, at that time, a fellow swamped in illusions, getting himself into the frame of mind of a conspirator? He had annexed himself to a general of the name of Yung, I think, and with the help of the general we were going to do amazing things, Gambetta and I — for I was a sort of understudy to him. It was going to happen at Lille. There's no need for me to depict for you Gambetta's conspiracies — they were screamingly funny. Naturally I had taken the matter very seriously, on account of Gambetta, on account of this general — because I was young and because, I must admit, it often happens that when one takes things seriously like that, well, you never know, they can become serious. Things are not serious in themselves.

MYSELF: No?

CLEMENCEAU: Certainly not. They're serious because of the conviction you put into them. However, I took this all very seriously, and gave each Deputy or Senator I brought along a slip of paper bearing a number and instructions for his particular job on the great day. We met in a café — near the Rue du Bac — on the site where the State Deposit and Consignment Bank now is. MacMahon stopped all that, fortunately. Otherwise it is obvious that we should all have gone to prison.

MYSELF: But you didn't apprise the delegates of the left of your plans?

CLEMENCEAU: No. Certainly not.

MYSELF: Then what happened in the committee?

CLEMENCEAU: Nothing. What always happens in committees, nothing ever happens. They just jabber away into the air. There were as many opinions as delegates, and no one was able to persuade anyone else, every man spoke for himself and only listened to himself. Just a muddle.[4] I've spent my life playing politics with people who didn't know what they wanted. Who didn't even know where they were and why they were there. Perhaps you haven't noticed it, but since I let go the reins, there is no longer a Parliament. There is no longer either a majority or a minority, nothing but vague thrusting. People no longer know around whom to group themselves and whom to follow. They need someone to tell them 'Do this or that !' Then they'd be for that man or against him. More likely against. For an Assembly looks at you askance if you tell it that it must do something. The present Parliament is nothing — that of fifty years ago didn't amount to much either.

MYSELF: Another question, sir; I want to bring you to 1919–1920 — to the subject of the Presidency of the Republic. You've been censured for not putting yourself forward as candidate for the Presidency of the Republic in 1920, and it is said that if you had done so, you would have been elected, which I personally believe. . .

CLEMENCEAU: But you aren't in the least informed on the matter. Think back to the time when I was shot at by that fellow — what's his name ? Cottin — I stayed here a week with a bullet in my back. Whereafter I got up and went to the Chamber still with my bullet. The newspapers reported that when I entered the room, the Deputies cheered. But mark this, Martet — when I entered, not a cheer was raised, not a single one. Yet, good God, I still had that bullet in my

---

[4] Clemenceau himself drew up the minutes — in a handwriting often quite illegible — of the sittings of the 'Committee of the Members of the Left of the Chamber of Deputies.' Here is the report of the meetings of the 8th November 1877; it was held in the morning at M. Léon Renault's. 'Present: MM. Proust, Louis Blanc, Clemenceau, L. Renault, Floquet, Lépine, Gambetta, Brisson, Albert Grévy, Goblet, J. Ferry, Lockrov, etc.

'The meeting is opened. Clemenceau is appointed secretary.'

A long and heated debate, led by Gambetta, follows, on the constitution of the Chamber and the 'griefs of the country' and the complaints of the Left against the Right for its electoral policy.—*Translator's note.*

body — with which a gentleman did me the favour, without any request on my part, of thanking me for what I had done for the country. . . I hadn't committed suicide !

Well, not one cheer. There you have the sentiments of the Chamber with respect to me.[5] At the public ballot they all voted for me solidly, of course, and with all their might — the country had its eye on them. But at the secret ballot naturally those gentlemen were out to get their own back. They dragged up heaps of reasons. It was rumoured that I was about to marry a mistress; then that I was very ill, half-senile — what about Deschanel, eh ? [6] — and that it would be tantamount to a state burial of me in the Elysée Palace, something to be avoided at all costs. I was consequently fed up with the business even before it began. Furthermore — from this point of view I am a little nearer the Republican spirit than all those fellows who present themselves for the presidency as for the Academy, with their polite calls, their gossip, their promises and undertakings — I hold that one doesn't become a candidate for a place like that. In any event that feeling's stronger than I — I've never been a candidate for anything. The proposal comes from the outside, not from me. Mandel, by dint of pestering me, obtained a paper from me in which I said that if my friends wanted to vote for me, I would submit to gentle pressure.[7] After this came the conference in

[5] On the 5th December 1918 Clemenceau ascended the rostrum of the Chamber to announce the surrender of Austria. M. Lauche shouted, 'Tell us about the Salonika Army ?' M. Camille Rebou, 'You've begun by criticizing.' While Deschanel was begging them not to interrupt Clemenceau, M. Raffin-Dugens was heard to fling out 'Say "Long live the Dictator" and have done with it.' Then Clemenceau resumed his seat. MM. Mayéras and Renaudel asked leave to put questions. M. Renaudel declared, 'Those who consider that the country expects its representatives to ask for the whole truth have a right to be heard.' There were murmurs. M. Renaudel proceeded, 'I know that in these enthusiastic sessions everything one says gets distorted . . .' MM. Bracke, Moutet, Longuet, and others offered shocked and grieved protests. 'There are already a number of them who won't forgive the victory' said Clemenceau that evening.

[6] It will be recalled that the late President Deschanel lost control of his mental faculties.—*Translator's note.*

[7] The newspapers of 15th January 1920 published the following paragraph: 'M. Clemenceau has formally authorized his friends to present him as candidate for

the Senate where the trial run was held.[8]  In view of the result I withdrew my name.[9]  You see, it's very simple.

MYSELF:  But why did Parliament dislike you so much ?

CLEMENCEAU:  My friend, for a very obvious reason: because, though in form I was addressing myself to Parliament, it was always to the country to which I spoke in reality.  My speeches always went over the heads of the Deputies and Senators and I always made them understand that, defeated or not, it was always the country which could, in the last resort, judge between me and them.  That's what I did in the Malvy Business.  When they told me, in 1916, 'You've only six votes,' I replied, 'That's of no importance.  The country will pass upon it.'  And that's what happened.

the Presidency of the Republic, stating that he was ready to accept the post if the Convention were to entrust him with it.  Consequently the friends of the President of the Council have decided to have voting papers printed in his name and put them before the members of the two houses who are to take part in the full Convention.'

On the 15th Clemenceau received one of the Deputies.  He told him 'Once I've been nominated by the full Convention, I shan't try to get out of it.'  He added, 'Entrust me with two more years.  I've won the war — the peace must now be won.'

[8] On the 16th January, in the Salle des Brosses of the Senate.  It was open to all the members of Parliament.  There were 812 votes.  Deschanel received 408; Clemenceau, 389; M. Poincaré, 16; M. Léon Bourgeois, 5; M. Jonnart, 3; Marshal Foch, 1.

[9] Immediately after the result of the vote was announced, the Cabinet ministers and Under Secretaries went to see the President of the Council.  A conference took place.  Clemenceau wrote the following to the President of the National Assembly: 'Mr. President,

I beg to inform you that I withdraw the permission I gave my friends to put me forward as candidate for the Presidency of the Republic, and that, if they go further and obtain for me a majority of the votes, I shall refuse the post so offered.

G. Clemenceau.'

The following day, at Versailles, 888 Senators and Deputies voted: Deschanel, 734; M. Jonnart, 54; Clemenceau, 53; M. Poincaré, 8; Marshal Foch, 8; M. Léon Bourgeois, 6.

The following events then took place:

On the 18th The Clemenceau cabinet resigned.  Millerand was called to the Elysée.

On the 24th of May Deschanel went to Montbrison to unveil the monument to Senator Emile Reymond.  At Montargis he fell out of the carriage window.

On the 21st September Clemenceau left for India.  Ignace, Mandel, Loucheur, Klotz, Raux, myself, and others went to see him off at the Gare du Lyon.  Waving of hats and handkerchiefs—and on the 23rd the Assembly elected Millerand President of the Republic.

Well, a Parliament doesn't like that sort of thing. A Parliament is always irritated with a man whose politics are national in scope. Furthermore they always held this against me, that I aroused a terrific distrust in my friends. I don't know why, but they were always in a terrible funk because I dragged them into places where they had no desire to go. It is obvious that they would have had no such fears with Deschanel. There wouldn't have been that business of the train. And the crossing-keeper's cabin,[10] all that extraordinary affair — like fiction in History, Martet — it was handled very nicely. He was charming, was Deschanel.[11]

MYSELF: One can't help wondering what would have happened if you had been elected.

CLEMENCEAU: There's nothing to wonder about, my dear fellow. I shouldn't have remained in office three months. What they wanted was someone who would let them alone. I shouldn't have waited a week before going off the deep end. You must realize that if I had agreed to take over that job, it wouldn't have been for the purpose of opening Horticultural Exhibitions. I should have done or tried to do something. You wouldn't have seen me giving my blessing to Locarno, to the reinstatement of those fellows who nearly did us in, and letting off traitors, spies, deserters, and other scoundrels of that kind. . . I should have jumped out of my coffin one fine day and said, 'No, I can't have that — I can't lend my name to that !' They chose Deschanel and they were perfectly right.

---

[10] After falling from the train Deschanel had been picked up by a crossing-keeper who was unable to believe that this man in pyjamas was the President of the Republic.

[11] When Clemenceau published *France before Germany* in 1916, he received this note from Deschanel:

*Dear Mr. President,*                                             *4th August* 1916

I've finished your book. It's magnificent. I can't deny myself the pleasure of telling you so. Etc. . .

Please accept, etc. . .

PAUL DESCHANEL

Do you see — the more I think of these things, of the kind of folly by which this country is possessed, as if victory had unbalanced it, the more it seems absolutely necessary that I write that book on Rome's decadence. It isn't that I like Rome, or feel any pity for her. What a vile people the Romans were at bottom — cold, surly, cruel, limited. I love Greece; I can't love Rome.

MYSELF: No they were complete opposites.

CLEMENCEAU: But there are some illuminating comparisons to draw and lessons to derive from them. They had their Deschanels — they had their Millerands. Millerand! When I remember that on leaving office I said to him, 'You're going to have matters in your hands now. I've been holding conversations with kings, cabinet ministers, and ambassadors for two years now; I'll tell you a little about what's been going on.'

He answered, 'It's hardly worth the trouble!'

I handed the Government of France over to him, I handed Europe over to him, Martet, and he took it as if it had been a pebble! Yes, and you may well say that when I needed somebody to govern Alsace, it was Millerand[12] whom I selected; he was still the best available. You see, my dear fellow, this world is far from perfect.

MYSELF: It was made too quickly.

CLEMENCEAU: Are you still coming to the Vendée?

MYSELF: More so than ever.

CLEMENCEAU: I should warn you so that you may warn your wife — the beds are a bit narrow.

MYSELF: We'll manage to squeeze in.

---

[12] I discovered amongst my papers a rather amusing document: an invitation in which, 'The President of the Republic and Madame Millerand beg that Monsieur Georges Clemenceau, Member of the French Academy, will honour them with his company at a soirée to be given in the Elysée Palace on Wednesday, January the twenty-fifth, at 10 o'clock.' In the upper right hand corner these two words appear in violet-coloured ink: '*In Uniform.*'

# XLII

## Jourdan

A LARGE yellow envelope on which a goose-quill has scrawled: *'Jourdan.'*
Four letters, all addressed to Clemenceau, tumble out.

### I

To Monsieur Georges Clemenceau, D.M. c/o M. Mataran
21, Bockmann Street, New York, U.S.A.

*Paris, 10th September 1865*

*My dear Georges:*

Your letter posted on August 21st arrived on the third of this month. I awaited it with impatience, as I hope you realize. I saw your father on his return from London — twice, in fact. I found him more cheerful and busy than depressed. It is true that he is reserved, and the stronger his feelings are the more he keeps them to himself. I needn't tell you that he freely resigns himself to your going away, but, underneath, he seems to be looking about for distractions in his lonesomeness and capable of finding them in the agricultural pursuits which so readily attract him. . . But regrets for what has been left behind shouldn't divert you from the duty of looking before you.

Your injunction was unnecessary and my slightly jealous friendship would have suffered too much from the commonplace piece of indiscretion which you fear to permit me to risk. I'm not surprised at the mood you're in. That's as it ought to be and I'm pleased because of it. It's a good thing to cling to your mother's petticoats and your father's affection, and I thank you for having shown me so simply the feelings which you can never have too strongly. I was deeply moved by what you told me of your impressions when you were saying good-bye to your father, and this gave me great pleasure, both for your sake and mine; for yours because I like to see you that way, knowing only too well that your pride will again assert itself, and for mine because, having never actually experienced these tender emotions, I like to think about them.

There is one point on which I am not in complete agreement with you. You say, 'You may well believe that I didn't write a word home about these feelings. . .' Why not? A word from the heart always does good, and it's no evidence of lofty virtue not to utter it to those who expect it but don't dare ask for it. To your mother, at least!

Your father described for me in detail, and very cheerfully, your interview with Stuart Mill. I thought that he would say a word about the commission with which you said he might entrust me, to find out about sending you your allowance. But he didn't speak of it, and as you well know, I on my side said nothing to him about it. This gives me cause for a complaint. You know your great fault — I remind you of it without ceremony. Men were made for you to walk beside, not over their heads, aristocrat that you are.[1] The less one has the right to ask, the more one demands; I'm like that, as you know. But why overlook speaking to your father about a thing that's already been arranged, and why on the other hand, tell Schmolk that I've been commissioned to pay

[1] The good Jourdan knew his Clemenceau well!

the freight on your cases of books from Paris to Havre, and to Sauve, the tailor's manager, that I am to send him some-thing every month on account of the 575 francs which you owe him,[2] when you haven't said a word to me about it ? This damned question of money makes me uneasy about you. You have too much — for your father has been very generous — to make it necessary to give up any large projects you may have, and you haven't enough to make it unnecessary for you to earn more. What are you going to do ? You may have to exercise great economy, dictated by a strong will. . .

Since your departure I'm quite alone and miss you more than I care to say.

I fled for four or five days immediately after you left, to go and kiss my wife. The trip did me good. Decidedly a devoted wife is a good thing and I feel myself realizing it all the more as I see so little else left to me.

I fancy that you have either remained in New York in the

---

[2] Clemenceau took away with him to America vast quantities of clothes and books.
Here are two bills for the year 1865.

OLD AND MODERN BOOKS
23, Boulevard Saint-Martin
ETIENNE SAUSSET
Successor to Achille Faure.

| | | |
|---|---|---|
| M. Clemenceau, Dr. 14 Juillet etc. etc. | 1 Challemel, Philosophie | 2.25 |
| | 1 Pouchet. Univers | 2.50 |
| | 1 Washington | 2.75 |
| | 1 Carlyle | 2.75 |
| | 1 Spinoza 3 vol. | 8.25 |
| | 1 Descartes | 1.75 |
| | 1 La Fontaine Fables | 3.50 |
| | | 6.— |
| | 1 De Maistre. La Pape. | 2.75 |

ASSOCIATION GÉNÉRALE
D'Ouvriers Tailleurs
33, Rue de Turbigo.

| | | | |
|---|---|---|---|
| M. Clemenceau, Dr. 23 Juillet 1865 etc. etc. | 1 Black frock-coat | 100. | Frcs. |
| | 1 Fleece-lined overcoat | 90. | " |
| | 1 Pair striped trousers | 38. | " |
| | 1 Pair of same | 35. | " |
| | 1 Pair wool trousers for summer | 32. | " |
| | 1 Pair black satin breeches | 38. | " |
| | 1 Black broadcloth waistcoat | 20. | " |

210 francs-a-week room which you found, or else that you went to Norwich, that you are going to set to work without delay and finish the translation of Mill's work on Positivism. It should be sent over in time for the new publishing season. It will be like dropping a card to your old friends. Lefort has left. Lafont has gone to live in the Batignolles quarter, and your Venus de Milo, who is now at home on my mantel-piece, sends you her Olympian greetings.

I should have a long letter from you in October; you will have recovered from the stupor which always goes with a great shaking-up, and in chatting with me about affairs, like a solicitor, and of the things that are going on under your eyes, like an intelligent onlooker, of yourself as a friend to a friend, you will give me a substitute for the brother and son I've never had. Don't forget me. My wife thanks you for your good wishes, and only complains of one thing, that you re-membered to send them so late.

Your devoted,

JOURDAN

## II

*The 11th November 1865*
*Pommier de Pin par Cour-Cheverny (Loir-et-Cher)*

*My dear Georges:*

I'm behindhand with this correspondence; I've had your let-ter since the 21st of October yet I'm only writing you now. You ask why my friendship and punctuality have failed? I've had a thousand things to do. Then I went to the country for a fortnight's rest and here I am at your disposal. You understand that to write you a casual word or two isn't in my line; I preferred to wait.

My wife's not getting on too badly; I'm quite well; my

affairs are in good shape; I'm satisfied; my mind is at ease. It's a good time for a chat.

Dear Georges, will you do me a great favour ? Let me 'tutoyer' you and treat you as a younger brother whom I love and for whom I have all the ambitions which my failings and my sense of proportion don't allow me to have for myself. You are far away and I miss you every day; you can grant me that much.

Before speaking with you for a bit about America, of which you are beginning to write so pleasantly, I should bring you up-to-date in news of the various friends or acquaintances you've left here, in so far as I know myself, for more and more I'm living the solitary life of a wolf.

Honour to whom honour is due. Pichat has a lawsuit on with Mangin. He is accused of an insult to religion and incitement to hatred and contempt for the Government by the quotation of some verses by Marc Monnier and their interpretation as follows: 'Agnes is the Church; Arnolphe the Pope; Horace Victor-Emmanuel and Paillasse is France.' The lawsuit seems absurd to me, but from that very fact I believe that it's a feud of long standing and that our friend will be badly nipped. The hearing will take place on the 16th.

Jobey wants to be remembered to you. He would like to have an exact description of the Federal and Confederate uniforms, with the distinguishing marks of rank. He is at grips with an American novel he's writing. I doubt whether he'll obtain fame and fortune from this work. He is better at singing about hunting and the table as a good liver than composing epic poems about the American Civil War.

There was a Convention of students at Liège. Regnard and Rey seem to have been the more or less fortunate heroes of the occasion. It seems that black crape was donned and swords flourished in honour of Materialism.

Politics are marking time and there's very little cholera

hasn't done to us.[3] A calmness prevails which outdoes the smooth surface of the Ocean when it sleeps. M. Hugo is singing about woods and streets.[4] I have no news about the second edition of your thesis, except that the thesis itself has been very favourably commented upon.

I wrote to Italy to try to get you a job as newspaper correspondent. Here is what the charming Mauro Marchi, who was re-elected at Cremona almost unanimously, answers, 'The Italian newspapers, even the most important ones, pay about as much attention to American affairs as they did in 1840, and, even if they are interested in them, are not in a position to pay a special correspondent. I'm sorry for your friend, but that's how matters stand. Mauro's answer, in view of the complete knowledge which he has of the Italian press and his friendship for me, shows me that it's hopeless to expect anything for you in that quarter. Can't we try somewhere else ? Who knows but what we might do something with the *Temps*[5] or the *Avenir*. You seem to have stumbled on a very good idea in wanting to do something for fame in the *Phare*. We should be able to get anything through Pichat.

It is unnecessary to tell you with what interest I read the second part of your letter. It was well said as well as well thought out. But you must take care of your eyes. We aren't handsome enough fellows to neglect those two lamps in which burns everything that's fine and good in you. The devil. I'm paying you compliments, so here I shall allow myself a very tiny stricture. . .

I like the picture of your Monsieur Forster: 'Customs have a higher value than law,' you say. 'The number of repressive laws which nullify themselves before taking effect is great. Over here it is the natural course of events.' Here is the answer; that course is the mark of a truly free country, which

---

[3] He was to die of it three months later.
[4] *Songs of the Streets and the Woods.* Appeared in 1866.
[5] We know that that advice was taken.

governs itself instead of receiving its impulses through external pressure. Law in such a country is much more an effect than a cause and one understands why it survives even after the reason which caused it has been replaced by another. I only think that you are wrong in saying, especially in reference to domestic life, that a social current is forming which has not yet been spoken of. In his second volume De Tocqueville[6] has an excellent chapter on this question. That's not to say that there has been nothing to analyse and note in the last thirty years. Far from it, but actually the movement you speak of has been observed. Amongst other things this movement clearly proves the powerful effects of a country's political institutions on its social economy. Just as there isn't the breadth of a hair between the political economy of the Institute of France and Carrey's yet these two systems, so similar and both regarded as true in two countries by their legislators, have produced quite different economic results.

I am not sorry about the great work of translating the book on logic — it would have required too much time and effort for a hollow honour and on conclusions which are always in dispute. I prefer the translation of Mill's book. It's more real. There has just appeared another work on utilitarianism, which has been translated in the *Revue Nationale*. It appears to be by a rejuvenated Bentham; I haven't read it yet.

My wife sends her affectionate greetings, and I too, with

---

[6] *Democracy in America* (1835)

I found amongst the memoranda which Clemenceau brought back from America two or three pages on which he scribbled spontaneously 'A few reflections' on 'Democracy in America.' 'It has been said that M. de Tocqueville's book had the rare good luck to please all parties. It's true, and I see a serious criticism in the fact. The book which pleases everybody is like a man who has no enemies. He may be honest, worthy, even interesting, but it is certain in advance that he lacks a centre, that he has no philosophy, and that even if by chance he stands for certain principles, he won't fight to the finish for any of them.' There are some interesting passages in these reflections. This one, for instance: 'When you do good, you stir up the ill-disposed against you. It is certainly less dangerous to do evil, for the hatred of well-disposed people, when they go as far as bringing themselves to hate, is infinitely less to be feared than that of the wicked, whom no consideration will soothe and whom no moral scruple will check.'

all my heart. Take care of yourself and send me exact instructions which I shall execute like a loyal soldier.

JOURDAN

## III

*Paris,* 10 *February* 1866

*My dear Georges:*

M. Dourlan, one of your former colleagues on the Committee, will bring you this letter. I had a visit from him, and at the same time learned that he was going to New York. I gave him a letter — I am not urging you to take him up. You know him better than I, and if I can judge by my personal impressions, he must be one of the friends whom you've missed and of whom you've thought. He has been overcome by a profound disillusion and is leaving to look for what one no longer finds here, men and a clean struggle in the full light of liberty.

He's not the only one in the grip of this new kind of upsidedown nostalgia. Rey left for Heidelberg two days ago, blessing his judges for having provided him so good an opportunity for seeking elsewhere all that life here is lacking. . . We've sunk lower than ever. I hated seeing Rey go; I used to see him every day and he had almost become a substitute for you. I like him so much because he reminds me of you by contrast every minute. I'm afraid he has nearly touched bottom. His head is in the clouds and his feet not firmly enough on earth. But he has a delicate temperament and a lofty character.

The newspapers are becoming more and more vile, and that makes me wonder whether, even if we succeeded in getting you a correspondent's job, you would want to take advantage of our success. It is generally thought that we shall insert a finger into Mexican affairs and settle them. The Latin races are being submerged; they have been for a long time, ever since the Reformation.

I'm waiting impatiently for your work on Mill. I hope that you will make use of me.

It didn't in the least make me shudder to hear that you want to study America in the light of the positivist method. Only I think, and Littré's book on Comte from which you quote is a proof of it, that that method has up to now been more negative than affirmative. It has been useful in overthrowing a priori presumptions, but I don't see what it has built up in the field of moral and political science, or to put it better, Comte and even Littré himself undertook to show its comparative impotence. This first observation is true. Now I'll run through the aphorisms which fill your last letter. They are too well put and thought out for you to have forgotten them. I'll only have, then, to quote from them here and there to enable you to follow the connexion.

I confess that I'm not at all convinced of what you say on the organism, its structure, and the environment in which it functions. It may be true for the organism in the ordinary sense, stomach, lungs, etc.; I doubt whether it's true for man, and the transition seems to me to be surmounted with too much facility. A man is something beside pure organism. I shall never sacrifice the idea of liberty to a materialistic or providential theory; it's part may be small but it exists.

The transition from individual to collective man remains a clumsy affair and you don't need a connecting link to explain it. I should like to believe in the law of heredity, but has it the infallibility you attribute to it ? If this law acts in so absolute a manner and if the environment only interferes to encourage or prevent the hatching of the transmitted germs, without adding anything of its own, the idea of progress would be difficult to grasp, and even, without speaking of progress, it would be hard to understand why, in the same country and the same century, two generations bear so small a resemblance to each other.

Everything that you say, after advancing these first points, seems to me well conceived and clearly reasoned. Thanks for having spoken to me of these things. Don't pay too much attention to my answers, work hard, and keep your affection for me. Tibi.[7]

JOURDAN

## IV

[In another hand]

*Paris, the 1st March* 1866

*Dear Friend:*

I have some very sad news to break to you. Your friend, I may say our friend, for I had learned to appreciate him in the little time we spent together, last Monday succumbed to a quite sudden attack of cholera.

Having gone to Brest the previous week, he brought back the fatal germ with him. In barely five days our poor friend was dead. I had seen him a few days before his trip. He had delighted me, as always, with his courtesy and good humour. We spoke of you, of how things were going in America, of France's future, which never seemed to be far from his mind and, despite the difference in our ages, despite the disillusions of all sorts, from which he had suffered more than I, it was he who was the optimist and I the pessimist. When I say optimist I perhaps exaggerate a little, for he did not conceal the difficulties in the present state of affairs. But he had that serene faith which never deserts those who have struggled passionately in a noble cause. Perhaps he also magnified his hopes a little, seeing how weak mine were. In any case he

---

[7] The letter is curious and truly high-minded. It shows how this somewhat sombre but subtle and conscientious mind was trying to round off the corners of the neophyte in Positivism.

had a healthy understanding of men and things. His conversation, in which the "I" invariably gave way to wider considerations, was usually to the point and full of fine shades. Bound to the past by his public actions and his private affections, he judged it without bitterness, yet without complacency. He didn't entertain that feeling of ridicule for the men of 1848 which most of them have kept toward one another, and he often laughed at their vanity while regretting their inadequacy.

His was in a word a clear-sighted and wise spirit, stripped of vulgar ambition, active, loyal, in fine a man who might have rendered great service and who cannot be replaced. For he was the only one of our contemporaries who didn't cherish illusions about the past and future of France.

I did not have the privilege of seeing Jourdan during his last illness. I only learned on Monday evening at five o'clock that he had taken to bed. I ran over to his house. He had just died. He had suffered a great deal during the last two or three days. But the attack was so violent that all feeling was soon dulled, and at the moment of death his nervous exhaustion was so great that he would have passed away in his sleep if his frightened wife hadn't awakened him. He was stretched out on his sofa like a convalescent. Wakened, or rather snatched from the comatose sleep which was prostrating him, he threw himself on his poor wife's bosom, saying, 'My poor dear, what a strange illness.' Then he collapsed and died.

A letter from you arrived on the evening before. It hadn't yet been opened before his death.

Good-bye, and my most cordial greetings,

TOULET

Poor Jourdan — a little place had to be found for him in these pages, where so many dead are lying.

# XLIII

## LIKE BEARDED WOMEN

CLEMENCEAU [*showing me a book lying open on his table*]: I'm engaged in studying the Carthaginians.

MYSELF: Ah, Mommsen.

CLEMENCEAU: It's interesting. It's written from a point of view altogether narrow and without horizons. That's what's good about it.

MYSELF: I've brought you two books; first this album of Druet's where you will find reproductions of some Monets. . .

CLEMENCEAU [*turning over the leaves of the album*]: Thanks. I'll look at it.

MYSELF: One thing I didn't know was the portrait of a man with an enormous umbrella and a tie like a bit of string. . .

CLEMENCEAU: Oh, that's fine! I didn't know it either. What a beak! You hardly know whether it's grotesque or magnificent. He did that under Manet's influence. It's obvious if he had wished to take up figure-painting, he would have done it as well as landscape and gone at it as profoundly and violently. This good fellow's done in a most frightening manner. And his trousers! The most expressive thing in the picture are the trousers. . .

MYSELF: Will you have finished your *Monet* soon?

328

CLEMENCEAU: It's being typed. I've only a few days' work left on it. I'll take it away to the Vendée. After that I'll attack the *Decadence.*

MYSELF: I've also brought you this book by Félix Sartiaux on the ancient civilization of Asia Minor. He's a man of intelligence and says things that will please you.

CLEMENCEAU: I know him. I believe that he has studied the subject seriously.

MYSELF: There are some pages on Miletus, Ephesus, and Pergamos which will interest you. . .

CLEMENCEAU: Asia Minor is a charnel house of dead cities. When you think of all those races who followed and exterminated one another — the Hittites, the Phrygians, the Lydians — Achilles and Agamemnon disembarked there when it was already very old.

MYSELF: They haven't excavated the hundredth part of it. What's so depressing is to see that the French School at Athens has altogether only a few thousands for its excavations, whilst the English, the Germans, and the Americans come along with millions, open work-shops. . .

CLEMENCEAU: My friend, there was a fellow, a French scholar, who bought the excavation rights at Pergamos — he sold them again to the Germans. [*Turning the pages.*] Oh, here's the Hera of Samos which is in the Louvre.[1] Shall I tell you a story about the Hera of Samos ? There's a little band around the middle of the trunk, with an inscription on it. If you want to read the translation of that inscription you have to go to London, my lad, to the British Museum, where they have a cast of the statue. I said to the Louvre people, 'Can't you put a translation of the inscription on the base of the statue ?'

---

[1] *Catalogue of Antique Marbles,* p. 41: Juno, draped, a statue which is probably the copy of an ancient ex-voto in wood in the form of a column; the head is missing: the dedicatory inscription is cut in a vertical line on the outside border of the robe. Gift of P. Girard. Temple of Juno at Samos.

They replied, 'There are a great many inscriptions already. The public complains that there are too many.'

And there you are, Martet.[2]

MYSELF: Sartiaux takes up the defence of the Decadence. He has a great respect for the Hellenistic period, which, he says, has been judged too severely and which has produced some fine things.

CLEMENCEAU: Which are they? In any case it didn't produce master spirits. Don't let them put it over on you! Look at the Parthenon. Look at the Erechtheion.

MYSELF: I'm a little lost with the Erechtheion.

CLEMENCEAU: Because you shouldn't try to take it in at a glance. It's two, three temples. You have the Caryatides. You have the east portico and the north portico. They brought those together for lack of room. Nothing ought to resemble Père-Lachaise as much as the Acropolis. A man wanted to erect a monument to his father — he stuck it there any old how. When the Propyleia was being built there was an idiot who tumbled from the roof and was killed. They erected a statue to him on the spot where he fell. You can still see the base of it.

MYSELF: As for the Parthenon, there is a metope at the Louvre.[3] It's pretty bad.

CLEMENCEAU: Yes, it's rather heavy. There's a horse who

---

[2] There is a letter which Babelon once sent him with reference to antique statuary, the one thing which probably gave Clemenceau the purest joys of his life: 'Monsieur le Sénateur, The Carthaginian sarcophagus of which I spoke in my lecture is in the Louvre, in the Salle des Mosaïques de Renan, on the ground floor; it's the room parallel to the garden museum designed by M. Duiardin Boumetz. There are two splendid sarcophagi, the finest that P. Delattre found; one is that of a Rab or high Priest of Baal Hammon — I didn't have the time to show it to my listeners. Both sarcophagi are at the far end of this room, which has for so long been under repair, on either side of the staircase. And when you go to admire them, Monsieur le Sénateur, I am sure that you will also admire to the same extent at least the label, on which the Governors of the Louvre tax all their ingenuity not to say that these sarcophagi were the gift of the artist. Believe me, etc.'
The Louvre labels have had a bad press.

[3] *Catalogue of Antique Marbles*, p. 44: Metope representing a centaur abducting a woman, tenth metope on the southern façade. Acquired by Fauval; Choiseul collection.

looks like a seal. But the Panathenea ! What serenity. And you must remember the fellows who made it were ordinary low-wage workmen. Phidias saved himself for the pediments. [*Silence.*] It's certain that Athens is worth more than Rome. Nevertheless, there was something to Rome — men like Tacitus and the younger Pliny. Moreover Rome or Athens, Athens or Rome, what interests me is the way in which races ascend, ascend — and at the end of it all what's left ? It's just the old story of the sun which over and over again sets mathematically into the water. If you want to form a judgment about anything you must take a view over the ages — must not be satisfied with ten years, or a hundred years. When you have ten or twenty centuries spread before you everything inevitably becomes clear, renews itself, and the same causes have the same effects; you see that the same mob which destroyed Athens destroyed Rome. Everything was said and done in vain — that's the way of the world.

MYSELF: Sir, I found amongst your papers notes which you took with the view of writing a book on women. I should like to ask you why you've always been an anti-feminist.

CLEMENCEAU: Oh, yes. I began that book when I was a medical student — a book of which I never wrote a line.[4] I merely set down the chapter headings. I wanted to study women, in relation to man, her conduct, her sphere, her development, to show to what she might lay claim, to what she might raise herself, physically and mentally — which are the same thing — outside the field of politics, naturally.

MYSELF: Why that exception ?

CLEMENCEAU: My friend, it's strength that determines all of this world's conduct. Whether for better or worse, that's how it is: a woman hasn't the strength. She is led by whoever wants to take the trouble. Amongst us she's led by the priest.

---

[4] A mistake. An article was written, which appears in the French edition, but has been omitted because of its length.

[*I made a gesture.*] Yes, indeed. And I see no need to give the priest any additional strength.

MYSELF: But are you as much afraid of the priestly peril as of the Bolshevist peril ?

CLEMENCEAU: The Bolshevist peril ? There is no Bolshevist peril. It's a thing of the moment. Don't you realize that for a time there will be killings and throat cuttings, and then everything will very quickly return to where it was before. Those things can't last. One must eat, after all. In ten years Russia will have a bourgeois government. She already has a bourgeois government. Every now and then they shoot a few individuals just to put people off the scent. But that only deceives congenital idiots. She has reformed her army and reopened her banks. One of these days you'll see the priests coming back. The circle will be closed. Since there have been men there has been Bolshevism. Every fifty or a hundred years it breaks out. Now and then it doesn't get anywhere. But in either event the martyrs to the good cause of Bolshevism can rest easy in their graves; they won't have had their heads broken for nothing. The principles which underlie a Revolution are not those which underlie a government or a state. Once violence has done its work you put it aside.

The priests are another matter. They make less noise, but they are more cunning, and, as regards our self-respect, our real liberty and dignity, as dangerous. I haven't told you about the answer I had before the war, from one of my father's farmers, a decent, respectable fellow. I said to him, 'You ought to vote for M. Untel. He's a republican.'

He answered, 'No, master, I shall vote for whomever the curé tells me to.'

MYSELF: Don't you find it odd and paradoxical that the right to vote is given to any lunatic or drunkard and that it's refused to Mme. Curie, for instance ?

CLEMENCEAU: As far as Mme. Curie is concerned you hit

CLEMENCEAU
*From a drawing by René Godard*

on an unfortunate example, my friend. I've observed her for some time, and seen her surrounded by a mass of people — queer folk — and taking part in all kinds of things that have nothing whatever to do with radium. I wonder if she isn't much more dangerous than the drunkard in question. When a person is intelligent, educated, and, into the bargain has a twist in his intellect, when he's lacking in fundamentals, that's a bad thing.

Now, if you tell me that the vote should be taken away from certain of the masculine sex, there, Martet, I grant you whatever you ask.

MYSELF: You must realize, sir, that a woman is usually a factor for reason and equilibrium in her home. . .

CLEMENCEAU: In domestic life, yes. And in her domestic life she should be given all rights, all security you like against the man, whose life of work and struggle makes him a beast three times out of four. But in political life you must have other qualities than reason and equilibrium. You must go out, get yourself insulted, roll up your sleeves, measure yourself against others, and, at the right moment, begin to take action. What do you expect! I can't see the woman-man. They produce an impression upon me — like bearded women. I should never have been able to marry a woman doctor. Medicine presupposes indifference and cold-bloodedness which were never intended for women.

MYSELF: Nevertheless, there are women who are feminine and none the less have good sense and judgment.

CLEMENCEAU: There are, my friend, that's obvious. But how many?

MYSELF: And how many such men are there, sir? I'm not a feminist, or if I am, it's not because I have unlimited confidence in women's political talent — I haven't yet come to that. It's because I distrust man's political acumen.

CLEMENCEAU: In that case I repeat: we agree!

MYSELF: I consider that from the moment one has taken the path of illogic — for universal suffrage, you will grant, is a step in that direction. . .

CLEMENCEAU: I do grant it.

MYSELF: Then logic demands that we follow that path to the very end, and, since we've given the vote to men of all sorts, intelligent or idiots, members of Temperance Societies or paupers, we ought to give it to women also.

CLEMENCEAU: Yes ?

MYSELF: Of course.

CLEMENCEAU: It's an odd logic that demands that you pursue it to an end in madness !

MYSELF: At bottom what frightens you is the priest, and you have that fear because you belong to a very Catholic country; if you had been born elsewhere, you mightn't have the same ideas.

CLEMENCEAU: At Saint-Vincent-sur-Jard the municipality rents an enormous piece of ground to the curé for forty francs a year. It's worth a thousand. I said to the Mayor, 'Why do you do it ?'

He answered, 'Well, I did talk to the curé about it. But he said, If you raise the rent, the bishop will remove me.

And there you are. The processions aren't yet too packed. I think that there are three or four important personages to take a stroll with the curé: a millionaire peasant called Bernard, a major of artillery, whose house is next to mine at the edge of the sea, Martin-Decaen and one or two others — I no longer remember who they are, but everybody goes to mass; the church is crammed. So it isn't very surprising to see the people marching at his beck and call like kids — and you'd like to organize the women the same way.[5]

---

[5] There are two letters which I found relating to Clemenceau's anti-clericalism. General Perraux wrote him from Dacre on 4th January 1905. 'Allow me, at the beginning of the New Year, to wish you success in the colossal job you've undertaken and are carrying on. I mean the struggle against the despotism of Rome.'

MYSELF: I wanted to ask you something else. The other day we were talking about Thiers. . .

CLEMENCEAU: I've told you what I thought of him. What do you expect me to think of Thiers ? There's no one who detested me more. There are two pairs of eyes that I remember: Thiers' and Marshal MacMahon's. When Marshal Mac-Mahon looked at me it was with the look with which the arrogant Hippolytus would have regarded a monster — a look filled with loathing.

MYSELF: But how did you happen to clash with the Marshal ?

CLEMENCEAU: I was secretary to the National Assembly; in this capacity I was invited to official banquets and receptions. That is if the Marshal was able to swallow me ! I walked about in the midst of all that grandeur with my usual charming smile. . . Thiers was a man who firmly abstained from having an idea, who literally had no perception of anything. During the Commune he did the same as he had done in the Rue Transonain, and with the same ferocity. And not only did he do it, but he boasted and crowed about it. Did I tell you about the abominable act he committed ? After having promised to leave the Parisians their guns, he took them away — which was the cause of everything that happened. . .

MYSELF: Perhaps it would have been no less unwise to leave them ?

CLEMENCEAU: Well, first, he shouldn't have promised to leave them and, secondly, he should have removed them intelligently. You don't handle mobs that way. He was one of those hide-bound fools who fancy that you can achieve something with an order written on a piece of paper.

MYSELF: And Galliffet ? Did you know him ?

And on the eve of his departure for the United States: 'Paris, 9th November 1922. Mr. President, the vicar of St. Gervais prays for a good voyage and a happy return for you. Accept my respectful greetings etc. GAUTHIER.'

CLEMENCEAU: No. He was also a swine.[6] You shouldn't forget that they were all like that. When the Versaillais entered Paris, they shot a deputy, Millière, whom of course they hadn't the right to touch. Much they cared ! They shot him on the steps of the Pantheon, after having tried to make him beg for mercy on his knees, which he refused to do. He said to them, 'You can kill me. Kill me. But you won't humiliate me.'

For six days they kept on shooting, wildly, blindly — it rested with the concierges:

'Are there any Communards in your house ?'

The concierge would answer, 'No. Oh, wait a minute ! There is one here, he looks like one of those scoundrels who pour petroleum about and set fire to it.' They dragged them out and bang !

How did I happen to come safely through all that ? I don't

---

[6] I found amongst the documents on the Commune which Clemenceau gave me these 'minutes' of a sort, where the 'swine' is painted to the life:

### GALLIFFET INQUIRY

IT APPEARS from the testimony of MM. Lelièvre, Bresnu, and Michot inhabitants of Chatou (Seine-et-Oise) that on 2nd April 1871, at eight o'clock in the morning three National Guards, an officer and a sergeant crossed the Seine together with the workers engaged on the Chatou bridge, then under repair, they came into the town.

They entered the establishment of M. Rieux, restaurant-keeper and wine-merchant, situated in the rue de Saint-Germain; they ordered a breakfast which was served to them a few minutes after their arrival. One Tranquard also an inhabitant of Chatou, a sergeant in the Fire Brigade left the place at the end of a short time to notify General Galliffet, who he knew was on reconnaissance in that country, of the presence of these wretches.

An hour later General Galliffet, at the head of fifteen cavalrymen, arrived before the Rieux establishment, arrested the National Guards, had them taken to a point several metres from the restaurant and lined up against a wall despite the pleas of these poor unfortunates; he gave the command to fire and they fell riddled by bullets.

The people, at the head of whom was M. Laubeuf, mayor of Chatou, attempted to protest against this horrible massacre; M. Laubeuf used words to this effect to General de Galliffet: 'General, these men are harmless, arrest them, take them away, bring them before a court-martial which will pass judgment on them, but spare us the horrible spectacle of needless butchery which nothing can justify. We beg you in the name of humanity.' The general's reply to this plea was, 'Shoot those rascals !' then turning to the mayor he said, 'I order you to be silent, and if you're not satisfied, I'll do the same to you.'

The paper goes on to say that Tranquard received a medal and was named Captain of the Fire Brigade for his services, but died of remorse.

understand it yet. There was at that time a brave woman —
my old friend Louise Michel. She was splendid before the
Versaillais. She told them, 'Don't think for a moment that
I'm afraid of you. I despise you. You're brigands, murderers.
I tell you so, and you can kill me if you want to.'

MYSELF: Didn't they shoot her?

CLEMENCEAU: They were afraid, by God. I'd known
Louise Michel when I was mayor of Montmartre and wanted
to separate Church and State. I had written a nice letter to
all the teachers, male and female saying, 'I don't ask much of
you. I merely want you not to require the catechism from
your pupils, and not to take them to the curé.[7] Amongst the
teachers there was only one who answered — Louise Michel.
She took the right attitude. Afterwards she was, of course,
guilty of stupidities. I became estranged from her. It proves
that with women. . . Like Séverine. Séverine was very nice,
very gallant. Now there she is, with all those people, and
every time she has a chance to throw her arms around a
traitor's or a spy's neck, she doesn't fail to do so and to

---

[7] Here is the letter. It is a lithographed circular.

'I hear that the priest of your parish has summoned you for tomorrow, Tuesday,
to celebrate High Mass with your pupils in his church.

In the first place I must remind you that, being a civil institution you are not
bound by the orders of your parish priest.

It is imperative that every person's liberty of conscience be scrupulously respected.
In summoning the children of your school to proceed in a body to any place whatever given over to the practice of any creed whatever, without consulting their
individual opinions or those of their parents, you would be bringing or seeming
to bring a regrettable pressure on their consciences.

It is the Municipality's duty to put an end to these abuses.

Like every other citizen, you are absolutely free to practise whatever religion
you may choose and in whatever way you choose. Your individual pupils have
the same absolute right to go to such church as they wish, with or without their
parents, so long as the latter consider it suitable. But it is impossible that you
should ever think of convoking them in a body to celebrate any religious rite. . .

You will observe that you are forbidden to take the children in your school to
catechism.

The children are free to go to catechism or not, with their parent's consent,
during their holidays. But I cannot allow you to devote the time belonging to
instruction to the dogmas of any religion whatever.

The mayor of 18th Arrondissement.
G. CLEMENCEAU'

Paris, 26th October 1870

23

assure the gentleman, with the greatest possible amount of publicity, of her unutterable respect for him. Say what you will, it doesn't make you want to be a feminist.

MYSELF: There's another distinguished person about whom I want you to say a word.

CLEMENCEAU: Oh. Who?

MYSELF: His Majesty Edward VII, King of England.[8]

CLEMENCEAU: Edward VII was a fine and, yes, charming, man, who really did all that he could. A gay dog, but like most gay dogs, a man of resource. One day he invited me to a party where there were twelve women, every one of whom had been his mistress, and amongst the number were several who were still pleasing to look at. You know that, nevertheless, his wife the Queen-Mother — who's still living, I think? — had great veneration for him. When I went to London, my car passed in front of her palace, and, in order to see me go by, she came out on the pavement. They told me that, so I went to pay my respects to her. Something gruesome and comic put in an appearance, a kind of old court servant, very gorgeously attired, with a flower in his buttonhole, bent double

---

[8] There is a very interesting letter addressed to 'His Excellency Monsieur Clemenceau, President of the Council of the French Ministry, Hans Belvedere, Carlsbad.' It bears the seal of the royal arms of England.

*Hotel Weymar, Marienbad*
*23rd August* 1908

MAJOR-GENERAL SIR STANLEY CLARKE presents his compliments to H. E. Monsieur Clemenceau and is desired by His Majesty, King Edward (Duke of Lancaster) to invite him to lunch at the Hotel Weimar on Wednesday Aug. 26th at one o'clock, and to beg him to come in ordinary travelling costume. His Majesty has also invited Monsieur Isvolsky.

IN THE *Times* of 24th December 1920, the editor in chief of that journal, who was formerly its special correspondent in Austria-Hungary, gave the details of a conversation which took place at Marienbad on 26th August 1908 between King Edward and Clemenceau: 'In the course of this lengthy conversation, M. Clemenceau had expressed his fears about the future of international relations and already foresaw a probable conflict. "England," he said, "has confidence in the power of her fleet to destroy the German fleet, but for France the danger of invasion is very real."'

Here the *Times* ends by reproducing in French Clemenceau's very words. 'It wasn't at Trafalgar, which was nevertheless a very brilliant naval victory, but at Waterloo, which was a small battle, that England broke Napoleon's power.'

by age, who came to do the honours almost on all-fours. After a time the Queen said to me, 'Do you realize that I went out into the street yesterday to see you go by ?'

She led me to a large portrait of her husband and pointing to it said, 'He was a splendid man. There's never been a better on earth.'

MYSELF: And George V ?

CLEMENCEAU: He's charming, too. They're all worthy people — what do you expect ? They do their job as best they can.

MYSELF: You haven't lost your memorandum on Foch ?

CLEMENCEAU: No. [*Indicating the drawer of his table.*] It's there. I'm letting it lie. You will profit from it. Have you been out in the country recently ?

MYSELF: Yes. The other day I went to a place called Champlieu. It's on the outskirts of the Forest of Senlis. I found there an old Roman city, with temple, a theatre, baths. . .

CLEMENCEAU: Of which nothing remains ?

MYSELF: Not much.

CLEMENCEAU: It's better so. Roman architecture gains a great deal by being in ruins. Do you know Pompeii ? That's worth the trouble of going to see. I saw a dead city like that in India, with streets and houses. I only wonder how these people managed to get into their own houses. There's only an opening high up and nothing to climb up by.

MYSELF: Perhaps they had ladders. . .

CLEMENCEAU: You've an answer for everything. Ruins. The world is paved with ruins. We take walks in cemeteries, and stroll amongst skeletons. I remember that at Tegea, where there is a vast temple to Athena — I wonder what it was doing there — a man came along looking for me. He said, 'I've a lucern field where you've only to stoop down in order to gather Tanagras.'

I went there with him. I picked up quantities of them — all broken, of course. . .

MYSELF: Why of course ?

CLEMENCEAU: Because business must go on. When Critias, son of Critias, brought his little statue to the priest, the priest smiled at him and said, 'Thank you, my friend.' He waited until Critias had returned home and broke the statuette. In this way the statuette business remained prosperous: the priests must have received a percentage. It's at Tegea that there is the little museum with that head. I've shown it to you twenty times. Come along all the same. [*He gets up.*] Come and see the head, Martet. [*We go into the study.*]

CLEMENCEAU [*showing me the cast of the Tegea head*]: What about it ? Eh ?

# XLIV

## SOME JEWS

*6th July* 1928

CLEMENCEAU is at work. I enter with my wife. We exchange greetings and sit down.

CLEMENCEAU: Well, Monsieur Martet.

MYSELF: It seems that we've lost a great financier.

CLEMENCEAU: Which great financier? Loewenstein?[1] If by any chance this great financier was a Jew. . .

MYSELF: As well as being a Jew he was occupied with money matters. . .

CLEMENCEAU: Not a bad death. A bit showy. . .

MYSELF: Empedocles. . .

CLEMENCEAU: Just what I was going to say. Speaking of Israel I've just had a visit from Edmond de Rothschild. He can still stand on his legs. . . Well, Edmond de Rothschild is, amongst Jews, a good Jew. He stayed a minute, and told me things which weren't devoid of good sense, which is rather rare in one who holds so great a power with money—even things which had an air of nobility about them. Edmond de Rothschild does not follow his ideas up systematically. Those thirty millions which he gave for laboratories — it's very don't you think, and he a Jew? And he's satisfied to be

from his aeroplane 4th July 1928, while crossing the Channel.

a Jew. One day I said something unpleasant about the Jews, whereupon he stood up, pounded on the table — yes, Martet — and said, 'Monsieur Clemenceau, the Jewish race is the greatest race in the world.'

And he began to talk to me about his Judas Maccabæuses. I rather like it, not the Maccabees, but that one shouldn't be ashamed of being what one is — it's the only way of being it decently.

D——² is another sort. He said to me, 'I've something like 110 or 140 millions — I don't even know exactly. And the boring thing is that I don't know how to spend it.'

I answered, 'It's senseless. Can't you become interested in a job ? Give the money to something worth while ?'

He assumed a knowing smile. 'Have you anything to recommend ?'

He reckoned that I was going to touch him on behalf of a person or a hospital. I said, 'No, I don't know any. It's for yourself — that your life may have some meaning.'

MYSELF: It's difficult to know both how to make and how to spend money.

CLEMENCEAU: That's what he said. 'My father only taught me to scrape and pinch. Can you realize that I'm distressed when my clerks write letters on headed paper ? I want them to write on scrap paper.' He recognizes it — that's something.

I had a curious experience this morning; needing a hair cut I sent for a barber. He came. He had a mouthful of gold teeth.

MYSELF: Schliemann would have liked that.

CLEMENCEAU: Yes. You know, you should see his Mycenean excavations. He's got a lot of cheek. He had said, 'You should find Agamemnon over there.' They dug, and found something which might well have been Agamemnon.

² Another Jewish financier.

MYSELF: Why not?

CLEMENCEAU: Quite. Schliemann said, 'But you ought to find two others.' They dug some more. They found a couple of other chaps. A triumph for Schliemann. The unfortunate part is that the next day they found a fourth, a fifth — an entire collection. . .

MYSELF: All the Atrides. Schliemann did archæology a very bad turn. He entirely pillaged Troy.

CLEMENCEAU: You must always be suspicious of the Boches; when they find themselves in front of a city, their blood tells — they demolish it.

[*We get up and move toward the door.*]

MYSELF: Have you read Sartiaux's book?

CLEMENCEAU: Yes. It's good. But there are two or three compliments to Christianity in it. It's a pity there ever was such a thing as Christianity. One might have lived so well worshipping Jupiter, Mercury, all those gallant deities who weren't jealous of opposition, and who, every time another god came along, squeezed up a bit to make room for him. Whilst your God. . . [*To my wife.*] Are you a Christian, Madame?

MY WIFE: Doubly so. I was baptized a Catholic and took my first Protestant communion.

CLEMENCEAU: And didn't you get married in the synagogue? You did wrong. You should bid for all the pictures.

[*We have arrived at the door. As we are shaking hands.*]

CLEMENCEAU [*looking at us*]: Are you happy?

MYSELF: We try to be. . .

CLEMENCEAU: What is happiness?

*30th July* 1928

A LOVELY soft blue sky across which glide enormous, lazy white clouds.

Machecoul. Challans, etc. . .

On leaving Saint-Vincent the car is swept by a puff of wind carrying the pungent odour of sea-weed. The road leads toward the sea. On the right an isolated hut — the famous Ocean Café for whose tenants Clemenceau wishes ruin with the least possible delay.

Then a little forest of pines in which the road becomes entangled. At the entrance is a notice, 'Private Property.' I rush in. There it is, what the post-cards of Jard and Talmont call, 'The cottage of M. Clemenceau.' A long farm-house with a tiled roof. In front of the house a confusion of flowers and shrubbery which grows mysteriously in the sand dunes. Beyond the garden the pale gold strand, and beyond the strand the smiling ocean dreaming in the sun.

A man in white is sitting on a bench facing the sea — it is Clemenceau.

He catches sight of us. 'Hello, there you are !' Without giving us a chance to say a word he asks, 'What do you think of my revolving fountain ?'

'Wonderful.'

'Wouldn't you think you were in the Parc Montsouris ?'

A man's head appears between two clumps of foliage. 'Hey,' calls Clemenceau, 'those spindle-trees must be cut down. They block the view.'

He turns to us. 'That's my gardener. He won't understand that I like to see the ocean. Come along and see your rooms.'

'Two ? That's a lot. . .'

'I told you the bed is as narrow as a canoe. Now come this way. Here are my cypresses. Look at them — they grow like weeds. Moreover everything grows in this grass.'

'There are two or three. . .'

'Say it — they're dead. That's because of a recent high wind. Turn round — what about that ? That blue thistle — those rose-coloured things ? That sort of fern with which the wind is playing — isn't it lovely ? And that — and that ? The sea and the sky. That lovely little cloud which looks as if it had been forgotten in moving. . .[1]

'There's an island away off on the horizon. Piétri maintains that it's Corsica. I think it's the Ile de Ré.'

On the left and way at the far end of the large bill-hook which is the shape the golden shore takes, is the headland of Groin. Distant ships. Gulls. The gentle sound of the waves breaking on the sand-bank. . .

'Come and do the tour of my castle. . .'

Behind the house lies a small enclosure of flowers which is protected by a broom hedge.

'In the morning I come and sit here,' says Clemenceau. 'I look and I listen. Tiny birds come and perch on the tips of the branches and sway and send forth their little chirps.'

We go into the sitting-room. It's a kind of large wood cabin which Clemenceau had built and which he filled with the furniture from Bernouville.[2] There are windows looking out

[1] Déménagement—the removal from one house to another.—*Translator's note.*
[2] Clemenceau had sold the property which he had at Bernouville in the Eure.

on the country and one on the sea. There are no foundations — it stands directly on the sand.

We cross the room and go out by a kind of manger of the Nativity, which Clemenceau has made his favourite corner. Tree trunks support the roof of branches. It opens out on the sea; the sound of the water-spouts and the waves are borne in gently by the breeze. . .

'So Stresemann is coming to Paris,' asks Clemenceau. 'Will they decorate the town with flags?'

He takes my arm. 'Come and see my nest. . .'

We take a few steps in the sand and suddenly he orders, 'Stop! Stoop down!'

He separates a clump of underbrush. I find myself staring into a downy crater filled with horrid little heads from which eyes stand out in the form of violet-colored tumours.

'It's cost me sixteen thousand francs to build dykes for my garden. Otherwise the ocean would have swallowed it. . .'

A terrace surrounds the shore. We walk through yellow iris. 'Just look at that. They grow all over the place; I can't sit down anywhere without an iris growing between my feet. . .'

We sit down on a wooden bench worn and scarred by the sea-winds.

'Let's dream,' says Clemenceau.

'About what?' I ask.

'The brotherhood of man.'

ALBERT appears behind the bench. 'Monsieur le Président, lunch is ready.'

'Splendid,' says Clemenceau. 'That dream gave me a hollow feeling. Let's eat.'

# XLVI

CLEMENCEAU DISCUSSES DOCTORS AND TOADS
WILSON SUGGESTS CEDING NEW YORK TO THE ITALIANS

*31st July* 1928

CLEMENCEAU is sick. At eight o'clock Albert brings breakfast to our room. I ask him.

'Monsieur Clemenceau is not up yet ?'

'Not yet.'

'Does he often get up as late as this ?'

'Never.'

I go out into the garden. I pass by his door and sit down in the little shed. The sky is overcast. Birds are flying low and perch on the hedges. Thus the morning passes. We lunch without Clemenceau. Albert informs us:

'He will not admit he tired himself out yesterday. The doctor has forbidden him to exert himself.'

In the afternoon I go for a stroll through the pine forest. On my return I pass his door.

'Martet !'

I go in. He is lying in bed fully dressed — in a white linen suit.

MYSELF: How do you feel, Monsieur ?

CLEMENCEAU: Like a man who hasn't yet succeeded in dying. [*He points to the little table beside his bed.*] There is your article on Foch.[1] Take it with you.

MYSELF: Is there a doctor in Luçon ?

CLEMENCEAU: Bah ! I don't know. . . In the good old days there used to be just one. A hospital interne. He never knew what to do. My mother once sent for him when she was sick. 'Shall I prescribe some of this for you, Madame ?' — 'Just as you wish, Doctor.' He knew nothing about illnesses or their cures. He was a really valuable safeguard to have about. He is dead. Now there are five or six of them. You know how at times mosquitos infest a place.

MYSELF: You don't want one of them called ?

CLEMENCEAU: What's the use ? I know what is the matter with me, I've absorbed too much digitahine.

MYSELF: What ?

CLEMENCEAU: I'll tell you. Only three drugs are known to the science of medicine. No more. But from time to time doctors have to make an impression upon their patients, so they call these three by different names. Digitahine is a sort of digitalia — the very latest word. When I was young it used to soothe my heart. Now it stimulates it. Don't try to understand all this. Also, there is another drug invented by that fellow . . . what's his name ? the one from Ardèche. . . Astier. . . No. . . Astier was cocoa. . . At any rate, it is supposed to be good. I asked my doctor. . .

MYSELF: Which one ?

CLEMENCEAU: The one from Geneva. The fellow who took Florand's place. I asked him what the symptoms of digitahine poisoning were. . .

MYSELF: What ! Do you want to poison yourself ?

CLEMENCEAU: I wanted to test him out. He answered: 'A weakening of the pulse and gastric disorders.' As far as a weakening of the pulse goes, I have no pulse at all. It's simpler that

[1] I will publish this article after Clemenceau's book on Foch has appeared.

way. And as for gastric disorders, I am beginning to think I have hit the toboggan. Men are divided into two classes, Martet. There are the hyper-tense and the hypo-tense. The hyper-tense usually die in their offices. Or when they are making love, as in the case of Felix Faure and certain other famous personages. Florand died during a consultation — a cerebral hemorrhage. He was examining a sick man. It made him a little panicky. The hypo-tense never die suddenly. They hang on pitifully. That's the fate which is reserved for me. God is testing me. Let him do so. [*He does not look at me as he talks; his eyes are fixed on the ceiling. From time to time he brusquely shoves his grey cap down over his ruddy face or else, impetuously, pushes it well back on his head.*]

CLEMENCEAU: I wanted to take you to Colombier. It is a magnificent opportunity.

MYSELF: Ah ?

CLEMENCEAU: Yes. When I am dead you will take me there. [*A silence.*] I would so like to die there. . . There would be no one around. [*He turns toward me, seeming to notice me for the first time.*] Why are you standing up that way ? Sit down. Where is that little wife of yours ?

MYSELF: I saw her in l'Etable de la Nativité. She was watching a toad which hopped from stone to stone; it looked like some little human monster.

CLEMENCEAU: A great deal has been written about toads. I don't see that they are any better than men. It is conceivable that they have souls. . . I do not know what magic you used to get into Piétri's good graces.

MYSELF: I'm so glad ! I like him very much. His affection for you is absolutely unselfish.

CLEMENCEAU: Corsica is an extraordinary country. You have never been to Sartène ? A sinister place; the walls have slits in them which may once have had the ambition to serve as windows, but now they are little more than loop-holes. . .

I was in a village down there and a lawyer made a speech to me. When he had finished he drew a revolver from his pocket and fired six shots into the air. I asked Piétri, 'What does he do that for ?' 'It's just a habit !' [*He pulls himself up in bed.*] You see how sensible it was to have the bed raised. I can see the sea. . . [*A pause.*] You have no news about Mussolini ?

MYSELF: I have heard that he wants to pass a law forbidding emigration.

CLEMENCEAU: The best law for him would be to feed his compatriots. I can remember poor Orlando at the Conference. . . He justified the seizure of Fiume because there were 100,000 Italians there. . . Wilson jumped up: 'There are two million Italians in New York ! You are not going to demand New York, are you ?' [*Brusquely he pulls his cap down.*] What time is it ?

MYSELF: Seven o'clock.

CLEMENCEAU: Take your article on Foch and go along to dinner. Tomorrow we shall see how I am feeling. I may request you to get out of here. It appals me to think of your wife with that toad. . .

# XLVII

## 'I Recommend Infidelity'

1st August 1928

ALBERT comes into our bedroom and throws back the curtains. Sunlight.

'Monsieur Clemenceau is better today, but he refuses to eat. The doctor is coming later.'

The room is small and has whitewashed walls. The floor is of broad spruce planks, the ceiling of narrow yellow pine, discoloured in spots where the nails have rusted. The bed, table, chairs, and bureau are likewise of coarse-grained yellow pine. In the walls hang three ancient mirrors; at the head of the bed there is a large Chinese painting on silk depicting several dragons with horrible gaping jaws.

At ten o'clock I go to see Clemenceau. He is lying in bed, fully dressed.

CLEMENCEAU: How are you?

MYSELF: Very well, Monsieur. . . And you?

CLEMENCEAU: I lay awake for hours last night trying to think of Madame Récamier's name. I could remember that her first name was Juliette and her maiden name Richard. . . But her husband's name? For the life of me I can't think of it. I'm almost positive it ends in 'et.' He was either a doctor or a banker. You know, there never was a more insignificant woman than Madame Récamier. She never said anything, never did anything. She just lay there in her chaise-longue. And in one corner sat Châteaubriand. I once knew a man who had known Châteaubriand. It was old man Bochet. His brother was administrator of the estate of the Orléans family. He had another brother who was a general and maybe a third who was a sailor. . . The administrator was a competent, rather intelligent fellow. As leader of a faction which could never hope to get anywhere, he adapted himself to circumstances with a certain common sense. As far as administering the Orléans estate went, I doubt whether he pocketed anything. The Orléans family had their wits about them. . . I met old Bochet back-stage at the Opera. He hadn't a penny and the women scorned him. . . As I was saying, Bochet used to see Châteaubriand; he was a little fellow and would never say a word. He just sat in a corner and played with his handkerchief. This old man in the corner reminds me of Madame Geoffrin's husband. In Madame Geoffrin's salon there was an old man who always sat in the same seat next the chimney and never said anything. One fine day he disappeared. A fortnight later someone asked Madame Geoffrin: 'There was a gentleman who always used to sit there. . . Who was he, anyway? What has become of him?' 'He was my husband, and he is dead.'

By the way, when did Châteaubriand die? I am under the impression he died somewhat before Julie. . . As for Julie. . .

MYSELF: Such a woman never dies. . .

CLEMENCEAU: Yes, before one can die one must have lived. [*I open the Larousse dictionary to Récamier.*]

MYSELF: First of all, Madame Récamier's maiden name was not Richard!

CLEMENCEAU: Ah?

MYSELF: No, Bernard. Her father was a banker.

CLEMENCEAU: Bernard. . . A banker. . . She was a Jewess !
MYSELF: She was born in Lyons.

CLEMENCEAU: Ah ! So that's the reason Herriot was interested in her.[1] I remember doing an article on his book in
which I said: 'How curious it is that a man should devote a
serious study to the least interesting woman who ever lived !'
He resented it. Some time ago he remarked to a sculptor who
was doing a bust of me and who was probably also doing one
of him: 'Clemenceau is spiteful. Oh ! he is a spiteful man !'
Poor Herriot ! Poor Châteaubriand ! [*He takes a drink.
Every fifteen minutes he drinks a large glass of water.*] But
the man I despise above all others is William II. He has ended
up self-satisfied and complacent. But all of the Boche kings
and emperors have found it rather easy to turn bourgeois.
One day I was in a hotel at Stuttgart. In one of the corridors
I saw a fellow all covered with gold braid surrounded by men
whose uniforms were also heavily braided. He had an air of
being absolutely self-satisfied. I might easily have taken him
for a Police Captain. It was the King.

I RETURN to see him about three o'clock. He is sitting up in
an armchair.

CLEMENCEAU: Go get your wife. I'm going to say good-
bye to you and then put you out. I'm no good any more.

[*I go out and return with my wife.*]

CLEMENCEAU [*to my wife*]: Never grow old. . . A man
who was here a little while ago told me there was nothing
the matter with me. While he was examining me I examined
him out of the corner of my eye; I could see that he wore
a blue shirt and had pince-nez glasses with a ribbon hanging
down. Take care ! A man who dresses like that will be unfaithful to his wife.

---

[1] Herriot, former Prime Minister of France and Mayor of Lyons, has written a
biography of Madame Récamier.

MY WIFE: I have warned my husband. An eye for an eye. . .

CLEMENCEAU: You would be unfaithful to him !

MY WIFE: Or else kill him !

CLEMENCEAU: I recommend infidelity; you are less likely to miss. There are those who cannot be killed. There are those who cannot die. [*Offering her his hand.*] Look at me !

# XLVIII

## The Cradle and the Grave

*15th August* 1928

I RECEIVED this telegram. 'WILL YOU LUNCH WITH ME WEDNES-
DAY AFTERWARDS GO TO COLOMBIER. CLEMENCEAU.'

This time it's raining. The roads are full of peasant women
in small white head-dresses and carrying large umbrellas.

I find Clemenceau in his bedroom.

'I'm better. But I had a bad go of it. The truth must be
admitted — I'm breaking up in every way. What did you
do with your wife? Didn't you bring her? She funked
the trip. I'm rereading a book which isn't at all bad — *Stories
of Merovingian Times.'*

'A bit theatrical. . . '

'It's all right. Have you seen my dog? No? Aren't you
curious? He's a Scotch terrier with a most sympathetic face.
I can't live without dogs. They have such silences. . .'

At noon we are eating.

'What do you think of this bass?'

'Excellent. You have travelled, sir. . .'

'A little. I know this world's roads fairly. . .'

'Have you ever seen a country where the food is as good
as in ours?'

355

'Never.'

'Recently I dined in a Chinese restaurant; it nearly killed me. . .'

'By Jove, yes. At Singapore they spread a Chinese banquet before me — sharks' fins, swallows' nests, and so forth. Those concoctions ought to be prohibited.'

I watched him devouring his food ravenously, fiercely. I can't help exclaiming, 'Oh !'

'What's the matter ?'

'You give the impression of having a capital appetite, I thought you were ill.'

'I want to die happy. Eat.'

After the stewed peach and coffee we make a start. Two pillows have been installed in the Rolls, and Clemenceau hollows out a place for himself in one of them. The rickety old vehicle lumbers forward with a whir. The struggle begins. Pot-holes and bumps. We negotiate the little hump-backed bridges at full speed. Clemenceau is hurled against me and I tumble over on him. Crash. Bang.

'I wonder if he's watching what he's doing,' says Clemenceau, referring to Brabant, the chauffeur.

Saint-Hilaire. Avrillé. Mouthiers-les-Maufaits and its covered market. Mareuil. The famous grove. The tangle of little valleys. The roads bordered with leafy hedges. The grey house roofed in rose-coloured tiles. Bonnezeau. Chantonnay. Brabant goes on, his head down. . .

Mouilleron. . . Rue Georges Clemenceau.

'That's the house in which I was born something like eighty-seven years ago. They've put up a plaque.'

The car stops before a large house with a flat and dreary façade. I glance at the plaque, 'The man to whom ascends the gratitude . . . etc.'

We go in. It is a bakery. One notices first a little shop full of six-pound loaves split in half. Then the Michonneaus,

CLEMENCEAU'S GRAVE

Father Michonneau, Mother Michonneau, the son and daughter-in-law.

We go into the sitting-room, a large square apartment whose windows open on the street.

'I've danced first-rate polkas there,' says Clemenceau.

Mother Michonneau drags me off. 'Come and see where he was born.'

We climb a little wooden staircase. On the first floor is a series of large square rooms.

Mother Michonneau pushes a door open. There it is. A bedroom. The window looks out on the back garden and the grape-arbour.

The next room (she opens another door) is where he slept when he was little. Through a third door is a third room, which he occupied when he was larger.

One would think that only he had lived in this house and that the house is full of him and him alone.

We go down again. Clemenceau chucked the old woman under the chin: 'I'm jealous of you.'

'Why ?'

'You've a handsomer moustache than I.'

When Father Michonneau complains of his feet, which make it difficult for him to get round, Clemenceau cried, 'You mustn't die before me !'

'I'll not let myself. I'll do all I can not to.'

'Hello !' exclaimed Clemenceau, recognizing a cupboard. 'I've been shut up in that.'

We leave. The grove is given life and dramatized.

Réaumur. 'The château is still there,' says Clemenceau. 'There are still descendants of the family in it. Probably they don't even know what a thermometer is.'

The valleys become deeper. Pousauges with its ruined keep. Le Boupère and its fortified church. Mouchamps. . . The Rolls becomes entangled in a road which is nothing but a dry ditch. It climbs, curves down. Suddenly: 'There's Colombier.'

Hay stacks. Mass of broken stones. In the midst of them is visible a large building pierced by narrow, widely-spaced windows, and by two dove-cote turrets. Back of it rises the squat tower which survives from the old château.

Men and women come up to him. He recognizes them.

'How are you ? Hello, there's Monsieur Georges.'

Jokes about life and the familiar old theme of death.

'Let's go in.'

A large square room with a beamed ceiling and an arms-rack over the mantel. You feel the sadness of dreary lives and of toil. Clemenceau looks all about him. He looks at the men who have called him 'Master,' at a child who is coughing.

All of his youth eddies through the four walls of this room, the great wood fire where he dried his damp clothes after hunting, the table where he devoured enormous dishes of food with his fifteen-year-old appetite; the rafters on the ceiling which he used to ask questions about the future. . .

Two or three words about the child's cough: ' I can no longer use a stethoscope — I can't hear anything. . .' He takes my arm. 'Come along.'

We again cross the courtyard, where the hens are pilfering and the dogs scratching themselves.

He points out an enclosure planted with trees.

'It's there.'

What's there ? He opens a door and we go in. A terrace planted with acacias which overlooks the bed of a stream.[1] In the centre of the terrace has been erected the Samos stele.[2]

'Stoop down. There's my father's grave. . .'

I stoop. It is situated on a lower level, on a kind of second terrace. A little iron frame, without a name. Weeds.

---

[1] The Petit Lay.
[2] It is the bas-relief made by Sicard after the stele in the Acropolis Museum.

'Mine is beside it. It's already dug.'

Trees. Many trees. There is a great simplicity about it, and yet at the same time a great arrogance. And a kind of peace as of the beginning of the world.

I remove my hat. Clemenceau nudges my elbow. 'Keep your hat on. It's nothing.'

Then pointing to 'his grave.'

'Take a look at it. There in a nutshell is all that you can say about me — a hole in the ground and a great deal of noise about nothing.'

# INDEX